AN ENGLISHMAN (AND HIS MOTHER) ABROAD

Neil Rathmell

Published by Southernwood Press

www.southernwoodpress.co.uk

Copyright © Neil Rathmell 2014

Neil Rathmell asserts his moral right to be identified as the author of this work.

ISBN 978-0-9928531-0-5

Printed and bound by Short Run Press Limited, Exeter.

All rights reserved. No part of this publication may be reproduced, stored in a retrieval system, or transmitted, in any form or by any means, electronic, mechanical, photocopying, recording or otherwise, without the prior permission of the publishers.

Neil Rathmell was born in 1947. He grew up in Yorkshire and now lives in Shropshire.

His first published fiction appeared in *Introduction 4 – Stories by New Writers* (Faber & Faber, 1972).

The Old School, a novel, was published by Faber & Faber in 1976.

He publishes a weekly literary blog which also features a selection of plays, poetry, essays and short stories.

nrathmell.wordpress.com

I live in a tall, thin house in a narrow passage in the middle of an English town. The windows at the back of my house overlook a courtyard with buildings on three sides, one of which used to be the town gaol. Prisoners once exercised in the courtyard, now the residents park their cars there. On the other side of the passage, opposite the front door, is a building which used to be a Methodist chapel and has now been turned into flats. From my bedroom window, I can see the stone tower of the school where Sir Philip Sidney, Elizabethan poet and courtier, killed at the Battle of Zutphen in 1586, was once a pupil. Now it's a library. Everything here used to be something else.

My father died a long time ago. My mother lived alone for thirty years but now in her ninetieth year she is living with me. Having spent the first few years of her life getting taller, she has spent the last few getting shorter. She never quite made it to five foot one and now she's down to four foot six. She has to stand on her tiptoes to do the washing-up. Her back is bent and she has to lift her head up to see where she's going. It gives her an air of determination. Just walking across the kitchen to get the tea towel, she looks as if she's setting out on a long journey. When she walks back with the towel in her hand, she has the look of a hunter bringing home his prey.

She is becoming mythical. As the humans in Ovid's poem are changed into trees or flowers, so she now is enduring a slow metamorphosis from life to death.

"I can't go on for ever," she says.

Sometimes, when she goes upstairs to bed, one step at a time, holding onto the banister, she says that God is cruel to keep her alive. But when she comes downstairs in the morning, she says with a smile, "Well, I've done it again!"

The physical space she occupies is shrinking. Every morning she unlocks the front door and puts her head outside, like a mouse looking out of its hole. The three stone steps outside our front door are her garden, shrunk from the garden she once had to a few plants growing in pots and hanging baskets. She doesn't have the strength to look after them herself, so I have become her gardener. All summer long, geraniums and fuchsias, busy lizzies and petunias, red and pink, purple and white, brighten the passage for the three or four hours that the sun shines on them. Sometimes she sits on a chair outside the door among the flowers, watching people come and go.

For a long time her sight, which was never good, has been getting worse. A few years ago she had glaucoma and lost the sight in one eye. A year or two before she came to live with me, she had a cataract operation on the other. The morning after the operation, when she took off the eye-patch, everything looked the same. She says that she sat on the edge of the bed staring in disappointment at the carpet until suddenly, like a misty landscape on an October morning, it burst into colour.

She was ten when she first admitted that she couldn't see the blackboard and started wearing glasses. The lenses were so heavy they kept sliding down her nose. She doesn't wear glasses anymore, but can't break the habit of lifting her hand every few minutes to push them back.

"God is good," she says, then adds, "and the devil isn't so bad if you treat him right."

Every morning, after I have gone to work, she does her chores. Her breakfast is a slice of buttered toast and a cup of tea. Sometimes she has another slice, but not often.

"It's only greed," she says.

She does the washing up, then mops the kitchen floor. While the floor is drying, she goes upstairs and sweeps her carpet with an old-fashioned carpet sweeper. Then she comes downstairs again, carrying the carpet sweeper in one hand, holding onto the banister with the other, and sweeps the carpets in the hall and the living room. When she has done her chores, she sits down in her sitting room to read.

Once a week, I walk with her to the old school that is now a library to change her books. When she is reading, the characters in the story are like real people to her. The first book she ever read was *Margot's Secret*, which her godmother gave her when she was a little girl. The old woman lived in an alms house in Leeds. All she remembers is that she dressed entirely in black, buttoned up from boots to chin with a bonnet on her head. *Margot's Secret* was the only book she had and she read it over and over again. She says she can still remember the feeling of wonder it gave her when she discovered there were two worlds, this one and a made up one. She didn't much like this one.

She was a lonely child, the youngest of three children, each born at seven year intervals. She was born on a small farm near Leeds, but when she was two her father died in the flu epidemic after the First World War. Her mother had to give up the farm and took her children to live in an off-licence in a street of back-to-back terrace houses. When the older children had grown up and she had saved enough money to live off the interest, she gave up the off-licence and rented a house in a village outside Leeds, taking her nine-year-old daughter with her. They lived together, just the two of them, until the girl got married and her husband moved in with them.

When she came to live with me, I thought she might find it difficult to adjust after thirty years of living on her own. But leaving her old house and moving in with me turned out to be as easy as finishing one book and starting another. When I come home from work I walk upstairs and see her sitting in her chair in front of the window, reading. She is so engrossed she doesn't even hear me come in. I can sit down on the other chair and watch her for several minutes before she becomes aware of my presence.

Sometimes she has other visitors. First it was a woman in a green dress, then two young girls in their night clothes, then a woman dressed all in black. The visitors disappear before she has time to speak to them. They come into her room when she is dozing but, when she opens her eyes and sees them standing there, they turn and walk away. Once she saw my father.

"What are *you* doing here?" she asked.

He did not reply, but turned and walked away like the others. She thinks the other visitors must have lived here before. How my father got there she can't say.

She had been living with me for three months when Rajpal came to visit. He bent down to touch her feet and then we sat and talked. We worked out that it was nine years since I had last visited him in India, six years after my first visit. Since then he has got to know my mother on his visits to England and the rest of my family when we spent Christmas with him in India. One of my daughters stayed with him for a few months, teaching at a school in Patiala. My divorce the next year, something that rarely happens in India, was a disappointment to him. Looking after my mother in her old age, something that everybody does in India, has helped to restore his faith in me.

"When will you come again?" he said.

I wish I could, but who would look after my mother while I was away?

"Bring her with you."

I told him that next year would be our combined one hundred and fiftieth birthday. My mother would be ninety and I would be sixty.

"You must come to India and celebrate mom's birthday with us," he said.

He asked me when her birthday was and, when I told him it was in February, he said the weather then would be perfect.

"Like summer in England. You must come!"

She told me later that she only agreed because she felt sure she would be dead by then and I would be able to go without her. She feels that she is a burden on me and tells me that she will be gone soon and then I will be free to do whatever I want.

"I can't last for ever," she says.

Fifteen years ago, on my first visit to India, Rajpal had arranged for someone to meet me at Delhi airport. Arriving early in the morning, I waited at the airport for someone to take me to Chandigarh, where Rajpal himself would be waiting for me. An hour later, I was still waiting. Outside, hundreds of people were gathered, their faces pressed to the plate glass windows, as if the airport terminal were a formicarium and they were studying the ants inside. As time went by, I began to feel that I had more in common with them than with my fellow ants, whose ceaseless movement had a sense of purpose which mine lacked. Alone and palely loitering, I stood out from the crowd.

"Taxi? Hotel?"

In India, hotel is pronounced *ho*tel, with the stress on the first syllable. If you stand by the side of the road for more than a minute or two in any city, someone will come up to you saying, "Taxi? *Ho*tel?" He will keep saying it until you go away. This word, repeated insistently, monotonously, like the call of a bird, has been imprinted on my mind since the day when I waited, at Delhi airport and later outside the bus station in Chandigarh, for someone to meet me.

"*Ho*tel? *Ho*tel?"

"No, thank you," I said, in a vain attempt to get them to leave me alone. "Someone is coming to meet me."

After an hour, my excuse, after so many repetitions, each greeted with incomprehension or disbelief (it was impossible to tell which), began to wear thin. After two hours, even I had stopped believing it. But this was my first lesson in the elasticity of time in India and the infinite patience of Indians. An Englishman resents having to wait, begrudging what he sees as a waste of his time. An Indian bears it with equanimity, welcomes it even, as if he has been given more time, not less. An unsolicited gift.

"Mr Neil?"

The welcoming party, it turned out, had been there all the time. There were two of them, students from the college in Patiala where Rajpal teaches. One of them picked up my suitcase and I followed them out of the airport. They had been waiting, Rajpal told me later, for an Englishman and his wife. He did not know how this misunderstanding had arisen but was able to correct it when they telephoned from the airport to tell him they had been waiting for two hours but there was still no sign of an Englishman and his wife, only an Englishman on his own.

The students belonged to Rajpal's Punjabi folk dance group. I met them again a few years later one summer afternoon in an English market square. The square, more accustomed to the skipping and jangling of blacked-up Morris dancers, was where Rajpal and I had decided to hold a Punjabi mela as part of our school exchange programme. The rhythm of the bhangra, the beating of the drums, the stamping of the dancers' feet on the paving stones, the reds and yellows of the dancers' clothes, were like a throwback to the merrier England of legend. The statue of Clive of India that stands on one side of the square had its back turned to the dancers. Rajpal, drawing my attention to the bird droppings on the statue, wondered whether the pigeons were Indian.

It was a long and largely silent journey from Delhi to Chandigarh on what, as I learned later, had once been the Grand Trunk Road, taking travellers on horseback and on foot from Calcutta in the south to Lahore in the north, but now in the process of being turned into a dual carriageway. We travelled by bus. One of the students spoke a little English, the other none at all. Conversation was soon exhausted and, after my overnight flight from England, so was I. In spite of my wish not to miss anything, I fell asleep.

They woke me when the bus stopped at Panipat. Everyone got off to buy tea. One of the students, who spoke a little English, told me we were halfway to Chandigarh. We would be there in another three hours. The afternoon sun was invisible, though its light was everywhere. Everyone got back on the bus and I slept again until it stopped in Chandigarh. They left me on the pavement outside the bus station.

"Professor Rajpal will meet you here."

I stood against the railings, my suitcase by my side, and waited.

"Taxi? *Ho*tel?"

On the other side of the busy road were the faceless buildings of Chandigarh, whose misfortune it was to be built at a time when architects had turned their backs on brick and stone, blinded by the dazzling vision of a future that was concrete. On this side of the road, overhanging the broad pavement, was a tree. Soon the noise of roosting birds grew so loud as to drown out the sound of the traffic.

"*Ho*tel? Taxi?"

I looked at my watch, but all I could do was ignore the importuning of the rickshaw drivers, listen to the never-ending crescendo of the birds and wait. The rickshaw drivers circled like jackals, hovered like vultures. The ceaseless twittering of the birds was like tinnitus in my ears. After an hour of waiting, just before I caught sight of Rajpal running towards me with a bunch of gladioli in his hand and heard about the day's second misunderstanding, which had caused him to wait for me at one side of the bus station while I waited for him at the other, I suffered the same fate as the statue of Clive of India. I had learned already, in the space of a few hours, two of the lessons that Englishmen must learn if they are to survive in India: forget about time and don't stand under a tree at sunset.

The difference between Rajpal and me is not merely a question of punctuality, but something much more profound. It was well expressed by a British writer called Flora Annie Steel who lived in India when it was part of the Empire and wrote about it when she came back with her husband to live in Macchynlleth.

'India holds a secret which we of the West have forgotten, if we ever knew it,' she wrote. 'She knows that "Time is not money, Time is naught." There is, then, no occasion for hurry, we can take our time in India.'

The truth of her observation became evident to me during the course of the first week that I spent there. Rajpal drove me from one school and government office to another to discuss with school principals, civil servants and politicians our plans for a school exchange. The cumulative delay in keeping the appointments that he made for us each day reached levels that in England would have put an end to our hopes but, in India, made no difference. I started referring to Rajpal as 'the late Professor Rajpal Singh'. It got a laugh, but it might have been me they were laughing at. Nobody seemed to mind.

One evening we arrived at a school where the principal, with her entire staff and all their pupils, had been waiting for us for five hours. The pupils had stayed behind after school to present for us a carefully rehearsed performance of traditional Punjabi songs and dances. In spite of their long wait, they sang and danced with what looked like unfeigned enthusiasm. The principal showed us round her school in the gathering twilight, as if five hours were five minutes.

Having no watch of his own, Rajpal would often turn to me, at the end, say, of a long conversation with someone we had met by chance in Jalandhar or Ludhiana, and ask me the time.

"Oh my God!" he would exclaim and run to the car.

At the end of the week, when he gave me a parting gift of a book and I realised that I had nothing to give him in return, I took off my watch and gave him that. The next time we met, he told me that he had worn it for a few days, but had to take it off in the end because it was making him unhappy.

We found a school to host our exchange (not, I am ashamed to say, the one we had kept waiting for five hours) and went on to organise more exchanges with other schools. But that first week of long car journeys, from Chandigarh to Patiala, Patiala to Sangrur, Sangrur to Ludhiana, Ludhiana to Jalandhar, Jalandhar to Amritsar, stopping for food at roadside dhabas, getting later and later every day, making overnight stops with Rajpal's friends (he had friends without number and called them, collectively, 'the friends'), though it was almost literally a whirlwind tour of Punjab, conducted in a whirl of dust, leaving behind a blur of half-remembered people and places, is yet the one that stays most vividly in my memory.

My week of missed deadlines that nobody expected to be met in the first place taught me that getting along in India is like learning to swim. You just have to let go and trust the water to keep you afloat.

Our Air India flight was delayed by twelve hours. Some passengers had spent half a day waiting at Birmingham airport for the flight to Amritsar, but we were not among them. My mother, who believes in providence, was grateful for whatever impulse caused me to check the airport website before we left. The suitcases stayed in the hall and we picked up the threads of another day (a gift!) until, at dusk instead of dawn, the time came for us to leave for the airport. I sent a text message to Rajpal and put the kettle on.

"I woke up this morning with a feeling of joy," she said when we were drinking our tea. "That's the only word I can find for it."

She sipped her tea and shook her head in disbelief.

"You shouldn't feel like this at my age."

Last Saturday morning, when we went to the market, she told all the stallholders where she was going for her birthday.

"I'll be ninety next week and I'm going to India."

Incredulous, they looked to me for an explanation, thinking she must have succumbed at last to the confusions of old age. But when I told them it was true, they looked back at her open-mouthed.

The woman at the vegetable stall said, "I never get further than Aberystwyth on my birthday."

The market traders all know her. She used to do her shopping in the market three times a week. When her eyesight began to fail and she could no longer see well enough to give them the right money, she gave them her purse and told them to take it themselves. When the walk into town became too much for her, she caught the bus instead. When even that was beyond her, she stopped going altogether and relied on me for her shopping. The market traders probably thought she had died or gone into a home. Now she comes to the market with me every Saturday morning and everyone is pleased to see her again.

At Christmas, when we bought some chicken wings from the poultry man, he wouldn't take anything for them and slipped a few more into the bag. "She's been coming to me for years," he said. "Tell her it's my Christmas present."

At the airport, I steer the luggage trolley towards the check-in desk. She walks beside me, holding onto my arm. She walks as slowly as Modestine, the donkey Robert Louis Stevenson lost patience with in the Cévennes, but all the impatience is on her side. She apologises for slowing me down. Stevenson was in too much of a hurry, always grumbling about something. Like Mrs Steel, I have learned one thing from India, if nothing else. Time is naught.

At the check-in desk they are handing out food vouchers to pacify grumbling passengers. We take the lift to the departure lounge, where we exchange our vouchers at one of the cafés. Most of the other people here are Punjabis, either going to visit relatives in India or going home after visiting relatives in England. I pass the time by observing the different ways in which Sikhs manage their uncut hair. A middle-aged Sikh, dressed like an English businessman except for a dark blue turban, keeps his beard in place with a narrow strip of cloth, like a chin strap. Every now and then he twists the ends of his waxed moustache with his fingers. If it were not for the suit, he would look like a maharaja. If it were not for the turban, he would look like a vintage RAF officer.

I count five other varieties of beard: long, straggly ones, streaked with grey; luxuriant, black ones, covering the whole face apart from the eyes; long, wispy ones, combed to a point, like candy floss on a stick; short, stubbly ones, worn by young men in jeans and trainers; and a long, thin, grey one which looks as if it has been stuck on, like a false beard in the Secret Agent disguise sets that boys like me used to ask for at Christmas.

When we go through security, my mother's walking stick has to be put into the X-ray machine along with our jackets and hand luggage. I take her hand and lead her towards the barrier, but a uniformed woman steps forward briskly and waves me back. She crosses her arms, takes my mother's hands and, walking backwards, pulls her through the barrier. My mother looks bewildered, as if she is afraid she might be swung round in an impromptu highland reel. I follow them through, retrieve her walking stick from the conveyor belt and take her hand again.

We find seats near the gate for our flight and sit down to wait. We have been at the airport now for nearly three hours. Our plane, we have been told, is on its way from Canada and should be here soon. I imagine someone standing on the runway looking out for it, as you might if you were waiting for a bus. The arrival of airline staff near the gate causes the waiting crowd to coalesce into a queue. A desk appears, barriers are erected and, a few minutes later, an air hostess wearing a green sari welcomes us onto the plane. She leads us to our seats and, thinking at first that she must have made a mistake, I discover one of the unexpected benefits of travelling with an aged companion. We have been upgraded to business class.

As the night wears on, we transform ourselves into a cargo of sleeping bodies wrapped in thin, grey blankets, like school children in a dormitory or patients in a hospital ward or corpses in a mortuary, dreaming earth-bound dreams while our bodies fly over the mountains. Behind us is a man with a hacking cough. In front, the engines throb and hum. But our seats are as wide as single beds and we have more leg room than we know what to do with. Flying around the world, we meet the sun coming back the other way. The night was no more than a line in a story or a stage direction in a play.

Time passes. It is morning. Enter air hostess with trolley.

Life in the sky carries on where it left off. The air hostess pours our tea. My mother tells her she's going to India for her birthday.

"I'll be ninety," she says.

The air hostess says she hopes she will put on Indian attire for the occasion and moves on to pour tea for someone else. Below us are the mountains of Afghanistan, ridged like the backs of emaciated cattle, creased like old leather. When the sun rose over Baghdad, we were still asleep. The captain announces that he is beginning his descent and soon, far below us, we see the villages of Punjab scattered across the plain, like knots in a skein of brown rope.

I help my mother down the steps onto the tarmac. The air is warm and meets us coming out of the plane like a cat rubbing against our legs. A little man in uniform runs up the steps to ask if we need a wheelchair and looks disappointed when his offer is refused. We climb onto the bus with the other passengers for the short drive across the tarmac to the terminal building.

We stand in line with our passports but before long we are singled out for preferential treatment by another little man who waves us forward to the front of the queue. The other passengers make way for us and urge us to go past, whether out of deference to my mother's age or respect for little men in uniform it is impossible to tell.

After we have passed through immigration, where the coincidence of my sharing a birthday with modern India is noticed by the officer who checks my passport, I find somewhere for my mother to sit and then join the crowd of people waiting to collect their luggage. There is only one carousel and the crowd around it is already three deep. I stand at the back. After a few minutes, the first case appears, followed a minute later by two more. We watch them going round and round, but no one claims them. Slowly, sporadically, more cases emerge through the flap to join the others on the moving belt. The crowd presses forward. The men waiting for their luggage look like hunters on a riverbank, spearing fish and throwing them over their shoulders. Their wives and children stand behind them ready to catch. The reason there are so many people here is that whole families are waiting to collect their luggage, mother, father, grandmother, children, all standing together. Recalling previous visits, I imagine each family driving home on a scooter, clinging to their luggage and each other, like a troupe of acrobats performing their act in the circus ring. The flow of luggage slows to a trickle. The crowd waits patiently. I am dismayed by an announcement advising passengers whose luggage is missing that it will arrive on the next flight and can be collected tomorrow morning. But no one seems to take any notice and a few minutes later more suitcases begin to appear. One family after another turns and walks towards the exit, pushing trolleys piled high with luggage. In the shoal of suitcases which is now tumbling out through the hatch, I see ours and watch with relief as they float towards me. I reach out to catch them, swing them onto my trolley and wheel it back towards my mother, who is waiting patiently where I left her half-an-hour ago.

The delayed flight means that Rajpal has been able to enjoy a good night's sleep instead of getting up in the middle of the night to meet us. To us it feels like early morning but it is already afternoon when he embraces me and stoops to touch my mother's feet. We follow him through the crowds and, sitting on our suitcases, wait outside the terminal for him to fetch his car. The air is warm. The sunlight is thickened by dust. The sky looks pale and far away. Between the airport buildings, beyond some trees, we glimpse the traffic on the road to the city. We sit and wait, neither of us speaking, and I wonder whether this is what she was expecting. Perhaps, after all, a few days in Aberystwyth would have been more sensible. Rajpal returns and, with a growing sense of apprehension, I take my mother's hand and lead her to the car.

We drive past fields green with wheat and yellow with mustard, past women carrying bundles of sugar cane on their heads, past men driving tractors or riding on carts. Before long, tractors and carts are joined by scooters, bicycles, hand carts, cycle rickshaws, motor rickshaws, buses, cars, lorries and pedestrians, all mixed together like the animals in the ark, every beast after his kind, and all the cattle after their kind, and every creeping thing that creepeth upon the earth after his kind, and every fowl after his kind, every bird of every sort. Along the side of the road are men selling goods of every sort from the backs of carts and the open fronts of shops in flat-roofed buildings like doll's houses. There are no pavements to divide them from the road, which flows and sometimes overflows like a river. I point things out to my mother, who has still not spoken, and wonder again if I have made a terrible mistake. Dust and chaos, cows ambling through over-crowded city streets. Lawrence Street, Amritsar. Rajpal slows down and points to our hotel.

"We're nearly there," I tell her. "Are you feeling alright?"

She keeps me waiting for her answer, staring out of the window at a street scene which, though I have seen it before, still looks strange. If it looks strange to me, what must it look like to her?

"I can't believe I'm here," she says, at last, in a voice more expressive of wonder than anything else. "It doesn't seem possible."

At the hotel, Rajpal leaves us in our room to wash and change. It is a large room on the third floor with two single beds at one end, a table and chairs at the other. She chooses the bed nearest the bathroom and says she hopes I don't mind sharing a bedroom with her. I sit on the edge of my bed, which is hard, like all beds in India, and think of the Whitehall farces I used to watch on television when I was a boy. I picture Brian Rix with his trousers round his ankles as the curtain comes down. Bedrooms have always been good places for

Englishmen to make fools of themselves.

Solitude is out of the question in India, another thing like time and the heat that makes an Englishman feel uncomfortable. I remember one of the English girls on an exchange visit telling me that the family she was staying with had gathered round her bed on her first night to make sure she went to sleep. Even the sadhus, the holy men, spend their lives wandering from town to town instead of hiding away like hermits. They attend their own funerals in symbolic rejection of material existence and travel free on the trains.

In Punjab, every day is a series of social encounters, with friends and strangers alike, and each encounter is an excuse to eat and drink. Almost wherever you go, someone appears at your elbow with a glass of water on a tray. In someone's house an invitation to sit down is followed by the appearance of a daughter or wife or servant bearing bowls of nuts or sweets. Depending on the time of day, tea may be offered or Coke or, in the evening, a glass of beer or Indian whisky. Half-an-hour later, someone brings you a plate of samosas. Whenever you empty your glass or finish the food on your plate, someone offers you more. You refuse, they look hurt, you relent and everyone is happy again.

Just as you are about to leave, your host's wife and daughters emerge from the kitchen, where they have been since your arrival, and he leads you to the table, where the women serve you the meal they have spent the last two hours preparing. Refusal is out of the question, even though you have already eaten more than you usually do all day, and in any case the food is delicious and you are pleasantly surprised by how much you can manage to eat. The women serve the food but do not sit at the table with you and this is something else that you get used to and learn to expect.

Rajpal joins us again and asks us if we are hungry. After some discussion, he calls room service and orders chicken tikka and cold beer for him and me, buttered toast and separate tea for my mother. Indian tea is made by brewing all the ingredients together in one pot for a long time. Separate tea means providing the ingredients separately, cup, spoon, tea bag, hot water, hot milk, sugar lumps, so you can make it yourself.

When the waiter comes, he brings separate tea, toast and chicken tikka, but no beer. Rajpal reminds him about the beer and he explains that the hotel has no licence. They have sent someone out for it. I make my mother's tea and spread the white Punjabi butter on her toast. We have just started to eat when the waiter returns with two bottles of Kingfisher.

When we have finished eating, Rajpal says he has arranged to meet a friend and suggests that we should join them in the hotel lobby when we have rested. After he has gone, I have a shower, leaving my mother to sit by the window looking out over the rooftops as the afternoon light starts to fade. The sun goes down slowly in England, dying like the embers of a fire that still burns in some dark corner of the sky. Here it drops like a stone. There is nothing between day and night but half-an-hour of twilight when the trees are full of quarrelling birds and the light drains from the plain as if someone has pulled out the plug.

Refreshed by my shower, I turn on the light and draw the curtains. We sit together for half-an-hour talking about the flight, the roads, the hotel. It is as if she is writing her diary, the story so far.

"If you hadn't found out about the plane being delayed, we might have spent the whole day at the airport. We'd have been there in the morning if you hadn't thought to look on that thing in your room. Some people must have been waiting there all day."

She looks up and points, in a familiar gesture, towards the place where she imagines her guardian angel to be.

"Someone's looking after us," she says.

I imagine the guardian angel arranging food vouchers here, upgrades there, generally keeping an eye on things.

"I still have that feeling of joy," she says. "I've had it ever since we left. When was that?"

"Yesterday morning."

She shakes her head in disbelief.

"I still can't believe I'm here."

Amritsar is famous for three things. Street food, the Golden Temple and the massacre at Jallianwala Bagh. A bagh is a garden and this is the one where, in April 1909, Brigadier-General Reginald Dyer ordered his men to shoot on a crowd of demonstrators. There was no way out. People climbed the walls to try to escape. Others jumped into a well. Hundreds were killed. Dyer said he had been obliged to teach a moral lesson to the Punjab.

"I think it quite possible that I could have dispersed the crowd without firing," he said, "but they would have come back again and laughed, and I would have made, what I consider, a fool of myself."

Thirty years later, at Caxton Hall in London, an Indian called Udham Singh shot dead Sir Michael O'Dwyer, who had been Lieutenant-Governor of the Punjab at the time of the massacre. Reginald Dyer had already died a peaceful death at his home in England. A report in The Times described it as 'an expression of the pent-up fury of the down-trodden Indian people'.

Udham Singh said, "He deserved it. He wanted to crush the spirit of my people, so I have crushed him."

He pleaded guilty and was hanged for murder.

Rajpal took me once to a Punjabi village, where I was made guest of honour at the village games. In the middle of the day, we sat in the shade and drank lassi from steel cups and ate saag and makki di roti, the former a dark green stew of mustard leaves served with white butter, the latter thick yellow chapattis. In the afternoon I sat as guest of honour on an armchair at the edge of a field and watched the bullock cart races. It seemed to me that the whole village was there but Rajpal told me later that one old man was missing. He had been a freedom fighter in the years before Independence and felt it an affront to his national pride to see an Englishman handing out the prizes at the village games. He had threatened violence. His friends thought it would be safer for all of us if he stayed at home.

If the assassination of Sir Michael O'Dwyer had taken place today, would it have been reported as sympathetically by The Times as it was then? The words of Gerry Adams on the assassination of Lord Mountbatten in 1979 seem to echo those of Udam Singh.

'The IRA gave clear reasons for the execution. I think it is unfortunate that anyone has to be killed, but the furore created by Mountbatten's death showed up the hypocritical attitude of the media establishment. As a member of the House of Lords, Mountbatten was an emotional figure in both British and Irish politics. What the IRA did to him is what Mountbatten had been doing all his life to other people; and with his war record I don't think he could have objected to dying in what was clearly a war situation. He knew the danger involved in coming to this country. In my opinion, the IRA achieved its objective: people started paying attention to what was happening in Ireland.'

How would my death at the village games have been reported?

'The former freedom fighter is reported as saying, "He was an Englishman. He should have known better than to hand out the prizes at the bullock cart races in a Punjabi village. He deserved it." What he did was an expression of the lingering resentment of a once downtrodden people.'

An Englishman cannot go far in India without being reminded who he is and where he comes from. Two hundred years of British rule left an indelible mark. It is most obvious in the cantonments that look like Cotswold villages transported to the foothills of the Himalayas, but it is everywhere, in place names and street names, churches and graveyards. Montgomery in Pakistan, Lawrence Road in Amritsar, the Gaiety Theatre in Simla. In Mussourie, the town in the hills where Rajpal went to college, there is a chapel that bears the same name as the one where my father was Sunday School Superintendent. Central Methodist Church, Mussourie. I took a photograph of it and brought it home to show to my mother.

I once visited the school in Sanawar where, in Kipling's novel, they sent Kim to make a man of him. It was founded by Sir Henry Lawrence in 1847 and, apart from its location in the foothills of the Himalayas and the red roofs of its buildings, looks very much like the English public school that I went to. Mine was a boys' school near Bradford and only later began admitting girls, but Sanawar was co-educational from the start, reputedly the first co-educational boarding school in the world. It was originally called the Lawrence Military Asylum, providing education for the sons and daughters of soldiers in the British and Indian armies. In those days perhaps it made men of the girls too, but not anymore. The girls I met during my visit told me they were scared of the monkeys.

Lawrence was killed at Lucknow in 1857. He was the British Commissioner resident in the city when it came under siege soon after the mutiny of Indian troops at Meerut and was one of the first casualties. We still call it the Indian Mutiny, but they call it the first war of Independence. Sir Henry Lawrence was there at the start, Lord Mountbatten at the end.

We find Rajpal in the hotel lobby, talking to a woman in a dark blue sari. He introduces her as Manisha and she puts her hands together in the traditional greeting. My mother hooks her walking stick over her arm so that she can do the same. She looks closely at Manisha for a few seconds and then says, "You're very pretty." She speaks with the licence of old age, as if she is simply stating a fact. Manisha is flattered. She invites us to her house to meet her family and we head for the lift.

I remember going to Leeds with my parents in 1958 to buy my school uniform from a shop with an old-fashioned lift operated by a man with a withered arm. I think of him when I read Hardy's story of the same name. The lift had an outer door and an inner door which the man opened and closed with a clang and a thud. The hotel in Amritsar has a modern lift. The lift shaft has a glass wall, so that we can see the street outside on our way down. We could operate the lift ourselves, but the hotel pays someone to do it. Perhaps it makes economic sense here to employ two people for every job that needs doing and one for every job that doesn't. It used to be like that in England. My mother remembers being told about a woman who came to the farm looking for a job for her son.

"I don't want you to pay him, maister," she said. "Just give him his meals."

We drive through the busy night-time streets of Amritsar to Manisha's house. There is something about the drive through the city that reminds me of riding on a ghost train. Perhaps it is the way we look out of the windows at a succession of unreal images, or the way we move through darkness into light and back again, or the way the car stops and starts without warning on its erratic journey through the city streets. We get out, not in a fairground, but in a quiet street of flat roofed houses behind high walls, each with a gate as high as the walls.

Manisha's house, though modern, is built in the traditional style and is unlike any house my mother has seen before. First there is the gate. It is not a garden gate for children to swing on, but a grown up gate, a gate descended from the gates of palaces, a gate which swings open as if by magic. India is full of gates. Every suburban family in India has a gate like this, with a servant to open and close it.

An English gate opens onto a garden, an Indian gate onto a courtyard. Sometimes there is a tree in the courtyard, sometimes plants growing in pots, always somewhere to sit, either a charpoi or, more often, plastic chairs. Manisha leads the way and waits for us at the door. My mother follows slowly, not wanting to miss anything, stopping to look at everything. With only one good eye, she has to get close to things to see what they are. Sometimes she puts her hands around her eyes like a frame to help her see more clearly. It reminds me of the way photographers used to disappear under a black cloth behind the tripod. Looking, like most other things in old age, is laborious. When I point something out to her, I have to wait until she locates it, turning her head from side to side.

"I've got it!" she says at last, as if she had lost something precious and has found it again.

She takes her time, determined not to miss anything, and we wait patiently for her, while we enjoy the cool night air. When she is ready, I take her hand again and we walk through the door into a room which, like the courtyard outside, can trace its lineage back to the maharaja's palace. The room is not like a room in an English house. If you knocked down the wall between your hall and your living room, you would be closer to it, though still some way off. This is the inner courtyard of the suburban palace, an open space with a marble floor and chairs ranged along the walls where family and guests can sit and talk. There are doors that lead to other rooms and a staircase that leads to a balcony with more doors, but there are no corridors.

At the top of the stairs is a little shrine with a statue and the remains of the morning puja, a bowl, a brass lamp, some petals, a snuffed out candle. Doing Latin at school I learned about the household gods of ancient Rome, the *lares*. Every home had its own god and a shrine to the genius loci. Shrines in English churches disappeared after the break with Rome in 1536. In any case, my parents were Methodists and sent me to a Methodist school, founded originally for the sons of Methodist ministers. (Rudyard Kipling's father, John Lockwood Kipling, one of the first pupils, nearly died there in an outbreak of food poisoning. If he had, there would have been no 'If'.) Shrines of any kind were outside my experience until I visited India.

Manisha invites my mother to sit, but she prefers to go exploring and sets off in the other direction. She looks like a picture in a story-book, an inquisitive little mouse with a walking stick, head thrust forward, nose twitching, whiskers bristling, curious and eager. We stand and watch until she has satisfied her curiosity.

We are joined by Manisha's daughters and, for a little while, it is they who are the centre of attention. One is twelve, the other ten and both are the kind of children you would be more likely to meet in Victorian literature than in real life. Neither speaks until she is spoken to. Modest and self-composed, they stand by their mother's side while she speaks for them. The younger one is sporty, the older one artistic. Manisha points proudly to a display of trophies on a shelf and sends the older girl for her sketchbook. My mother, who sometimes finds children irritating, especially the noisy English kind, is charmed by these Indian girls. We look through the sketchbook while its owner looks on with a detachment beyond her years, as if none of this has anything to do with her.

When we have finished with the sketchbook, the girls take us to see their baby brother. I take my mother's hand and we follow the girls across the room, through a door into another room with a double bed, which looks as if it has not been made since it was slept in last night. One of the girls lifts a corner of the rumpled sheet to reveal the sleeping baby. I bring my mother closer to the bed and, not knowing what she is supposed to be looking at, she moves her head this way and that until, suddenly, she sees it. She could not have been more astonished if the baby had appeared by magic.

"Oh!" she gasps, her face breaking into a delighted smile. "It's a baby!"

A little later, Manisha's brother-in-law comes home from work. He greets us and then goes upstairs to his room. The household consists of Manisha, her husband, his brother, their parents and the three children. Eight people, three generations, one house. As common in India as it is rare now in England. The family eats together every day. They snatch food in ones and twos and threes at various times between getting up in the morning and coming home in the evening, but every night they sit down together for the main meal of the day and when they do, Manisha says, she and her daughters prefer to eat from the same *thali* or tray, from which the three of them help themselves. I wonder whether they sit separately from the men, the father and his two sons, and think again about Manisha's elder daughter and that air of quiet detachment which she carries with her, a preparation perhaps for life as an Indian woman.

We say goodbye to Manisha and her daughters. When we go out of the gate, I point out to my mother a lemon tree growing by the side of the road. The pale fruit is half hidden behind long, dark leaves.

On the way back, we stop for a walk in Ram Bagh, a garden in the grounds of what was once the summer palace of Maharaja Ranjit Singh, *Sher-e-Punjab*, Lion of the Punjab. When the East India Company took control of the Punjab after the Sikh wars that followed Ranjit's death in 1839, they gave Ram Bagh a new name, Company Garden, but now it's called Ram Bagh again.

Ranjit Singh's story bears comparison with that of better known conquerors. Alexander the Great, for example. Alexander was sixteen when he inherited his father's kingdom. Ranjit was only twelve. Alexander was twenty-one when he conquered the Greeks. Ranjit conquered Lahore when he was nineteen. Alexander was twenty-three when he conquered the Persians. Ranjit conquered Amritsar when he was twenty-two. Alexander founded lots of new cities and called them all Alexandria. Ranjit created a Sikh army to defend the Punjab so that Muslims, Hindus and Sikhs could live together peacefully. Alexander was taught by Aristotle. Ranjit was illiterate. Both were superb horsemen, both were short. At a little over five feet, Ranjit was the taller.

The British did a deal with Ranjit Singh. He got the Punjab, they got everything else. They met at Amritsar in 1809 and signed a treaty which lasted until Ranjit's death. Their patience rewarded, the British took over. After the first Sikh war, another treaty was signed at Amritsar. The British got Kashmir and the Koh-i-Noor diamond. After the second, they got the lot.

Ranjit Singh's descendants led sad lives. His son, Duleep Singh, was the last Maharaja of Punjab and the first Black Prince of Perthshire. Ranjit having gained his kingdom when he was twelve, Duleep lost it when he was eleven. The East India Company took away his empire and made an Englishman of him. He converted to Christianity when he was fifteen and went to live in England. They put him up at Claridges, then gave him a house in Wimbledon, a castle in Scotland and an estate in Norfolk. Queen Victoria doted on him and he lived the life of a playboy. He died in Paris and wanted to be buried in the Punjab but the British thought that would be unwise, so they buried him beside his wife and son in the graveyard at Elveden

Church in Suffolk.

His mother, the Maharani, was put in prison after the war but managed to escape, disguised as a maid. She left a note for the British saying, 'You put me in the cage and locked me up. For all your locks and your sentries, I got out by magic.' The British confiscated her jewellery and cancelled her pension. Perhaps they thought she had made fools of them. She lived in Kathmandu until her son brought her to England, where she died.

Duleep Singh had eight children, six by his first wife and two by his second. Frederick was an archaeologist, Victor was a gambler, Edward died when he was thirteen, Sophia was a suffragette, Catherine enjoyed a long-standing relationship with her German governess, Pauline was illegitimate, Irene committed suicide and Bamba went mad. None of them had any children.

The trees Ranjit Singh planted in his garden two hundred years ago are still there today, but it is dark tonight and we can't see them. We climb into the car and Rajpal drives us back to the hotel.

My mother and I are both awake at two o'clock in the morning. I hear her get up to go to the bathroom. When she is back in bed, I get up and drink a glass of water. We exchange a few words, then close our eyes and try to sleep, but it still feels as if it is too early to go to bed. It may be two o'clock in the morning here, but in England it's half-past-eight yesterday evening. On the other hand, it's nearly two days since we had a good night's sleep.

I imagine the planets and their moons like gears in a complicated machine, all turning in different directions at different speeds. We only have ourselves to blame for trying to beat the machine and getting ahead of ourselves. The only thing to do now is to stay in one place until we meet the earth coming round again. I lie on my back with my eyes closed and wait while the earth slowly turns.

Morning times its arrival perfectly. When I open my eyes, my mother's bed is empty and I can hear her in the bathroom. Someone has slipped a copy of The Times of India under the door and, a little later, someone brings tea. Early morning tea in India is known by its colonial name, bed tea. Feeling rested and refreshed, we sit on the armchairs to drink it and look out of the window. Our room is at the back of the hotel and has a rather desolate view over the flat roofs of apartment blocks and offices. The sun is shining through the dust and two workmen sit talking on the roof of a building a hundred yards away. They are the only people we can see. But even these ordinary sights are astonishing to my mother, because they are sights seen in India.

"I never thought I'd make it," she says again.

I sit with the newspaper on my knee and my mother talks about the things that happened yesterday, bringing her diary up to date. She talks about the things we saw on the way to Amritsar, the scooters, the bicycles, the rickshaws, the people, the shops by the roadside. Then she talks about our visit to Manisha's house, the two girls, the baby on the bed, the lemon tree growing outside. She asks me questions to make sure that she remembers everything properly and understands who everyone was.

"I didn't know you were taking me to see a baby," she says, remembering how surprised she was when she saw it.

Leaving her to her thoughts, I turn back to the paper and read about the state elections which are due to take place all over India in a few weeks. Someone has been shot and killed at an election rally in a town called Beas, not far from Amritsar. One of the candidates is implicated and someone has a video of his brother carrying a gun, but the police don't seem to be doing much about it. Other stories are all about the activities of Cong and SAD. Cong is short for Congress, which is the party in power in Punjab. SAD stands for Shiromani Akali Dhal, the party in opposition. There is also an article about something called fake encounters, but I have no time to find out what this means before Rajpal arrives to take us out for breakfast.

We drive a short distance from the hotel, turn down a side road and stop outside a café which is reputed to sell the best kulcha in Amritsar. Punjabis generally eat dahi and paratha for breakfast. Dahi, which is served with every meal, is curd. Freshly made from buffalo milk, a bowl of dahi is smooth and shiny, like white linen falling in folds. The curds have a slightly sour taste which is cool and refreshing. A paratha is a kind of flat bread, fried and served with white butter. I have eaten paratha for breakfast every day on previous visits, sometimes plain, sometimes made with flour and potato mixed with spices, in which form it is called alu paratha, but I have never tasted kulcha or even heard of it.

I help my mother out of the car, over the rough ground at the side of the road and up the steps into the café where, at the other end of the long room near the counter, two or three groups of people are sitting at plain wooden tables. They look round curiously when we come in and, when they see my mother, they smile and point her out to each other. We sit down at an empty table and a waiter quickly steps out from behind the counter to take our order.

When breakfast is served, my mother refuses the dahi, which looks to her like milk that has started to go off. She pulls a face and shakes her head. But she agrees to try the kulcha, which is reassuringly solid and looks as if it has been properly cooked instead of just being left to its own devices. She eats a little and leaves the rest.

After breakfast, we set off for the long drive to Chandigarh. I sit in the back with my mother to keep her company and, as we drive through the streets of Amritsar, we look out of the windows at the colour and confusion which surround us. I remember the story Rajpal told me about a Chinese politician who, when he got back home after a visit to India, told his Maoist colleagues that he now believed in God.

"If God did not exist," he said, "how could anything in India ever get done?"

The roads in India bear a superficial resemblance to the roads in England. There are roundabouts and traffic lights, cars drive on the left, there are policemen at crossroads. But it soon becomes clear that these features are purely symbolic and have no practical application. Roundabouts and traffic lights are treated as inconvenient obstacles, cars drive on the left sometimes, policemen stand at crossroads just to keep a general eye on things, they don't actually do anything.

On Indian roads, size matters. The only rule is to give way to anything bigger than you. The hierarchy starts with lorries and descends through buses, cars, tractors, auto-rickshaws, scooters, bicycles, horse carts, donkey carts, bullock carts, bicycle rickshaws, hand carts, cows, women carrying bundles of sugar cane on their heads and other miscellaneous pedestrians. There are further subdivisions based, for example, on the number of passengers (anything from one to four on a scooter) or size of load relative to size of vehicle (huge sacks of cotton on the backs of lorries bulge out over the road like an

Englishman's beer belly, bamboo poles turn a rickshaw into Boadicea's chariot). There are wild cards too, such as elephants or camels.

The use of the horn is obligatory, not to vent your frustration, as in European cities, but simply to let people know you are there. Every lorry carries three legends written in florid script on its tailgate: Use Dipper at Night, Horn Please, Wait for Side. The latter simply means that you should not try to overtake until the driver has pulled over to make room for you, which he will do eventually if you blow your horn long enough and keep blowing it until you are safely past.

The noise of the horns is like an orchestra condemned always to be tuning up and never actually playing anything. The notes vary from the trombones and euphoniums of the buses and lorries to the flutes and piccolos of the scooters and auto-rickshaws. Only motor vehicles have horns. Drivers of carts and pedal vehicles just have to listen and keep their wits about them. Cycle rickshaw drivers are constantly looking over their shoulders.

As we negotiate another roundabout, at which nobody gives way to traffic coming from the right, I wonder whether there are any rules at all and, if there are, whether anybody obeys them. But as I watch the cars and scooters and rickshaws nudging their way onto the roundabout, I realise suddenly that there *are* rules and that *everyone* is obeying them. They are not the rules of the road, they are the rules of the pavement. On Indian roads, drivers behave like pedestrians. If the vehicle in front is going slowly, you go past it. It doesn't matter which side you pass it on, so long as you don't bump into it. If someone stops, you go round them. If you come to a junction, you don't stop and wait, you just slow down. Driving down Lawrence Road in Amritsar is like walking down Oxford Street in London.

This insight transforms apparent chaos into a beautifully choreographed dance, in which the bicycles, scooters and rickshaws are the corps de ballet, the cars are the principal dancers and the buses and lorries are the prima ballerinas. They weave their way in and out, twisting and turning, going fast, going slow, graceful and skilful. Even the noise of the horns begins to sound like Stravinsky.

The long road from Amritsar to Chandigarh takes us past green and yellow fields that disappear into a haze of dusty sunlight. The fields are crossed by the faint lines of hidden ditches and sometimes by the bolder line of a canal reflecting the blue of the sky. There are houses shaped like boxes set back from the road behind brick walls, with hens scratching in the dust outside and goats standing clumsily on two feet, stretching their long, sinewy necks into the branches of the trees. Beside the road, pale brown cow pats are stacked in rows to dry in the sun, making patterns so intricate and varied, so pleasing to the eye, as to turn these stacks of dung, dried for burning, into works of art. A woman squats in the sun, a shawl covering her head, tossing a cow pat between her hands to shape it before adding it to the stack.

We drive through small towns, on roads lined with flat-roofed, open-fronted shops and carts piled high with fruit and vegetables that glisten in the sun like smears of paint on an artist's palette. Every few miles, between the towns, a square chimney marks the site of a brickworks, with a track leading from the road to the brickyard and a huddle of buildings round the chimney. We stop to watch some men making sugar by the side of the road. One of them is working the machine to crush the sugar cane, another is standing beside a trough of boiling syrup, stirring it with a wooden pole. They watch us watching them over the slabs of dark brown jaggery laid out to dry in the sun. In England it was water that drove the manufacturing processes, the mills, the tanneries, the breweries. Here it is the sun.

My mother sits beside me in the back of the car and we talk about the things we see. She remembers when there were fewer cars in England and drivers blew their horns to warn people they were coming.

"You always used to blow your horn when you came to a roundabout," she says.

The little brickworks out in the country remind her of the soap works beside the beck in the village where I grew up. The patchwork of fields and ditches remind her how fields used to look when she was a girl.

"I feel as if I've been here before," she says.

A few minutes later, I feel her hand squeezing my arm and look round. She is sobbing.

"Thank you," she says. "Thank you so much."

When I was five, my older sister died. She was eleven, in her first year at grammar school. The pain she had been experiencing, diagnosed by the family doctor as ear ache, got worse and he called in a specialist. She was lying in bed at home the last time I saw her. My father took me into her bedroom to say goodnight before I went to bed. He must have known that it might be the last time I would see her. All she did when I went in was to put her arm across her face and turn away. The next day, the specialist operated on her brain but the operation was not a success. My father must have gone with her in the ambulance, leaving my mother at home with me. We had no telephone, so she must have had to wait for him to come home before she knew that my sister had died. One of them must have told me. I remember hearing my father say that the bus conductor had let him stand on the platform, away from the other passengers, because he couldn't stop crying.

The other thing I remember clearly is, at bedtime, saying to my father that we would have to try to forget her. I must have been trying to puzzle things out for myself and that was the conclusion I had come to. My father said no, we should try to remember her. We did, of course, but we never spoke about her. I did not go to the funeral. Perhaps it took place on a school day and they decided it would be better if I went to school as usual. My sister's death was like a guilty secret that nobody ever mentioned. I felt unable to talk about her because nobody else did. My parents kept their grief to themselves. My mother blamed herself but never talked about it. She kept her feelings to herself and for a long time she never left the house.

It was a year or two after our visit to India that she broke her silence. It was St Patrick's Day and she told me that was the day Heather died. She mentioned it almost in passing and I was surprised. Even to hear her use my sister's name was unusual. A minute later, I saw her mouth trembling and she began to sob. I put my arm around her and sat beside her, saying nothing. I wanted to sob too, never having been able to share with her my own grief, but more than anything I felt happy that she was now able to do so. When she had recovered her composure a little, she began to speak.

"It was so sad for a little girl to have to die when she was still growing up."

The tears were now running down both our cheeks, like a dried up spring starting to flow again after years of drought.

"I'm alright now," she said. "Don't worry about me."

My father missed the first few years of Heather's life. He got his call-up papers early, she was four when he was demobbed. I have his old bellows camera and a box of glass plates wrapped in war time newspapers. Most of them are photographs of Heather. They are what my father, a printer by trade, called negs. One day, I will ask someone to make prints from them, so that I can see them properly. She was a chubby little girl with rosy cheeks, but you have to work that out for yourself from the black and white negative.

My father was a chubby little man with rosy cheeks when he died of a heart attack at the age of sixty-one, but in one of the glass plates, cigarette in hand, dressed in army uniform, he looks thin and rather suave, in the Fred Astaire mould. I remember him as being always light-hearted, but that changed towards the end of his life. When I was seven or eight, he started his own business, renting premises in the village where we lived at what had once been the Liberal Club. There was a billiard table upstairs. The business did well to begin with and he moved to larger premises in Leeds. But within ten years, the business was losing money and he had to sell up and go back to working for somebody else.

He was never a business man. The business had the same effect on him as my watch had on Rajpal. He should have been an artist. He had a talent for drawing and, when he left school at fourteen to be apprenticed to a printer, attended evening classes in Leeds. The headmaster of his elementary school had tried to persuade his mother and step-father (his father was killed in the war) to let him arrange an apprenticeship for him with a commercial artist, but there was a family connection of some kind with the printing firm and in any case printing was a good trade. When work was slack at the printers, they made use of his artistic talent by giving him sheet music covers to design. We had some in the piano stool at home, but they have been lost or thrown away since he died. He was a pianist too and played the organ in chapel.

He had, according to my mother, a very simple faith. Talking now more often about Heather, she told me that, after she died, he said she would not be lonely in heaven because her grandmother was already there. Towards the end of his life, she said, his faith began to waver.

By then, he had suffered two strokes. All this was happening when I was too preoccupied with my own life to take much notice of his. I had been to Cambridge, got a job a hundred miles away teaching English at a grammar school, had some stories published, got married. It never occurred to me that he might have needed help or that I might have been able to offer it.

On Friday 13 December 1974, I was asked to go to the school office to return a telephone call. When I did, I was put through to a doctor who told me that my father had died of a heart attack. I never saw him cry or listened to him as, in the last few months, I have been able to listen to my mother. One day, she told me that she had dreamed about him the night before. In her dream, he had come to her, with tears streaming down his face, to say that he couldn't work anymore. At first, I thought it was just a dream, but then I realised that she had been dreaming about something that had really happened.

She talks sometimes about lives wasted, blighted, meaning not just theirs but the lives of ordinary people growing up in England in the early years of the twentieth century. How different their lives would have been, she says, growing up now.

"Excuse me, sir, may I click your photo?" asks a young woman outside the restaurant near Jalandhar where we stop for lunch. She is very pleased when I say yes and even more pleased when Rajpal offers to take a photograph of her standing between my mother and me. We all smile for the camera.

"You're such a beautiful couple," she says.

By now a crowd has gathered, among them an excited group of schoolgirls, all eager to get a closer look.

"Hello!" say the bolder ones, coming to the front, while the shy ones hide at the back and peep out.

They are like children in England playing 'What time is it, Mr Wolf?' But my mother doesn't scare the children away with a shout of 'Dinner time!' when they get too close. She's having far too much fun being the centre of attention.

"Hello!" she says.

"Hello!" chorus the girls, excitedly.

Now that the ice is broken, they ask us our names and tell us theirs. But all they really want to do is look at her. Perhaps she looks to them, as she sometimes does to me, like a picture in a storybook. So when their teacher arrives with a camera, they all want to be in the picture. Once again, we smile for the camera and, when the picture is taken, their teacher thanks us and leads them away. But they keep sneaking back for another look. We walk for a while in the grounds of the restaurant before we go in for our lunch and, whenever we see them, they wave and giggle and run away again.

The grounds are set out like a Punjabi village and there are people demonstrating traditional crafts outside some of the houses. We watch a potter making pots on a wheel which he spins with his hand and a weaver making a carpet with home spun thread which he twists together with his fingers. Two boys put on a puppet show and a conjuror makes coins drop from our noses and doves appear from nowhere. A waxwork bride sits in a doli, its poles resting on the shoulders of four waxwork men. It is all for the benefit of Indian tourists, nostalgic for the villages their grandparents grew up in. On our way into the restaurant, an elderly Punjabi coming out stops to talk.

"I come from Wolverhampton," he says, shaking my hand.

Jalandhar is about halfway between Amritsar and Chandigarh. The second part of our journey is quicker than the first, on the dual carriageway that used to be the Grand Trunk Road. For Kipling, it was 'such a river of life as nowhere else exists in the world'. It used to be the Great Road, *Sadak-e-Azam*, and once went as far as Kabul. The East India Company took it over and called it the Grand Trunk Road. It was fifteen hundred miles long in Kipling's day. It was sometimes called the Long Walk. Now they call it the GT Road, pronounced 'Jeety'.

The Long Walk is a short drive which brings us soon to the outskirts of Chandigarh, a city built for modern times. *WELCOME TO CITY BEAUTIFUL!* say the signs on the broad, tree-lined road, beside which migrant workers from Uttar Pradesh and Bihar have pitched their tents. Chandigarh was Nehru's dream after the nightmare of Partition, which left the Punjab without a capital. The beautiful city of Lahore was now in Pakistan. Amritsar, Ludhiana, Jalandhar, Patiala and Ambala were beautiful too, with temples and forts and palaces, but none of them could take the place of Lahore. What was needed, Nehru said, was something new, a city 'unfettered by the traditions of the past', a city that would be 'a symbol of the nation's faith in the future'. Three architects were employed to build it, Albert Mayer from America, Matthew Nowicki from Poland and Le Corbusier from Switzerland.

Chandigarh, like Milton Keynes, was built for the motor car. It has long, straight roads and a solar system of roundabouts. It has shopping centres with car parks, offices with car parks, government buildings with car parks, parks with car parks. It has a university and a man-made lake. The Shivaliks, the foothills of the Himalayas, are within easy driving distance. Chandigarh was planned on paper and built with concrete. The original city plan was divided into forty-seven sectors, but no one wanted to live in Sector 13, so it was re-named Sector 48.

The architects forgot to make room for the migrant workers, who build their shanty towns now on the pencil lines between the sectors. The city authorities offer them land and lend them money to build proper houses, but the people from Bihar and Uttar Pradesh (UP, pronounced Youpi) don't want it. How can people like them live in Chandigarh, among the office workers and the civil servants, the teachers and the university lecturers, people on government pensions, people who can read and write? So they go on living on the rough land beside the roads, doing the jobs educated people don't want to do, and take their wages with them when they go back home. The workers are invisible, the tents they live in a smudge on the architect's drawing.

When we first met, Rajpal lived with wife and son in an old house in Patiala. Now they live in a new house in Chandigarh (Sector 48). Kuldip and Gorky are waiting to greet us. My mother met them when they came to England for a dance festival. Gorky was a little boy then. Now he's a student in his last year at college, in jeans and T-shirt, with fashionably short hair and stubble. His mother, a college lecturer like Rajpal, wears, as all Punjabi women do, traditional Punjabi clothes. While Rajpal and Kuldip show us to our rooms, Gorky drives off to spend the night with a friend in Patiala, promising to be back tomorrow for my mother's birthday.

I help her to unpack and make sure she knows where everything is. We go back to the sitting room and meet Rajpal coming in with food from a roadside stall, pieces of freshwater fish fried in batter with a bowl of mint chutney to dip them in. Still wary of unfamiliar food, my mother won't try the fish and Rajpal begins to worry about how little she has eaten today. I tell him that she never eats much, a slice of toast for breakfast, a sandwich for lunch and a small helping of whatever I cook for dinner in the evening. When we sit down to our evening meal later, she eats just enough to persuade our hosts that she will not starve, a little rice, a piece of chicken, a spoonful of dhal, a morsel of chapatti.

"Mom has very small appetite," says Kuldip, chuckling. "In India we call it 'sparrow feeding'."

My mother looks at me, not understanding what Kuldip has said.

"Kuldip says you're eating like a sparrow. Have you had enough?"

"Yes, thank you," she says, turning back to Kuldip. "That was very nice. No more. I've had quite enough."

Kuldip laughs again and asks her if she likes what she has seen of India so far. Again, my mother turns to me and I repeat the question.

"Very much," she says. "It's the best thing that's ever happened to me."

Sitting on the veranda, drinking tea in the early morning sunshine, she puts her hand on my arm and tells me again how wonderful it is. She has slept well and we are both starting to feel as if time has slowed down to let us catch up. It is nine o'clock in the morning and it feels, more or less, like nine o'clock in the morning.

"I still have that feeling of joy inside me," she says. "And I know you'll think I'm silly, but I still feel as if I've been here before."

Birthdays in India, Rajpal told us at breakfast, are celebrated in the evening. Until then, the day is just an ordinary day. But sitting in the Indian sunshine on her ninetieth birthday, feeling joyful, makes this an extraordinary day for my mother. I wish her a happy birthday and give her my present. She gives it back to me to undo the wrapping paper, because she can't manage this herself, then I give it back to her so that she can finish unwrapping it, then she gives the wrapping paper back to me and, finally, she holds the present in her hands. It is a book called *Daddy Long-Legs* by Jean Webster, one of the books she remembers reading when she was a girl. This is a signed copy. 'Jean Webster, New York, 1915.'

Every few minutes, hawkers on bicycles pedal slowly down the road, calling their wares. Their call is a tune with two notes and sounds like a sing-song iambic pentameter: low high low high low high low high low high. They all seem to sing the same tune and, as we can't understand the words, we don't know what they are selling until they ride slowly past the gate. Some of them pull carts behind them, stacked with fruit or vegetables, some just tie their goods onto the bicycle. The toy seller has dolls and balloons dangling from the end of a pole tied to his crossbar, making him look like Don Quixote with a spear fastened to Rocinante's saddle.

Kuldip hears the fruit juice man in the distance and comes outside to ask if we would like some. He stops at the gate and we choose, on her recommendation, orange and sweet lime. While she goes inside to fetch the glasses, the man drops the fruit into a contraption fastened to the back of his cart. He turns the handle, the pulp drops into a bucket hanging underneath and the juice drips into a jug. Kuldip returns with glasses and he pours the juice into them. It is the colour of a Van Gogh sun. It feels as warm in my throat as the sun does on my face.

Inside, one of the migrant workers from UP is cleaning the house. Tasks which the English do on their hands and knees, Indians do squatting. When I take our empty glasses into the house, the barefoot cleaner is scuttling across the room like a tiny crab in a rock pool, sweeping her cloth from side to side over the marble floor. She looks at me sideways as I go past, but does not return my smile and looks away again, frowning slightly.

When I go back outside, my mother has her hands together, as if she is greeting an Indian friend. But her eyes are closed and I realise that she is praying.

"Well," she says, when she opens her eyes, "I've done it. I've lived to be ninety. I've done better than either of them."

She means her brother and sister. Her brother, the oldest, died in his seventies. He came in from the garden, where he was building a wall, went upstairs and dropped dead. His wife downstairs heard him fall.

"What have you done now, Jack?" she called up to him and, when she went upstairs to find out, he was already dead.

Her sister, married three times and now alone again, sat in a chair for the last two years of her life with her dog, Ruby, at her feet, looking out of the window at her garden. She was a few months short of ninety when she died.

"Who'd have thought I'd live longer than either of them?" she says, shaking her head over another of life's unfathomable mysteries.

In the distance I can hear music playing, faintly at first, then louder, drums beating, flutes wailing, until round the corner comes a bullock cart decked with red flags and silver bunting. The bullock has a garland round its neck and there are flag poles at the corners of the cart. Between the poles sits a pink and blue tent, the kind you see in pictures of the Crusades. More flags fly from the tent poles. The music is coming from inside the tent, but there are no musicians. The raucous sound comes from a cassette player with the volume turned up as high as it will go. A man walks beside the cart and two women go from gate to gate asking for money. The cart passes our gate and the women stop outside and hold out their hands, but I have no rupees to give them. They shrug their shoulders, turn round and walk away.

It is hot in the sun and we decide to go indoors. I sit and read the paper and my mother falls asleep in her chair. The Tribune, Chandigarh's English language newspaper, brings me up-to-date with the shooting in Beas and other election news. Cong and SAD candidates swap allegations and file complaints. The police have been put on alert. One of the men has been charged with murder but both of them 'continued to attend political rallies today'. A woman has been kidnapped. The situation is 'tense but under control'. A 'heavy police posse' has been deployed. The man who was killed in the shooting has been cremated.

His death seems less important than the politics that caused it. The front page story continues on page five, ending with a few lines about the dead man and his mother.

'The fatherless Dilbag Singh (32), a resident of Mehsampur village who was killed in firing by Congress men yesterday, had come to India from Dubai last month. He was to go back after the elections. His shell-shocked blind mother Kans Kaur, who could not attend the cremation of her son, said it would be difficult for her to meet both ends since her sole breadwinner had been killed. The deceased leaves behind his wife and an infant girlchild.'

Tributes have been paid to Mahatma Gandhi on the fifty-ninth anniversary of his assassination. Phone charges are coming down. The Himachal unit of the All-India Scheduled Caste and Scheduled Tribe Federation has submitted a list of thirty Christian converts who want to become Hindus again. The Sardar Sarovar Dam in the Narmada Valley has been finished, forty-five years after Nehru laid the foundation stone. Irfan Pathan has been picked for tomorrow's one-day match against the West Indies. Traffic was held up in Haryana yesterday by villagers protesting that their names had been left off the BPL list. A body is to be exhumed in the fake encounter case. I remember that BPL means 'below the poverty line', but I still don't know what a fake encounter is.

I put the newspaper down and go upstairs to sit on the balcony outside my bedroom, leaving my mother asleep in her chair. The horizon is never far away on the plains of north India. Across the road is a patch of rough ground, then another road, then an embankment carrying a railway line, then sky. I sit in the shade and watch the traffic go by on the road in front of the embankment. The road is too far away for me to hear the noise of the traffic, which makes the silent procession of vehicles look like a scene from a puppet play. I imagine someone just below the horizon moving cardboard cut-outs across a painted backdrop. Rickshaws, buses, lorries, cars, scooters, bicycles appear stage left, cross the stage and disappear stage right. The same pictures keep returning. A man in a turban sitting up straight on his scooter, a man on a bicycle leaning over the handlebars, a woman on a scooter with her dupatta blowing in the wind, a man on a scooter with a woman sitting side-saddle behind him, a cycle rickshaw, a battered bus, an ancient lorry. On the embankment behind, the railway line is deserted until, not a train, but a group of three small figures appears, three women with shawls over their heads, silhouetted against the sky. Slowly, they make their way along the railway line, while the traffic on the road below them keeps up its endless repetition. If it was a puppet play, this is where the story would begin.

I stand up to go downstairs but, before I do, I rest my hands on the balcony rail, looking down at the street below, feeling the sun on my head and the backs of my hands. The street is empty. Some children are playing behind the gates of the house next door. Clothes are drying in the sun, their varied colours turning verandas and balconies into children's paint boxes. An old woman comes out of a gate and walks slowly down the road. She carries a long stick, which she grips in her bony hand like a staff. A thick, grey shawl covers her head, reaching almost to her feet. Her face is as grey as the shawl, her dark skin creased like leather. If my mother is a little mouse with a walking stick, this old woman, alone on the empty road, ambling peacefully along, is her neighbour, the cow.

I go downstairs and find her still asleep. The beginnings of stories still in my mind, the women walking along the road, the old woman with her staff, I remember the book of Punjabi folk tales written by Flora Annie Steel, the woman who put into words what Rajpal had already shown me when he gave back my watch. They are stories she collected while she was living in India towards the end of the nineteenth century and they are quite unlike English folk tales, or at least the kind of tales that English children read. Mrs Steel wrote some of those too. Her *English Fairy Tales* was illustrated by Arthur Rackham, whose pictures are now all that the book is remembered for. Her Indian book was illustrated by J.Lockwood Kipling and perhaps, who knows, lay behind some of the stories written by his more famous son, Rudyard. Her introduction to *Tales of the Punjab told by the people* sets the scene.

'It is sunset. Over the limitless plain, vast and unbroken as the heaven above, the hot cloudless sky cools slowly into shadow. The men leave their labour amid the fields, which, like an oasis in the desert, surround the mud-built village, and, plough on shoulder, drive their bullocks homewards. The women set aside their spinning-wheels, and prepare the simple evening meal. The little girls troop, basket on head, from the outskirts of the village, where all day long they have been at work, kneading, drying, and stacking the fuel-cakes so necessary in that woodless country. The boys, half hidden in clouds of dust, drive the herds of gaunt cattle and ponderous buffaloes to the thorn-hedged yards. The day is over, – the day which has been so hard and toilful even for the children, – and with the night comes rest and play. The village, so deserted before, is alive with voices; the elders cluster round the courtyard doors, the little ones whoop through the narrow alleys. But as the short-lived Indian twilight dies into darkness, the voices one by one are hushed, and as the stars come out the children disappear. But not to sleep: it is too hot, for the sun which has beaten so fiercely all day on the mud walls, and floors, and roofs, has left a legacy of warmth behind it, and not till midnight will the cool breeze spring up, bringing with it refreshment and repose. How then are the long dark hours to be passed? In all the village not a lamp or candle is to be found; the only light – and that too used but sparingly and of necessity – being the dim smoky flame of an oil-fed wick. Yet, in spite of this, the hours, though dark, are not dreary, for this, in an Indian village, is *story-telling time*; not only from choice, but from obedience to the well-known precept which forbids such idle amusement between sunrise and sunset.

'But from sunset to sunrise, when no man can work, the tongues chatter glibly enough, for that is story-telling time. Then, after the scanty meal is over, the bairns drag their wooden-legged, string-woven bedsteads into the open, and settle themselves down like young birds in a nest, three or four to a bed, while others coil up on mats upon the ground, and some, stealing in for an hour from distant alleys, beg a place here or there.

'The stars twinkle overhead, the mosquito sings through the hot air, the village dogs bark at imaginary foes, and from one crowded nest after another rises a childish voice telling some tale, old yet ever new, – tales that were told in the sunrise of the world, and will be told in its sunset. The little audience listens, dozes, dreams, and still the wily Jackal meets his match, or Bopoluchi brave and bold returns rich and victorious from the robber's den. Hark! – that is Kaniya's voice, and there is an expectant stir among the drowsy listeners as he begins the old old formula –

'Once upon a time…'

PRINCE HALF-A-SON

Once there was a king who had seven wives but no children. All he really wanted was a son, just one would do, but his seven wives had given him no children at all. His heart grew heavy and he took to spending his days in solitude, lying on a battered old charpoi under a mango tree in the palace gardens.

One day a faqir walked through the gardens and stopped to ask him what it was that weighed so heavily on his heart. When the king told him his troubles, the faqir took pity on him and decided to help him.

"Here," he said, holding out his stick. "Take this stick and throw it twice into the branches of the mango tree. At the first throw, five mangoes will fall. At the second, two will fall. Give each of your queens one mango to eat and they will each bear you a son."

The faqir turned and walked away, leaving the king looking up into the branches of the tree with the stick in his hand. He drew back his arm and threw the stick as hard as he could. It clattered among the branches and five mangoes fell to the ground. He jumped to his feet, picked up the stick and threw it again. This time, two mangoes fell to the ground.

The king was so pleased that he ran to where the stick had fallen, picked it up again and threw it into the tree a third time. But this time, the stick remained lodged in the branches and the seven mangoes flew back up into the tree and hung there, just out of reach.

The next day, at the same time, the faqir came back and the king told him what had happened.

"That's what comes of being greedy," said the faqir. "Surely seven sons are enough for anyone!"

The king hung his head in shame and looked so miserable that the faqir decided to give him another chance.

"This time," he said, "do exactly as I told you. If you don't, you can lie here for ever for all I care."

He turned and walked away and, as he did so, the stick that had lodged in the branches of the tree fell to the ground. Quickly the king picked it up, stepped back and threw it up into the tree. Just as before, five mangoes fell to the ground. He picked up the stick, threw it again and watched as another two mangoes fell. This time, he picked up the mangoes and carried them into the palace, leaving the stick where it lay under the tree.

He went in search of his wives so that he could give them each a mango to eat, as the faqir had told him. One by one, he gave them their mangoes, but his youngest wife had gone out walking, so he put her mango in a cupboard until she returned. By the time she got back, a little mouse had nibbled away half the mango, but she ate the other half anyway and enjoyed it as much as the other queens had enjoyed theirs.

Just as the faqir had told him they would, his queens all bore him a son. But when the youngest queen's son was born, he was only half a boy. He had one eye, one ear, one arm and one leg. Looked at from the side, he was as handsome as the other little princes, but from the front, it was plain that he was only half a boy. So they called him Prince Half-a-son.

But that didn't stop him from doing everything that his brothers did. He grew up with them and everywhere they went, he went – or rather hopped – too. Everyone in the palace made jokes like that, but he just shrugged his shoulder and pretended not to hear.

One day, when his brothers were preparing to go out hunting, he asked his mother if he could go with them.

"How can you hunt?" she said, with tears in her eyes. "How can you pull a bow, with only one arm?"

"That doesn't matter," said Prince Half-a-son. "I can play at hunting, even if I can't really do it. Don't worry about me. But please will you make me some sweets to take with me and share with my brothers?"

But with only half a son, the young queen felt as if she was only half a mother and she was too busy feeling sorry for herself to hear what he was saying. So he went to one of his aunts and asked if she would make him some sweets to take with him. She said she would but when she told the other queens what she was doing they decided to play a trick on Prince Half-a-son and fill the sweets with ashes instead of sherbet. Then, so that everyone could enjoy the joke, they told their sons what they had done.

"Make sure you watch when he puts the first sweet in his mouth and gets a mouthful of ashes," they said.

So when the seven – or rather, six and a half – princes stopped to eat their sweets, the six who were in on the joke nudged each other when they saw Prince Half-a-son put the first sweet in his mouth and, when they saw him pull a face and spit it out, they all burst out laughing.

"My aunt must have made a mistake," he said, his mouth smeared with ashes. "This sweet doesn't taste very nice. Perhaps she opened the wrong jar for the filling. Please, let me have one of your sweets to take the taste away."

The other princes held out their bags of sweets but, when he reached out his hand to take one, they snatched the bag away and laughed even more.

Later in the morning, they came to a field of melons and, one by one, the princes tried to squeeze through a gap in the thorn hedge that surrounded the field to help themselves to some of the ripe, juicy melons. But the gap was very narrow and the only one who could squeeze through was Prince Half-a-son. The other six heard him licking his lips as he sat on the other side of the hedge eating one of the delicious melons.

"Throw some over to us!" they said.

"Remember the sweets!" mumbled Prince Half-a-son through a mouthful of melon, wiping the juice from his chin. "It's my turn now! Mmm! This melon is delicious!"

"It was only a joke," his brothers said. "We won't do it again, honest! Please throw some over."

He chose the most unripe melon he could find and threw it over the hedge, wishing he could see the expressions on their faces when they bit into the sour fruit.

"Only a joke!" he said, when he heard them spitting it out.

But the six princes had the last laugh, because one of them went in search of the farmer and told him that someone was stealing melons from his field. The farmer came running, caught the thief red-handed and tied him to a tree to teach him a lesson. Still laughing, the princes turned and walked away. But a few minutes later, their brother caught up with them and they looked at him in surprise.

"How did you escape?" they said.

"Aha!" said Prince Half-a-son. "That's my secret!"

The brothers thought that the farmer must have come back and untied him, in case the king was angry with him, but they were wrong. The truth was that Prince Half-a-son had the magical power of being able to make a rope do anything he wanted. So when everyone had gone, all he had to do was say, "Break, rope, break!" and he was free.

Soon, they came to an orchard full of plum trees. One of the princes kept lookout while the others climbed the trees to pick the fruit, but the branches were too thin to bear their weight and the only one who could reach the plums was Prince Half-a-son. The others gathered underneath the tree, looking up at him where he sat on a branch eating one juicy, yellow plum after another.

"Throw some down for us!" they shouted up to him.

"Remember the sweets!" he said, spitting plum stones onto their heads. "It's my turn now!"

When the lookout saw the farmer coming, he told him there was a boy in his orchard stealing plums and they all ran away while the farmer pulled their brother down and tied him to the tree. But all

Prince Half-a-son had to do was say, "Break, rope, break!" and soon he was hopping along behind them again. They were so annoyed that, when they came to a well and stopped for a drink, they waited until he was leaning over to reach the bucket, then took him by the leg and tipped him over the edge. They didn't wait to hear the splash but turned at once and ran back to the palace.

Prince Half-a-son landed on a ledge halfway down the well. When he looked up he could see the sky like a bright new silver coin above his head and when he looked down he could see the water like a shiny old black coin below his feet. When night fell, he heard a sound and looked up and a pigeon flew past him down to the bottom of the well. A minute later, he heard another sound and a serpent slithered down the wall on the other side. A minute later, he heard another sound and a one-eyed demon climbed down the wall hand over hand. Being only half a boy, it was easy for him to stay hidden on his ledge halfway down the well and listen.

The pigeon, the serpent and the one-eyed demon all lived together in the well. Every day they went about their business and every night they came back and sat at the bottom of the well, boasting of their exploits, each trying to outdo the other.

"I have the emperor's daughter in my power," boasted the one-eyed demon. "I am draining her of life and soon I will kill her."

He gave a wicked laugh, as demons do.

"I could make her well again if I chose," cooed the pigeon.

"How?" said the demon.

"By making her eat my droppings, which are magic and can bring people back to life."

"That's disgusting," hissed the serpent. "Who would want to eat your droppings?"

"Everybody would," said the pigeon, "if they knew how good they were."

The serpent uncoiled himself, admiring his scales, which glistened like diamonds in the moonlight.

"Anyway," he said. "The emperor's daughter is no concern of mine. I have the treasures of seven kings underneath me."

"So you keep telling us," said the one-eyed demon.

The three of them went on like this all night long, while Prince Half-a-son sat on his ledge and listened. When the first light of dawn began to trickle into the well, he pressed himself against the wall and held his breath as the pigeon flew past him, followed by the serpent, swimming up the wall like an eel, and the one-eyed demon, scuttling over the stones like a lizard.

Not long after they had gone, a camel-driver came to draw water from the well and let down the bucket. When it reached the bottom, Prince Half-a-son took hold of the rope and held on tight. The camel-driver felt a heavier weight than usual when he began to wind the bucket up again and leaned over the wall to see what was wrong. When he saw half a boy looking up at him, he was so frightened that he let go of the handle and ran away. The bucket began to fall, but all Prince Half-a-son had to do was say, "Pull, rope, pull!" and the rope wound itself up again and he was soon out of the well.

He set off at once to the palace of the emperor and announced that he had come to cure the emperor's daughter. The emperor's servants let him in, but they warned him that, if he failed, the emperor would have him put to death.

"Many men have tried and failed," said the emperor when they brought Prince Half-a-son to him. "What can half a man do?"

But Prince Half-a-son, who had a handful of the pigeon's droppings in his pocket, was not afraid. He made a bargain with the emperor. If he failed, the emperor would have his head. But if he succeeded, he would give him his daughter's hand in marriage and half his kingdom as a reward.

"After all," he said, "I'm only half a man, so half your kingdom will be enough for me."

Everyone was amazed when the emperor's daughter took the medicine that the stranger gave her and immediately grew well again. The colour came back into her pale cheeks and her dull eyes began to sparkle. The emperor had no hesitation in keeping his side of the bargain and preparations were quickly made for his daughter's marriage.

But when the other six princes heard what had happened, they were jealous and started a rumour that the stranger who had cured the emperor's daughter of her mysterious illness was not a prince, as he claimed, but the son of a poor sweeper. When he heard this rumour, the emperor sent for the stranger and accused him of deceiving him.

"Give me half-a-day and a train of mules to prove that I am who

I say I am," said Prince Half-a-son.

"Very well," said the emperor. "But if you can't prove it, you'd better stay away, because if you come back without proof, you will lose your head after all."

Prince Half-a-son had remembered the boast of the serpent, that he had the treasures of seven kings under him. He went to the well, dug up the treasures, loaded them onto the mule train and drove them back to the emperor's palace. When he got there, he told the emperor who he really was and how it came about that he was only half a man.

"I know who it was who started these rumours about me," he said. "It was my brothers. They were jealous and wanted to stop me from marrying your daughter."

When the emperor heard this, he let it be known that the other princes would not be welcome at his daughter's wedding and had them escorted out of his kingdom, with a warning never to return.

On their way home, the brothers gathered at the well.

"This is where our half-a-brother dug up the treasure and became rich," one of them said. "Let's climb in and see what we can find."

So they climbed down into the well and began to search for treasure. They were still searching at dusk when the pigeon, the serpent and the one-eyed demon came back to the well. The one-eyed demon was very angry, because the emperor's daughter was well again.

"Someone has stolen my princess," he said, stamping his feet.

"Never mind that," said the serpent, looking down into the well. "Someone has stolen my treasure."

"Never mind that," said the pigeon. "Someone has stolen my droppings."

The six princes heard voices and looked up to see who it was, but it was too late. The pigeon flew down first and started cooing. The serpent slithered down next and wound himself round them so they couldn't move. Then the one-eyed demon climbed down hand over hand and ate them all up, one by one.

In the evening, I sit beside her on the settee, surrounded by roses. There are other presents too, but nearly everyone has brought roses. Around her neck is a pearl necklace and on the table facing her sits Ganesh, the elephant god. Birthday guests stand in groups around the room, talking and eating. One of them, a grey-haired woman with a gentle, earnest face, sits beside us, waiting for my mother to answer the question she has just asked her. It is not an easy question and there is a long silence before my mother speaks.

Earlier, we were left alone in the house, while Rajpal and Kuldip went shopping. They were late back, hurrying in with boxes and parcels and plastic bags, and for the next few minutes we sat in our chairs listening to the sounds coming from the other rooms until, just before the guests were due to arrive, the preparations were finished and it was time for the birthday to begin.

"Happy birthday, mom!" said Kuldip, giving her the first of the roses. There was a birthday card too and a parcel for me to help her unwrap. Inside was a box and inside that a pearl necklace with ear rings to match. Her ears are not pierced, so she could not wear the ear rings, but she said that she had always wanted a pearl necklace. I helped her to put it on.

Then there was another parcel, this one too big for her to unwrap even with my help. So I did it for her. She must have seen the look of incredulity on my face when I saw what was inside. It was a picture in a frame. I held it up for her to see. She moved her head this way and that.

"Oh!" she gasped, when she made out at last what it was. "It's me!"

It was her portrait in oils and an excellent likeness. A little mouse with white hair, leaning forward, eyes bright, nose twitching. Hermione's statue. The Picture of Dorian Grey with a happy ending. Rajpal knelt down beside her and explained that he had commissioned the portrait from a friend of his called R.M.Singh, who is a well-known portrait artist.

"You will meet him later," he said.

He propped the portrait on the sideboard, poured two glasses of Indian whisky and proposed a birthday toast.

"To mom!"

Within half-an-hour most of the guests had arrived. Sitting on the settee is a peasant girl who has just been told that she is really a princess. Taken from the woodcutter's cottage, where she was abandoned as a baby and brought up by the woodcutter and his wife, she has been brought to the palace, where a procession of lords and ladies kneel before her and lay gifts at her feet.

First to arrive are two young women, friends of Kuldip. They put their hands together and stoop to touch her feet before giving her their roses. They are both dressed in black salwar kameez. One has a pink silk dupatta around her neck, so long it reaches to the ground and floats after her when she walks away. The other has a dark brown Kashmir shawl wrapped around her shoulders and arms. Both have long black hair and skin that gleams like burnished copper. She looks from one to the other admiringly and tells them how beautiful they are.

Next to arrive are a big man with a thick, grey beard and his small, round-faced, smiling wife. The big man looks like a shepherd and his wife looks like a fairy. In the story, they would be the king and queen of a small, far off country. The two young women would be the daughters of a rich merchant.

The grey-haired woman with the kind face comes next. Instead of roses, her gift is a little box wrapped in paper. My mother and I play our usual game of pass-the-parcel until I take off the lid and place the little blue box in her hand. Inside the box is a little glass elephant.

"This is Ganesh. Ganesh is elephant god. People believe he helps them when they are starting some new adventure. He is god of new beginnings. This is why I thought I should give him to you on your first visit to India."

Dressed in a white sari, with a white shawl wrapped around her shoulders, the grey-haired woman with the quiet voice and gentle eyes is the wise woman, the old nurse, the fairy godmother.

A young couple are next to appear. He is short and slight with a big, black beard and a white turban. She is small too, dressed in peach, her black hair tied back. Both look very happy as they walk towards us.

"They're in love," my mother says later. "You can see it by the way they look at each other."

Rajpal introduces them. "Mom," he says, "this is R.M. Singh, who painted your portrait. You may call him Rahi. And this is his wife, Sangeeta."

They put their hands together and, as she reaches out her hands to them, they come closer and lean towards her. She takes both their hands in hers. First she thanks him for the portrait. Then she turns to his wife and looks closely at her face.

"Very beautiful," she says.

She turns back to the artist.

"And you," she says. "Very handsome."

We talk about the portrait. I tell him that, when Rajpal asked me to send him some close-up photographs of my mother, I had no idea what he wanted them for. It never crossed my mind that they would be used for someone to paint her portrait. In fact, I had forgotten all about them.

"I wanted to give her earrings," he says. "Two little pearl earrings. But no one could tell me whether she wore earrings or not, so I decided not to."

"Perhaps you should have done. They would have suited her."

When she finally releases their hands and lets them go, I explain to her about the earrings.

"Everyone wants to give you pearls."

"I've always liked pearls. How did they know?"

Seeing them standing at the other side of the room talking to each other and still smiling, I wonder what they would be in the story. Two dolls that fall in love, perhaps. He could be a paint brush, his turban like a blob of white paint. She could be a fairy cake covered in peach coloured icing. I imagine them dancing in a ballet, like the Nutcracker and the Sugar Plum Fairy.

Kuldip brings in the birthday cake. I help my mother to the table and everyone gathers round to sing Happy Birthday and watch her cut the cake. There are two candles, one in the shape of a nine, the other in the shape of a nought. Rajpal lights them.

"Happy birthday to you! Happy birthday to you! Happy birthday to mom! Happy birthday to you!"

With two breaths and to much applause, she blows them out. Someone gives me a cake knife, I put it in her hand and we pose for the cameras. There is more applause when she cuts the first slice. Carrying her plate, I help her back to the settee and then go back to fetch a slice for myself. Victoria sponge is as popular in India as chicken tikka is in England, like mutual gifts we gave each other on parting. When the cake is finished, its place is taken by dishes of rice and chicken and vegetables to which we help ourselves.

It is then, while everyone is busy eating, that the grey-haired woman with the gentle eyes and quiet voice comes to sit with us again and asks her question.

"You have lived a long time," she says, looking earnestly into my mother's eyes. "We are all your children. You are our mother. Please tell us what you have learned from your long life. We should learn from you. Young people should learn from old people."

My mother thinks for a long time before she answers. She looks as if she is afraid she might lose her kingdom and be sent back to the woodcutter's cottage if she gets it wrong. The grey-haired woman holds her hand and looks into her troubled eyes as she searches her soul for the answer.

It is a question that could only be asked in India. In England, no one expects old people to have anything interesting to say or even to be capable of rational thought. In television interviews, centenarians are asked to give their secrets for long life. Everyone expects them to say something amusing about cigarettes or beer or sex.

I sip my whiskey and wait patiently for her answer, as the Greeks waited for the oracle at Delphi. But when the answer comes, it lacks oracular ambiguity. It is, in the end, just a frank admission of ignorance.

"I don't think I've learned anything."

In the silence, the grey-haired woman waits, knowing there is more, which there is.

"Only there must be a reason for it all. There must be some purpose. I can't believe that everything just happens by accident. Someone must have planned it."

One by one, the guests come to touch her feet again and say goodbye. When everyone has gone, my mother tells me it has been the best birthday she has ever had.

"I feel ten years younger," she says.

"Three more birthdays like this," I say, "and you'll be younger than me."

I am woken at half-past-four in the morning by the sound of a band playing outside the window. The music is loud and raucous, as if some drunks have raided the barracks, stolen the regimental band's instruments and set off to march through the streets intent on waking everyone up. I lie in bed, waiting for them to go away, but the noise grows louder and, after a while, I get up to look out of the window.

In the street below, in the half-light of morning, stands a small band of musicians, wearing red and blue uniforms which fit so badly they might have been stolen too, playing loud enough to wake the dead. Perhaps they *are* the dead. Perhaps my mother has died in the night and this infernal band has come to escort her to the grave. I can think of no rational explanation for the appearance of a brass band in a suburban street in Chandigarh at half-past-four in the morning. I let the curtain fall and go back to bed. A few minutes later, the sound of the music recedes as the band resumes its march to wherever it is going, in this world or the next. I can still hear them playing when I fall asleep.

Cold water drips from the shower. I turn the tap first one way then the other with no observable result. Most Indian houses have showers, but not many of them seem to work. This is probably because nobody uses them, preferring to wash in the traditional way with a jug and a bucket of water. At the Lawrence School in Sanawar, there was a magnificent cast iron bath in the bathroom, but this was a relic of colonial days. In India a bath is not something to sit in while listening to the radio or drinking a glass of wine. Taking a bath means pouring water over your head. To this end, the bathroom is furnished with a tap, a bucket, a jug, a wooden platform to stand on and somewhere for the water to drain away. Sometimes there are two taps, but the difference between them is usually that one of them works and the other one doesn't. Most plumbing in India is just for show. A jug, a bucket and a tap that works is all anyone really needs. Ignoring the shower, I pick up the jug and fill it from the other tap, which works.

Downstairs, my mother is sitting on her bed, waiting for me to fasten the pearls around her neck. The February sunshine promises a day more like June in England, and we go outside to sit on the veranda. We talk about the weather as all English people do because the weather in England offers endless possibilities for conversation and no Indian does because the weather in India does not. George

Formby's 'Turned out nice again!' would not work as a catch-phrase in India.

"When your father came home after the war," my mother remembers, "the weather was awful. He used to say, 'Is it always like this here?' He couldn't get used to it after Italy."

He was a sapper in the Royal Engineers, printing maps for the Royal Ordinance Survey. His maps must have helped to bring the troops from Monte Casino to Rome, which is where he was when the war ended. It was there he met Maria, whose name was familiar to me throughout my childhood. They exchanged Christmas cards every year, the stamps going into my stamp collection, and she visited us once when I was nine or ten, bring her nephew with her, on their way to a holiday in the Lake District. She never married. If there was a story to be told, I never knew it and it died with him. Stories have to be made up to make up for life's deficiencies. I wrote to her when he died, but she did not reply.

The street sellers are already out on their bicycles crying their wares. Kuldip hears the vegetable man coming and goes out to the gate to stop him. We follow her outside and watch as she makes her purchases, choosing from the potatoes, carrots, onions, aubergines, cauliflowers, tomatoes, chillis and bunches of green herbs which he has on his cart. It is made like a bicycle rickshaw, with a box for vegetables where the passenger seat should be. Old planks have been nailed to the sides of the box to make it deeper and old sacks have been used to line it. The vegetable man, small and thin, with dark skin and short black hair, weighs the vegetables on a pair of scales which he holds up like the scales of justice outside the Old Bailey.

After breakfast, we go for a walk along the road, where children play behind the gates and washing dries on the balconies, to a small park at the end with grass and flower beds and swings. We go through a gate in the iron railings and walk slowly along the footpath looking at the flowers. An old woman sits on a bench, two children play on the swings, a young woman sits with her baby on the grass. The Indian sky is pegged to the roofs of the houses like a pale blue canopy. The sun floats out of reach like a child's boat on a lake.

When we have walked all the way round, stopping every few paces to admire the flowers (roses, marigolds and dahlias, flowering improbably in February), we find a bench near the gate and sit down.

We talk about last night's birthday party and she says again that it was the best birthday she has ever had. She talks about the roses and the pearls, Ganesh and the portrait. We try to imagine how Rahi must have felt when he saw her for the first time, having painted her portrait from photographs. She asks me again who everyone was. She remembers the woman with the grey hair and how intently she looked at her. I tell her that when I first met her she was living with her father, an old man who spent his days in a book-lined study in their little house in Chandigarh, studying the Sikh scriptures. He is dead now. When she wasn't looking after him she was organising a project to give poor children the chance to read books and listen to stories. She used to go out to the villages with a troupe of singers and actors to hold workshops for children. Last night she told me about a story she is writing about a little girl whose father beats her mother. The little girl makes friends with a sparrow and between them they help her father to see that what he is doing is wrong.

"Children see these things happening and they don't understand. The story might help them to understand."

I remember the place *Margot's Secret* and *Daddy Long-legs* had in my mother's unhappy childhood, but I think they had more to do with escaping than understanding. As she gets older, her memories of that time grow more vivid. She dreams about the shop where they lived after her father died and wakes up feeling lonely and miserable, as if she's still living there. Her mother protected her, because she was the youngest. When she could afford it, she took her away from the council school and paid for her to go to a private school instead. It was run by two sisters and the fee was two guineas a term. She was even lonelier there. The other girls invited her to their birthday parties, but she was too ashamed of where she lived to invite them to hers. When her brother got married and left home, she went to stay with him sometimes and hated it when the time came to go home again.

When both the older children had left home and she had saved enough money to live off the interest, her mother gave up the shop and rented a little house in the village near Leeds where, twenty years later, I was born. My mother left school when she was fifteen and found a job in a factory. Her poor eyesight caused her to make so many mistakes that she was sacked at the end of the week. After that she stayed at home with her mother, who never re-married and suffered either from migraine or depression. Sometimes she did not speak for days or even weeks. She lived long enough to know my sister, but not me. My mother found her one day during the war lying dead on the floor. The doctor said it was a brain haemorrhage. She lived in her shadow as a girl and has lived ever since in the shadow of her own unhappy childhood. But now, after ninety years, sitting in the sun on a park bench in India, she looks at me and says, "If I was in paradise, it couldn't be better than this."

It is the birthday of a Sikh saint, Rajpal says when I ask him if there really was a band playing in the street at half-past-four in the morning. This, he says, is an old tradition. The devotees walk through the town and, when people hear the band playing, they come out to join them. Soon there is a long procession winding its way through the streets to the gurdwara. But the tradition, he says, is dying out. It started in the villages, where people get up early to work in the fields, but the office workers of Chandigarh are less enthusiastic. In fact, he says, the authorities are thinking of banning these early morning processions through the quiet suburban streets. I wonder whose side I would be on in the case of the Sector 48 Noise Abatement Order (Saint's Day Processions). It reminds me of people in England who retire to the country and complain about the ringing of the church bells or the crowing of the cocks. A less controversial ban, he says, is the one the Election Commission has imposed.

"Listen!" he says, dramatically, holding up his hand.

The sound of a car going by, the distant call of a street vendor, nothing else but the sound of our own voices.

"Until this ban came in, all you would hear all day long would be the loudspeakers on the motor rickshaws playing music and political slogans."

It is the quietest election Punjab has ever known. Apart from the occasional burst of gunfire in Beas, hardly a sound has been heard.

In the afternoon, we drive to the Rose Garden. Rajpal drops us at the entrance and then drives off to park the car. We stop to read a notice which tells us that this is the largest rose garden in Asia, with fifty thousand rose trees and one thousand six hundred species. From where we stand, we can see the rose beds fading into the distance under the trees, like rolls of red and yellow silk spread out on the grass. My mother is feeling tired after our morning walk and the drive through the city, so I take her hand and we walk slowly along the footpaths between the rose beds, stopping occasionally to sit on a bench in the warm afternoon sunshine.

The Rose Garden is the St James's Park of Chandigarh, where office workers come to eat their lunch, mothers to play with their children and students to sit on the grass and talk. Its real name is Zakir Gulab Bagh, after Zakir Hussain, who was President of India in 1967 when the garden was opened, but everyone calls it the Rose Garden. Or rather, Rose Garden, Punjabi being one of those languages, like Latin and Russian, in which nouns stand on their own two feet, without an article to support them. When Punjabis speak in English, they usually forget the, to them, unnecessary article.

The Rose Garden is as surprised by my mother as my mother is by roses that bloom in February. The little, old, white-haired English woman walking among the roses attracts so many curious glances that she could be species number one thousand six hundred and one. So many people have turned to look at us on our walk through the park that, when we sit down on a bench to wait for Rajpal, we don't pay any attention to the young woman sitting on the grass behind us. But when we see Rajpal walking towards us and I stand up to meet him, she stands up too. She waits politely until we have finished speaking before catching his attention and speaking to him in Punjabi. He turns to me and explains.

"She has been sitting here for some time," he says, "wanting to speak to you, but she is too shy and not sure if her English is good enough. So now she asks if I will introduce you."

He does so and the pleasure which both she and my mother take in this sparks off a love affair which lasts from here to the park gate. Rajpal asks the young woman to take us there while he brings the car and she readily agrees. She walks by my side and I ask her a little about herself, explaining her answers to my mother. I understand her better than she understands me, but we get by. When Rajpal arrives, she opens the car door and helps my mother in, then stands back and waits until we are ready to go. She puts her hands together and my mother does the same as we drive away. Thinking that she was someone Rajpal knew, she is even more moved when I tell her that she was a complete stranger.

We stop at Sukhna Lake on our way to have tea with Rahi and Sangeeta. Sukhna was once a stream running down from the foothills of the Shivaliks, but when Chandigarh was built it was dammed to form a lake. At night, you can see the lights of Kasauli, a hill station on the road to Simla, reflected in the water. Daylight is fading now and the air is cool. It is too early to see the lights of Kasauli and too late to see the hills through the dusty veil which falls across the plain at twilight. We walk for a few minutes by the side of the lake, my mother as usual attracting many curious looks, and then return to the car. She is tired and, on the journey from Sector 6 to Sector 48, she closes her eyes and falls asleep.

Our visit starts with alu tikki and ends with bhangra. Rahi and Sangeeta meet us outside the apartment block where they live, greeting my mother with hands pressed together before stooping to touch her feet and then taking her hands in theirs. She embraces them. They are all smiles. It is like watching three butterflies dancing together on a sunny morning. I take her hand and we climb the stairs, slow as caterpillars, while the young couple fly ahead and wait for us at the top.

"Ik, doh, tin, cha, punj," she says, counting her way up the last five steps. "I'm there! I've done it!"

Everyone laughs and claps their hands. If this was a story, it would be the story of the caterpillar that wanted to be a butterfly.

Once upon a time, one step at a time, ik doh tin cha punj, a little caterpillar climbed up the steps to a house where two beautiful butterflies lived.

"Hello, little caterpillar," said the Red Admiral, smiling kindly.

"We're just going to have tea," said the Painted Lady, spreading her beautiful silky wings. "Would you like to join us?"

"Yes, please," said the little caterpillar, who thought she had never seen anything so beautiful in all her life.

We go in and sit down. First there is a gift to be unwrapped, then food to be eaten. I help with both, unwrapping a hand-painted papier maché bowl and eating my mother's alu tikki. These little potato cakes served with chutney are too spicy for her. She helps herself to cake and pastries instead. This is the third Punjabi home she has visited and it is different from either of the others, less Punjabi. The furniture is elegant, there is a bathroom with a bath, paintings and prints on the walls, the alu tikki is served on a white plate with two swirls of chutney, one red, one green. Only the sound of Indian music playing somewhere in the distance reminds us where we are.

My mother, having shown off her knowledge of Punjabi by remembering the lesson I taught her and counting from one to five, still finds it difficult to remember people's names. The sounds get muddled in her head and come out in the wrong order. She solves this problem by giving them names of her own and I explain to Rahi and Sangeeta that she has decided to call them Ratty and Señorita. They seem pleased with their new names.

After tea, Ratty takes us to the room which he uses as a studio.

"Yesterday morning," he says to my mother, "I was finishing your portrait here. The paint was still wet when you saw it."

He shows us a book of stories about the life of Guru Nanak for which he did the illustrations. His water colours depict scenes from stories re-told for English-speaking Punjabi children by a second-generation Canadian Punjabi. Each of the stories ends with a moral.

'Love conquers all creatures.'

'Rituals alone have no spiritual value.'

'Truth cannot be seen through the veil of illusion.'

'Always allow others to share in your good fortune or its fruits will not be as sweet.'

It reminds me of the books of bible stories I used to read at Sunday School when my father was Sunday School Superintendent. The stories were different but the pictures and the morals were the same. Nanak, I think, has a look of Jesus about him. There are goats instead of lambs, mullahs instead of Pharisees, a vanishing at the end instead of a resurrection, but the style is the same.

While my mother turns the pages and looks at the pictures, Ratty brings out a portfolio of his work. He has been commissioned to illustrate another children's book about a little boy's adventures in a mysterious underground world. These pencil drawings of crumbling tunnels, dangling roots and scary creatures are nothing like the sunny water colour world he painted for Guru Nanak. Nor are the portraits of famous people (and one of my mother) which make up the rest of his portfolio. He shows us the photographs he worked from when Rajpal asked him to paint her portrait and explains how he included details from each of them in the finished painting. He gave her a new jacket and tells us again that he had wanted to give her pearl earrings. My mother has her new pearl necklace around her neck and we all agree that, if he had followed his instinct and given her the earrings, it would have looked just right.

He makes her a gift of the Guru Nanak book when we leave. A young woman in one of Jane Austen's novels could not have been more thrilled by a gift from an admirer but would have found it easier to hide her feelings. In tears, she reaches out to embrace him. Then she turns to his wife and, for the next two or three minutes, the old woman and the young couple hold onto each other as if they are drowning.

When at last we make our way down the stairs, we discover the source of the music which has been playing since we arrived. On the grass behind the apartment block is a marquee where a wedding is being celebrated. From where we stand at the foot of the stairs, we can see the shadows of the dancers silhouetted on the wall of the tent like moths inside a lampshade. In a spontaneous expression of pure joy, caught up in the rhythm of the bhangra, my mother lifts her feet and starts to dance. I take her hand and we dance together down the path, while the others laugh and clap.

The Legend of Guru Nanak

When Nanak was born in 1469 at a town called Talwandi, not far from Lahore, he didn't cry, he laughed.

"I've never known anything like it," the midwife said. "Babies always cry when they're born. It's the first sound they make. But not this one. This one laughed!"

"It's true," said Nanaki, the baby's sister. "I heard him. It made me laugh too!"

Tripita, the baby's mother, told her husband, Kalu, to send for Hardyal, the pandit. When Hardyal came, he asked a lot of questions and studied his astrological charts and made his calculations on a piece of paper.

"Was the baby born before or after midnight?" he asked, looking up from his charts.

"What difference does it make?" asked Kalu.

"If the baby was born before midnight," said the pandit, "he is destined to be a wealthy man. If he was born after midnight, he will be a saint."

"He was born before midnight," said Kalu.

"Are you sure, daddy?" said Nanaki.

"It was after midnight," said Tripita.

"What name should we give him?" Kalu asked.

Hardyal thought for a few moments and then said, "You should call him Nanak Nirangkari."

"That's a nice name," said Nanaki.

Kalu frowned.

"It's a name for Muslims as well as Hindus. Why not another name, one that only Hindus use?"

"If you don't like it, choose your own name," said the pandit, gathering up his papers and preparing to leave.

Kalu paid him and the baby was named Nanak Nirangkari.

When he was seven, Nanak went to the school where the other Hindu boys went and began to learn Sanskrit. The teacher, a Brahmin called Gosal, took him from his father, sat him down at the back of the room and gave him the alphabet to learn. He sat there quietly for the rest of the day, studying the alphabet.

A few days later, when his friends called for him on their way to school, they found him sitting under a tree reading a book.

"What are you reading, Nanak?" they said.

Nanak held up the book so that they could see.

"You can't read it really," they said. "It's in Sanskrit. You're just pretending to read it. What's it called anyway?"

"I can read it," said Nanak. "It's called Bhagavad Gita and it's a holy book. Listen! I'll read it to you."

The boys sat down on the grass in front of him, as if he was their teacher and they were his pupils, while he read to them. They listened patiently for a while until one of them put his hand up. Nanak stopped reading and, like a teacher, asked the boy what he wanted.

"Well, Nanak," said the boy, "what I want to ask is, what does it mean?"

"Yes," said another, "how do we know you're not just making it up?"

"That's right! He could be just making it up! How would we know?"

"I bet he's making it up! It sounds like gobbledegook to me!"

"I'm not making it up," said Nanak.

"Bet you are!"

"Bet I'm not!"

"Prove it then!"

But before the argument could be settled, one of them realised that they were late for school and they all ran off, leaving Nanak sitting alone under the tree. To save themselves from a beating, they all blamed Nanak for making them late.

"Sir, he's sitting under a tree, sir, pretending to read a book and he won't come to school."

"We tried to persuade him, sir, but he wouldn't come."

"Sir, shall we go and fetch him, sir?"

As excited as if the teacher had given them a holiday, they raced out of school, back to where Nanak sat cross-legged under the tree. His eyes were closed and the book lay on the grass beside him.

"Sir says you've got to come to school."

"He says we've got to bring you back."

"He says you'll be punished if you don't come."

"He says he'll tell your father."
"You'd better come or you'll get a beating."
"Two beatings."
"Come on."
"You've got to come."
"Nanak?"

Nanak had not moved and his eyes were still closed. The mystified boys looked from one to the other.

"What shall we do?"
"I don't know."
"Do you think he can't hear us?"
"I don't know."
"Nanak, can you hear us?"
"I bet he's just pretending."
"I bet he can hear us really."
"What shall we do?"
"I don't know."

At a loss, they stood and scratched their heads, until one of them came up with an idea.

"I know! Let's pick him up and carry him."
"Yes!"
"Good idea!"
"Come on!"

So they picked him up and carried him on their shoulders back to the school. There they set him down on the floor in front of the teacher, where he sat cross-legged, his eyes still closed, as if he was still under the tree.

"This is the book he was reading, sir," said one of them, holding it out.

The Brahmin took the book and looked at it. The boys looked at each other, waiting for the teacher to speak, waiting for the beating they knew Nanak was going to get, a little scared now, because a beating is always scary, even when it happens to somebody else. They watched in silence as the teacher closed the book and looked down at Nanak.

"So," he said, "I give you the alphabet to learn on Monday and on Friday you are reading the Bhagavad Gita in the original Sanskrit. Nanak is a great scholar, boys! We have a genius in our midst!"

They all laughed, taking the teacher's sarcasm as permission to join in with their own taunts and jibes.

"Five days to learn Sanskrit!"

"He must be a genius!"

"Amazing!"

"Incredible!"

"Well?" said the teacher.

The boys fell silent again, looking at Gosal. His hand was raised, ready to bring the book down on Nanak's head. They watched with bated breath, waiting for the blow to fall.

"Shall I read it to you?" said Nanak, opening his eyes.

Before Gosal could reply, Nanak had taken the book from his hand. He opened it at random, read one of the verses, then closed it again.

"If you don't understand Sanskrit," he said, "it means, 'O Arjuna, there is nothing greater than me. Everything that exists is joined to me like pearls on a thread.'"

"Is that right, sir?" said one of the boys.

The teacher nodded. Nanak opened the book again and read another verse.

"Which means," he said, when he had finished reading, "'There and then, Arjuna, son of Pandu, could see the whole universe, variously divided, situated in one place within the universal form of Lord Krishna, the lord of all lords.'"

The boys looked at the teacher.

"That's right," he said. "That's absolutely right. Yes, perfectly correct. Very good, Nanak. Very good indeed."

The boys didn't know whether to be disappointed that Nanak had escaped a beating or pleased that he had scored a victory over the teacher.

Nanak bowed politely to the discomfited Brahmin, before turning and walking out of the door back to his place under the tree, where he sat every day, reading and meditating, while the other boys went to school.

One hot day, Nanak fell asleep under the tree. The sun went on with its travels across the cloudless sky and soon the shadow of the tree, like a silk sheet pulled by an invisible hand, slipped from Nanak's face onto the grass, leaving him in the full glare of the sun. As the shadow slid away over the bumps and hollows of the fields, something rippled under it, a long, thin, rippling shadow underneath the shadow, until the invisible hand, like the hand of a magician, whisked the sheet away to reveal, slithering across the grass towards the sleeping Nanak, a long, green, hissing King Cobra.

More than twice the length of the sleeping boy, the snake reared up and looked down at him, swaying from side to side, hissing softly. The shadow of the snake moved silently from side to side on the grass, like the wind rippling across a field of wheat. Slowly, the snake slid around the sleeping boy, like a rope unwinding, until the sun was behind it. Then it reared up again until the shadow of its hood fell across the boy's face and there it stayed, quite still, more like a snake carved out of wood than a real cobra. Protected from the sun, soothed by the gentle hissing of the snake, which sounded like the rustling of the leaves in the tree, Nanak slept peacefully.

Some men out riding saw the unmistakable shape of a cobra under a tree and stopped. One of them dismounted and walked slowly across the field. He stopped when he saw a body lying on the grass beside the cobra. Cautiously, he walked towards them. The cobra's head swung round and he stopped again. Slowly, the snake lowered itself to the ground, as if it was disappearing into a hole, and slid away.

Nanak opened his eyes and found himself lying in the shadow of a man. He rubbed the sleep out of his eyes and saw that the man was Rai Bular, the chieftain of Talwandi.

"I dreamed you were a snake," he said, sitting up.

"You weren't dreaming," said Rai Bular.

"I must have fallen asleep."

"It was a King Cobra."

"Yes. I know. I must have seen it in my sleep. I was hot and then I was cool again. I think it was shading me from the sun."

Rai Bular walked with Nanak back to his house and told his father what he had seen.

"Your son is blessed," he said, "and by his presence among us, Talwandi is blessed too. By God's grace he is your son. You should not think of him as your son but as a guest in your house. Give him whatever he wants, Kalu, and never raise your hand against him."

Tripita served them tea and Nanaki helped her.

"I knew my brother was a saint," she thought.

Kalu told Rai Bular about the pandit's predictions at Nanak's birth.

"He can read Sanskrit too," said Nanaki.

"Sanskrit is all very well," said Rai Bular, "but Persian is better. I will pay for him to attend the Muslim school. Leave it to me. I will speak to the mullah."

So Nanak, a Hindu boy, went to the Muslim school and soon he was as proficient in Persian as he was in Sanskrit.

When Nanak was nine years old, his father made preparations for him to receive the janayoo, the sacred thread worn by high caste Hindus. He arranged for Hardyal to perform the ceremony and sent out invitations to all his friends and relations. When the day came, everything was done according to custom, with recitations from the Vedas and the ritual bathing, after which Nanak put on a new dhoti and was presented to the guru.

Hardyal was about to place the thread around his neck when Nanak raised his hand and asked him to wait.

"Before you put it on," he said, "tell me what difference this thread will make to my life."

"Without it," Hardyal explained, "you cannot be purified. You must wear the thread around your neck and never take it off."

He tried again to put the janayoo around the boy's neck but Nanak put his hand up again to stop him.

"I don't understand," he said. "Does everyone who wears the thread live a pure life? Which is more important, the thread or the life?"

"It is the custom," said the pandit. "Wearing the janayoo helps you to remember what the scriptures teach."

The people who were gathered around looked from one to the other, from the Brahmin to the boy, the boy to the Brahmin, wondering where this would lead.

"In that case," said Nanak, "put another thread around my neck, one that will never get dirty, one that will never need to be replaced."

Hardyal looked puzzled, staring at the janayoo which hung from his hand.

"Another thread? But this is the only one I have."

"In that case," said Nanak, "I must find my own."

"Your own? How can you find your own?"

"This thread," said Nanak, taking it from the Brahmin and holding it loosely in his own hand, "is maya. An illusion, placed between us and God's truth, like everything else in this world. Wearing this thread will only make it harder for me to wear the real thread."

He took Hardyal's hand and hung the thread over it.

"The real thread," he said, "is the thread of truth. That thread never gets dirty and never has to be replaced. That thread is the one I will take with me when I die."

The ceremony ended there but the guests still enjoyed the feast and Nanak's father gave Hardyal and the other Brahmins the customary gifts, the diksha which he was obliged to pay to the guru to mark his son's initiation.

Nanaki felt a little cross when she watched her father doing this. In her opinion, it was the pandit who should have paid diksha to her brother. There was no doubt in her mind who was the guru and who the sikh.

Nanak had a friend whose name was Bala. He was a good Hindu boy, always obedient and well behaved, and Kalu often wished that Nanak was more like him. At any rate, he was always pleased when he saw them together, hoping that some of Bala's good qualities would rub off on his wayward son.

"It's all very well Hardyal saying that he will be a saint and Rai Bular telling me that I should never chastise him," he thought, "but what's a father to do with a son like that? Why can't he be more like Bala? Sometimes he makes me so angry, I just want to slap him. I can't help myself."

On his way to work one day he saw Nanak sitting under a tree, with his eyes closed. Struggling to control his anger, he rushed towards him, his hand raised above his head ready to strike.

"Is this what I keep you for? Is this what I feed you for? What kind of son are you? Just a lazy, good-for-nothing boy who deserves a beating!"

Nanak opened his eyes and looked at his father in surprise, thinking that he looked like a dog straining at the end of a chain.

"I'm sorry, father," he said. "Please tell me what you would like me to do and I will do it gladly."

Kalu's arm fell to his side and his anger subsided.

"All I want is for you to be like other boys and think about your family."

"I do think about my family," said Nanak. "But let me prove it to you. Tell me what you want me to do for you and I will do it."

"Here," said Kalu, after a moment's thought, putting twenty rupees into his son's hand, "take this money into town and show me that you understand how to do business. Use the money to strike a good bargain. See how much profit you can make on twenty rupees. My father set me the same challenge when I was your age and I came home with... Well, let us see if you can do as well as I did!"

He laughed to himself and then added, as an afterthought, "And take Bala with you. He is already helping his father with the family business. He will give you good advice."

Nanak and Bala, hand in hand, set off to walk into the town. On the way, they came upon a group of holy men sitting by the roadside. One of them was reading aloud, some were sitting on the ground listening to him, others were sitting apart, meditating. Nanak stopped, put his arm around Bala's shoulder and whispered eagerly into his ear.

"I know what I'm going to do!" he said. "I'm going to give the twenty rupees to these sadhus. In return, they will give me their blessing. What a bargain!"

Bala looked doubtful.

"I don't think that's the kind of bargain your father had in mind," he said.

But Nanak was already kneeling on the ground at the feet of the man who was reading, holding out the money in his hand and begging the sadhu to take it and buy food for himself and his friends. The sadhu shook his head.

"What use is money to us? Keep it for yourself or give it to someone else."

Nanak stood up and Bala took his hand, breathing a sigh of relief. He turned to walk away and Nanak reluctantly followed him. But after a few paces he stopped.

"Wait here," he said and went back to the holy man.

"Santji," he said, "please take this money. My father gave it to me and told me to use it to make a good bargain. I can't think of a better bargain than to exchange it for your blessing."

The sadhu laughed.

"Twenty rupees for one blessing?" he said. "Is that a good bargain?"

"Oh yes!" said Nanak, eagerly. "A very good bargain!"

"Your friend is not so sure," said the sadhu, looking at Bala, who was sitting on the ground with his chin in his hands.

"He's my friend," said Nanak, "so he wants to please me. But he wants to please my father too. He is the kind of boy who wants to please everyone."

"What about you?" said the old man. "Who do you want to please?"

"I want to please God," said Nanak.

The sadhu looked at him thoughtfully, combing his long, white beard with his thin, brown fingers. Nanak waited patiently and at last the old man spoke.

"Our vows don't allow us to take money," he said. "Go with your friend into the town and spend your money wisely. If you can spare a little rice or a few eggs to give to us on your way back, you will have my blessing."

Bala did his best to make sure that his friend was not cheated in the market.

"Tell me what you want and leave the talking to me," he said.

Nanak waited patiently, holding the bag of rupees in his hand, while Bala haggled with the shopkeepers, using all the tricks he had learned from his mother, laughing, scowling, cursing, complaining, cajoling, flattering, turning his back, shrugging his shoulders, until he got the price he wanted. Then he turned to Nanak and told him how much to give.

"Give him ten annas. That's all it's worth."

"Two rupees. It's daylight robbery, but give it to him anyway."

"This man would rob his own mother. If you think it's worth it, give him half what he asks. Even that's too much."

"Five rupees? Ridiculous! Give him one. Take it or leave it!"

By the end of the morning, they had bought enough to feed a small village and a cart to carry it on. Bala was especially pleased with the cart.

"This was such a good bargain!" he said, smiling with pride as the two of them pushed the over-loaded cart back along the road to Talwandi. "Just think what you could do with it! Your father will be very pleased with you, Nanak."

Nanak smiled happily too and, when he saw the holy men further down the road, he pushed harder.

"There they are, Bala!" he said. "Quick! They're waiting for us!"

"Careful!" said Bala, as the cart bounced over a stone. "Slow down! If you go any faster, you'll have the cart over!"

After they had left the holy men, Nanak pushed the cart and Bala walked by his side.

"I thought you were just going to give them a bag of rice and a few eggs," he said. "I didn't know you were going to give them the lot."

"We've still got the cart," said Nanak. "I thought you said my father would be pleased with the cart. You said it was a bargain."

"Loaded, yes," said Bala. "Then it was a bargain. Now your father will say, 'Is this all you got for twenty rupees?' You call that a bargain?"

Nanak was still glowing from his last encounter with the holy men, but it upset him to see his friend looking so unhappy.

"Why don't you sit on the cart and let me push you?" he said.

But Bala preferred to walk.

When they came to the edge of the village, both boys stopped.

"Do you want me to help you push the cart to your house?" said Bala.

"It's alright," said Nanak. "I can manage. You go home now. Your mother will be expecting you. I think I might just sit here for a while."

Bala knew his friend would get a beating from his father and it made him feel bad to leave him. But there was nothing he could do to help him, so in the end he went home. The sun was at its height and, after a while, Nanak curled up under the cart and fell asleep.

The elephants were stampeding. He heard them trumpeting in the distance. He heard their feet stamping on the ground, louder and louder. There were screams and shouts from the village. An elephant's trunk wrapped itself around him and dragged him out from under the cart. Then the elephant lifted its head and bellowed and struck him across the face with its trunk and knocked him to the ground. He looked up and saw his father. Bala was behind him, crying.

"I'm sorry, Nanak! I had to tell him."

His father pulled him to his feet and slapped him again and again, on his head, his face, his arms, his legs. Nanaki was hanging onto his arm, begging him to stop.

"Please don't hurt him! Please don't hurt him!"

The big hand slapped him again and again, harder and harder.

"I had to tell him!"

"Please don't hurt him!"

"Stop! What are you doing? Stop! Stop!"

Kalu looked over his shoulder and saw Rai Bular hurrying down the road from the village.

"Stop this at once! Leave the boy alone!"

In his temper, Kalu turned his back on Rai Bular and raised his hand again to go on with the beating. But Nanaki was in the way now, trying to protect her little brother, wiping the tears from his eyes, and their mother was on her knees begging him not to hurt them. Rai Bular seized him by the arm and pulled him away.

Tripita took the children home, leaving Kalu with Rai Bular and Bala, who told the village chieftain about the twenty rupees.

"Here!" said Rai Bular, counting out twenty coins and putting them in Kalu's hand. "Now you have your money back! Now are you happy?"

Kalu felt ashamed and tried to return the money.

"I just want him to be like other boys," he said. "A son should work hard so that he can look after his parents. Bala works for his father. Why can't my son be more like Bala?"

"I've told you many times," said Rai Bular, "Nanak is different from other boys. He will be a saint one day. You should be happy about that. I would be proud to have a son like Nanak. I would even have him come and live in my house as my son, if it were not for the fact that he is a Hindu and I am a Muslim."

"Please," said Kalu, holding out the twenty rupees that Rai Bular had put in his hand, "take it back. I don't want it."

But Rai Bular refused and when Kalu walked back home, watching Bala run off in front of him, he didn't know which weighed more heavily on him, Rai Bular's money or Nanak's saintliness. When he got home, he put the money in a box and tried to forget about them both.

Not long after, Nanak's sister was married to a man called Jai Ram and went to live with him and his parents in Sultanpur. Nanaki was happy in her new home, but she missed her brother and often thought about him as she went about her work. Jai Ram always knew when she was thinking about him from the expression on her face, which was happy and sad at the same time. She liked to talk about him and Jai Ram liked to listen, partly because he wanted to please her and partly because the happy-sad expression made her face even more beautiful than it already was.

Once, when he was listening to her talk about Nanak, he had an idea. He thought about it for a few days and then, when he had made up his mind, he told his father. Next, he spoke to the man in charge of the modikhana, the granary where he worked for the nawab, Dhaulat Khan. Finally, he spoke to Nanaki.

"Nanak must be missing you as much as you are missing him," he said. "Next time you go back to Talwandi, why not ask him if he would like to come and live here with us? He is my brother now and my parents will make him welcome. I have even found a job for him."

Tripita was sorry to lose her son, but she knew it was for the best. Kalu raised no objections. When Nanaki left with her brother to go back to Sultanpur, he took Rai Bular's twenty rupees out of the box and told her to give them to her husband. It was a weight off his mind.

Nanak rose before the sun every morning to bathe in the river and spent a long time at his prayers before leaving with Jai Ram to walk to the modikhana. There, he did his work diligently, sitting on the floor beside the sacks of grain, putting the weights on the scales, scooping out the grain and pouring it into the pan until the scales balanced. There was a boy whose job it was to lift the pan off the scales and pour out the grain. Someone else took the money and someone else wrote it down in a book. Everyone had his own job to do, so there could be no mistake or, if there was, there could be no doubt who was to blame. All day long, men went in and out of the store room with sacks on their backs and people from all over the city came in to buy grain, sitting cross-legged in front of the scales, watching with keen eyes until the scales balanced. In the evening, when his work was done, Nanak found a quiet place, under a tree or on the bank of the river, where he could sit and meditate. So his days passed.

One day, a poor man came to buy some grain. When Nanak asked him how much he wanted, the man held out a coin.

"Whatever this will buy," he said. "It's all I have."

Nanak put the weights on the scales and began scooping grain out of the sack and into the pan, counting each time he emptied the scoop.

"Ik, do, tin, cha, punj…"

When he got to thirteen, tera, the scales balanced, but Nanak went on counting.

"Tera, tera, tera."

Another scoop and another and another.

"Thirteen, thirteen, thirteen."

"Stop!" said the man. "Don't give me any more. I won't be able to pay for it."

He watched the scales, waiting for them to tip.

"Tera, tera, tera…"

The heap of grain grew bigger. His eyes grew wider. He looked at Nanak.

"Tera, tera, tera…"

He looked back at the scales. They were still balanced. Nanak stopped counting and leaned back. The boy took the pan off the scales. The man held out his sack and the boy poured the grain into it. Someone took the coin out of his hand. He picked up the sack, heaved it onto his shoulder and walked out.

When he reached home with his sack full of grain, his wife was afraid. She thought he must have stolen it and begged him to take it back.

"What will we do if they arrest you?" she said. "How will we manage then?"

He told her what had happened. It was a miracle, he said. The man who weighed the grain had counted to thirteen and the scales had balanced and after that there were a lot more thirteens and none of them had made any difference. But she didn't believe him.

"He must be cheating the nawab. Some kind of fraud they have cooked up! They must all be in it together! And you will get the blame!"

They decided to grind up the evidence and eat it as quickly as they could.

Nanak's way of counting soon became well known among the poor people of Sultanpur and the villages all around. It wasn't just that every tera brought them more grain than they could afford to buy, it was the way he turned his counting into a song. Tera, tera, tera, he sang, over and over, tera, tera, tera, spinning like a coin, tera, tera, tera, two faces blurring into one, because tera has two meanings.

"Thine, O Lord!" he sang, as he poured the grain into the marvellously, magically, miraculously balanced scales. "All is thine! Thine! Thine! Thine!"

Dhaulat Khan, the nawab of Sultanpur, first heard about the miracle in the modikhana from one of his servants.

"His name is Nanak," he said, as he rubbed soothing ointment onto the soles of the nawab's feet. "He is still young, only just a man, but the poor people love him and some people say that he is a saint."

"I'm not surprised they love him if he's giving away my grain," said Dhaulat Khan. "As soon as you've finished rubbing my feet, I shall have it looked into."

Nanak sat alone in the room where they had left him, with a guard outside, while the officials from the treasury went carefully through the accounts and counted the sacks of grain in the store house and then counted them again. A crowd gathered outside the closed gates of the modikhana. On the other side of the gate, Jai Ram paced up and down, wondering what he would say to Nanaki.

The guard opened the door and Dhaulat Khan walked in. Nanak stood up.

"Everything is in order?" he said.

Dhaulat Khan nodded.

"Everything is in order. The accounts tally. There is, if anything, more grain in the store than there should be, not less. Now tell me..."

"All this counting and weighing," said Nanak, interrupting him. "When you receive a gift from someone you love, someone who loves you, do you count it? Do you weigh it? If you did, would it not be an insult to the person who gave it?"

"Yes, it would," said the nawab. "It would be a great insult. But..."

"So why do you insult God," said Nanak, "by weighing His gifts? If you tried to count the grains of God's harvest, I think you would hear Him laughing. Ik, do, tin, cha, punj... You would soon run out of numbers."

One morning, when Nanak went to bathe in the river, he heard music playing. He recognised the sound of the rabab and, through the water that ran down his face, he saw a man walking along the river bank, drawing a small, curved bow backwards and forwards across the strings of the long necked instrument. He thought the man looked like a bird singing its morning song, calling to its mate across the river. The man stopped and sat down. Nanak stood in the water and watched as he put down the bow and used his fingers to pluck the strings, spinning music out of the rabab like a woman spinning cotton. The prayers which Nanak usually said to himself as he bathed began to fit themselves to the music and, bending again to pour water over his head, he began to sing.

The man's name was Mardana. He was a Muslim and, like his father and his father before him and his father before him, he earned his living by playing the rabab. He was a few years older than Nanak, with a wife and a young daughter. After their first meeting on the river bank, the two men became friends and they often met there in the early morning.

Sometimes Bala joined them too, usually bringing with him a present for Nanak from his mother. If she saw him in the market, she would call to him and say, "Bala, please come to my house later. I have something for you to give to Nanak next time you go to Sultanpur." Bala and Mardana became good friends too.

One morning, when Mardana went down to the river, he saw Nanak's clothes lying folded on the bank as usual, but there was no sign of Nanak. He sat for a while, playing his rabab, looking across the river. Once, he thought he heard him singing and stood up to look down the river, where the sound seemed to be coming from, but there was nobody there, just a heron standing motionless in the water and a vulture flapping slowly across the fields. He looked again at the neatly folded clothes and sat down to wait.

"Where is Nanak?" said Bala, surprised to see Mardana sitting on the river bank, for it was now late in the morning. "I went to look for him at the modikhana but no one has seen him."

"I have been here since sunrise," said Mardana. "His clothes are here, but where he is, who knows?"

"He will be meditating in some quiet place," said Bala. "You wait here. I will go and look for him."

Bala walked along the river bank, first one way, then the other, asking everyone he met on the way if they had seen Nanak, but no one had. Soon, the rumour began to spread through Sultanpur that Nanak had drowned. Jai Ram organised a search party and Dhaulat Khan sent messengers to all the villages. Night came and there was still no news of Nanak. When Jai Ram went home, his meal was ready and Nanaki was waiting for him at the door.

"Don't worry, Nanaki," he said. "We will find him tomorrow. As soon as it's light, we will go on searching."

"I'm not worried," said Nanaki. "There is no need to go looking for him. He will come back."

After three days, the search was called off and everyone gave him up for dead. Jai Ram tried to console his wife but she just smiled and told him not to worry.

"He will come back," she said. "I know he will."

"I hope you're right," he said, even though he knew that she would never see her brother again.

The next day, he came back.

"I knew he would!" said Nanaki, running with Jai Ram and Bala down to the river, where Mardana sat on the bank playing his rabab and Nanak sat beside him, lost in meditation. Word quickly spread through the streets and alleyways of Sultanpur.

"Nanak is alive! Nanak is alive!"

Soon there was a big crowd on the river bank, listening to Mardana, watching Nanak, waiting for him to speak. The murmuring of the crowd was so quiet it sounded like the wind blowing across the plain. Jai Ram, Bala and Nanaki sat together on the grass, speaking in whispers.

"I don't understand," said Jai Ram, leaning closer to Bala. "We looked everywhere for him."

"He must have found somewhere to hide," said Bala, leaning closer to Jai Ram. "Some secret place that only he knows about."

"Perhaps he was here all the time," said Nanaki, speaking so quietly that no one heard her, "but you couldn't see him."

Nanak opened his eyes and saw, to his surprise, that everyone in Sultanpur seemed to be sitting on the river bank, watching him. He heard a noise like birds twittering and looked around to see where it was coming from.

"He's opened his eyes!"

"He's opened his eyes!"

The murmur of the crowd rose to an excited crescendo, then fell again.

"Hush!"

"Hush!"

Mardana went on playing and Nanak's thoughts shaped themselves to the music. His first thought was a thought about a thought. But thinking, he thought, was not the way. His next thought was a thought about not thinking. But not thinking, he thought, was not the way either.

Only Nanaki knew what he was thinking.

"He is thinking," she thought, "that for three days he has been sitting here and no one could see him."

"Yes," he thought, "that is what I am thinking and I am thinking that it is the same with God."

Like butterflies, his thoughts chased each other round and round until, at last, they flew away. Then, when there were no more thoughts, he sang them.

Dhaulat Khan was disappointed when he heard that Nanak had given up his job at the modikhana. He sent one of his officials to offer him a more senior position, that is to say, one where he could earn more money for less work, but Nanak turned the offer down. All his days were spent in meditation now and he knew that very soon the day would come for him to leave Sultanpur and begin his travels.

One afternoon, when Dhaulat Khan was smoking his hookah and enjoying all the pleasant sensations that went with it, he heard angry voices in the courtyard outside.

"What now?" he thought, with a sigh.

A servant opened the door and asked if he would receive a deputation.

"Who is it?" said the nawab crossly. "What do they want?"

Hearing that most of the city's leading Muslims were outside, including the qazi himself, and that they wished to make a serious complaint about Nanak, he relinquished his hookah, laying the pipe aside as gently and regretfully as if it were the hand of a young girl, and told the servant to send them in.

"'There is no Hindu, there is no Musulman!' This is what he has been saying," the qazi explained. "It is an insult!"

The nawab looked puzzled.

"No Hindu? No Musulman? What does he mean?"

"He means to insult us," said the qazi. "That's what he means!"

Dhaulat Khan thought about this while the deputation of mullahs and farmers and market traders muttered angrily among themselves. He liked Nanak and wanted to find out for himself what he meant by these rather puzzling words. The saintly Nanak, he thought, would surely be as slow to give offence as these people were quick to take it.

"Come!" he said. "It will soon be time for afternoon prayers. Let me send for Nanak and see if he will pray with us in the mosque."

Feeling sure that this simple suggestion would soon clear up the misunderstanding, he dismissed the deputation, sent one of his servants in search of Nanak, returned to his hookah and raised the pipe once more to his lips.

Nanak was waiting at the mosque when the nawab arrived.

"Come!" said Dhaulat Khan. "Come and join us in our prayers. Afterwards you must explain to me the meaning of this saying of yours. What is it? No Hindu, no Musulman! Some people seem to have taken it the wrong way, but I'm sure that when they hear it from your own lips they will understand what you mean by it and then we can all be friends. But first, will you come with me into the mosque and pray with us?"

He took Nanak into the mosque and led him to where the others were kneeling on their prayer mats, waiting for the prayers to begin. Dhaulat Khan knelt too, but Nanak remained standing.

"I will pray with you," he said, "if you will pray with me."

The nawab felt slightly irritated. Here he was trying to smooth things over and all Nanak could do was make more difficulties. What did he mean anyway? What were they all there for if not to pray? But he kept his thoughts to himself and let Nanak do as he wished. If he chose to stand there in silence while everyone else was kneeling and reciting the prayers, that was his affair. He was soon lost in his own thoughts and forgot Nanak altogether. When the prayers were over and he stood up to leave, he was surprised to see Nanak standing behind him.

"Nanak-ji!" he said. "I'd forgotten you were there! Come! Let us walk together and talk about this saying of yours."

But as soon as they emerged from the mosque, they were confronted by an angry crowd, all demanding that he should punish Nanak for insulting them and their religion.

"First he denies our religion, then he insults us by refusing to recite the prayers!"

"It's a disgrace!"

"He said he would pray with us! What did he do? Stood in silence while we were all kneeling in prayer!"

Dhaulat Khan held up his hand. His irritation with Nanak quickly returned. Some people just couldn't be helped!

"Well?" he said, feeling rather as if he were holding the dogs off and might just be persuaded to let them go if Nanak couldn't see that he was trying to be helpful and oblige him by returning the favour. "Well? What do you have to say? I think it's time you explained yourself."

Nanak smiled.

"The explanation," he said, "is very simple. I told you that I would pray with you if you would pray with me. So tell me, how could I pray, if no one else was praying?"

Nanak's reply caused outrage. Everyone started talking at once.

"Not praying?"

"What do you mean, not praying?"

"We were all praying!"
"You heard us!"
"Everyone was praying!"
"Everyone except you!"

The nawab held up his hand again. Things were going from bad to worse.

"Come, Nanak-ji!" he said. "It's true! We were all praying! You heard us!"

Nanak shook his head.

"I heard the sound of your voices," he said, "but I could hear no one praying."

A shout went up again and again the nawab held up his hand.

"Go on," he said.

"Who shall I start with?" Nanak asked.

"Start with me," said the nawab.

"Very well," said Nanak. "You were reciting the prayers like everyone else, but your mind was elsewhere. In your thoughts, you were in Kabul buying horses for your stud. Am I right?"

Without waiting for Dhaulat Khan to reply, he turned to the qazi.

"And you," he said, "you were thinking about that newborn foal you had to leave behind when it was time for afternoon prayers."

The qazi opened his mouth and closed it again. Nanak looked from face to face in the crowd, but everyone avoided his eye. Dhaulat Khan burst out laughing.

"No Hindu, no Musulman!" he said. "Just men with other things on their mind! Of course! Who could deny it?"

They all went their separate ways and, the next day, Nanak set off on his travels.

"Whoever it was," she says, "made a wonderful world."

We are sitting on the veranda in the morning sunshine after another walk to the park at the end of the road, where we sat on one of the benches and watched the gardener digging weeds out of the grass with a long, flat bladed trowel. Like the cleaner we had left in the house, he sat on his haunches to do his work, thrusting the blade into the soil and tossing the weeds onto one of the green heaps that covered the grass like worm casts. For her it brought back memories of a lifetime's gardening, first in the houses where she lived with her mother, then in the houses where she lived with my father, then in the houses where she lived alone.

"I always used to garden on my knees. I can't garden standing up like some people do. Adam was a gardener and God who made him sees that half a proper gardener's work is done upon his knees. The Glory of the Garden. Rudyard Kipling. I don't suppose children learn poetry at school any more, do they? It was a regular thing with us. England is a garden and such gardens are not made by saying 'Oh how beautiful!' and sitting in the shade, while better men than we go out and start their working lives by grubbing weeds from gravel paths with broken dinner knives. I still know it off by heart. Not bad for ninety."

What better place could there be, I think, for my mother to recite one of Kipling's poems than a park bench in the Punjab? We sit in the sun, watching the gardener. People come and go. The sun climbs higher.

"I just feel as if I want to scoop it all up and take it home with me."

Tired when we get back, she sits on the veranda and closes her eyes. I go inside to read the paper. The editorial in this morning's Tribune explains the meaning of fake encounters.

'The judicial inquiry into the alleged killing of innocent people in fake encounters to claim rewards will hopefully bring out the truth. In the case, which rocked the state, an innocent boy was killed by a special unit of the Jammu and Kashmir police in a fake encounter. It was claimed that he was a Pakistani militant. This was done to claim a reward the police officer was entitled to. For an ordinary person, it is beyond belief that an agency entrusted with the responsibility of maintaining law and order will go to such low depths to win a monetary reward. It is amazing that the lure of lucre is such that the police can say two hoots to all ethics and civilised behaviour.'

I make my way through other items about the elections ('Paramilitary forces to be deployed in Beas... Disabled at rally thrashed by policemen'), statistics from a survey into election bribes ('As many as 58% respondents found alcohol as the most favourite allurement whereas 30% opined that all kinds of intoxicants, including smack, were distributed, and 12% said poppy husk was the preferred one in their respective areas'), allegations that some candidates have been buying the votes of poor people by paying their bills for them ('Adding that her husband is an alcoholic and that she makes both her ends meet by picking rags, Seelo says that she has no option but to sell her vote'), an eye-catching headline (MANIFESTLY SIMIAN IN UTTARAKHAND – about a manifesto pledge to take action against troublesome monkeys in a hill town) and a story about a drunk policeman who was caught trying to enter the Prime Minister's house in Delhi ('When confronted, the constable told the guards that he was going to have his dinner') before coming to the matrimonial adverts which fill several pages of today's paper.

There are two sections, Brides Wanted and Grooms Wanted, with further subdivisions for caste.

Wanted, educated, beautiful match for handsome, clean-shaven Ramgharia Sikh boy, 29, 5'10".

Respectable Saini Sikh family seeks beautiful, slim, smart professionally qualified match for their handsome clean-shaven boy, 5' 7".

Beautiful, slim match for handsome, educated Khatri Sikh boy 26, 5' 9½", branded hotels in Canada, property in Jalandhar.

Beautiful, professional match for Goel handsome boy, 1.8.81, 5.30 a.m., Ambala City, 5' 8", B.Tech., MBA.

All the boys are handsome and all the girls are beautiful. Every advertisement provides the same details, like the shipping forecast on the radio. Beauty, height, qualifications, caste, profession. Sometimes date and time of birth are given too, for astrological purposes. I imagine the mothers in search of a match for their grown-up children ticking off the boxes on their personal checklist before they make their choice. Bingo!

I wonder when arranged marriages, outside royal circles, became a thing of the past in England. My guess is that most marriages in England were more or less arranged until about a hundred years ago.

Perhaps the end of the arranged marriage in England was the beginning of the end of marriage itself. Marriage, after all, is a social institution and personal feelings are only part of the story, along with property, inheritance, social obligations, family and status. How much simpler it must have been, particularly for shy Englishmen, when marriages were arranged for them by their mothers.

Wanted, beautiful, slim match for clean-shaven boy, 15.5.47, 2.30 p.m., Leeds, 5' 6½", MA Cantab.

Among the things that my mother has told me since we came back from India is that when my father proposed to her she turned him down. Two boys were competing for her favours. She preferred the one from the Salvation Army, her mother preferred the one from chapel. She did as she was told.

"I never loved him," she said. "He was a good man, but I never loved him. He would have been better off with somebody else. It was a shame."

He wrote to her every day of the six years he was away during the war. He wrote poems for her too, she says, but she kept neither the letters nor the poems. She can't remember when or why she threw them away. They just disappeared.

I put the paper down and remember that my mother is still outside. I go out to the veranda and find her sitting on her chair in the sun. I ask her if she would be more comfortable in the shade, but she shakes her head.

"I'm enjoying it. I like the sun."

"You might get sunburn."

"Not at my age. I'm too old. A bit of sunshine won't hurt me."

"Your face is looking a bit red."

"Leave me alone. I'm alright."

"It's too hot for me."

"Not for me."

"Fear no more the heat o' the sun, nor the furious winter's rages, thou thy worldly race hast run, home art gone and ta'en thy wages."

"I'm not dead yet."

Perhaps, I think, when you get to her age you start to enjoy some of the advantages of death, with none of the disadvantages. I leave her, fearless in the sun, and go inside. Putting the newspaper down, I look on Rajpal's bookshelves for something to read. Some of the books are in Punjabi, some in Urdu, some in English. Among them, I recognise one that Rajpal showed me on a previous visit, when he was living in Patiala. I take it off the shelf, sit down and open it.

ROMANTIC TALES FROM THE PUNJAB
With INDIAN NIGHTS' ENTERTAINMENT
COLLECTED AND EDITED FROM ORIGINAL SOURCES BY
THE REV. CHARLES SWYNNERTON, F.S.A.
One of H.M.'s Indian Chaplains Retd.
WITH NUMEROUS ILLUSTRATIONS BY
MOOL CHUND OF ULWAR

I turn to the introduction and read the author's assertion of the authenticity of his sources.

'I owe none of these stories to the labours of other writers. I owe none of them to books whether in English or in the vernacular of ancient or of modern times. I owe none of them to such sublimely venerable creations as the Rig Veda, the Puranas, the Mahabharata, the Ocean-stream of Stories, the Panchatantra, or the Jatakas. In those ancient works variants of some of these Punjab tales of course do occur, for all flow from a common and still more ancient source. But this collection claims, like that of Sir Richard Temple, to have been taken down without exception from word of mouth.'

The stories themselves are told in simpler but no less elegant style, as the author himself explains.

'I have striven to couch my translations in language as simple as the language in which the stories were told, an observation which is true of the prose generally but also true of the measured rhythm, of those passages which recur again and again in the nobler legends, passages which the wandering bards invariably sing, lifting up their voices to the accompaniment of their heirloom instruments of stringed music.'

Sir Richard Temple, who was Mrs Steel's collaborator in her book of Punjabi Folk Tales, wrote elsewhere in less complimentary terms than the chaplain about the wandering bards from whom they both took their stories.

'Many as the vices and faults of these people are, the bhat, the marasi, the bharain, the jogi, the faqir and all of that ilk are in truth but a sorry set of drunkards as a rule – tobacco, opium and a little food sufficing for their daily wants – and I have found that a small payment, say one or two rupees for each separate song and their keep in food and an abundance of their favourite drugs while employed, has amply satisfied them, and in some cases have been inducement sufficient to send other of their brethren to me.'

Temple is the scholar, Swynnerton the romantic. A few pages further on in his introduction, I come to a passage in which he describes hearing, in the company of a friend (reminding me of evenings I have spent with Rajpal), the stories he is about to tell. The passage is worth quoting if only for the extremely long and beautifully constructed sentence with which it ends – a marvel of Victorian literary engineering.

'It was at the little village of Ghazee on the eastern or left bank of the river Indus, thirty miles above Attock and upwards of a thousand miles north of Bombay, that many of these tales were written down from the mouths of the simple narrators themselves. There, at the solitary bungalow of my old friend Thomas Lambert Barlow, within sight and hearing of the majestic river of history and romance, quite close to the ancient ferry over which Alexander the Great threw his bridge of boats, nor yet far south of the great mountain rock-fortress, the Aornos of Arrian, the capture of which virtually laid the Upper Punjab at Alexander's feet, and the site of which has only just been finally discovered and fixed by that distinguished orientalist and explorer, Sir Aurel Stein, there in a district exclusively pastoral which comprises within its area the fabled mountain-ridge of Gundghur, the stronghold of the last of the giants, in the midst of many a ruined temple and fallen fortress pertaining to a former faith and a nobler race, we used to sit late into the night round the leaping log-fire in winter, under the starry sky in summer, and enjoy hearing as much as the villagers enjoyed telling the tales which had charmed their forefathers for scores of generations.'

One story stands above all others in the Punjabi imagination, a love story called *Heer Ranjha*, which some call 'The Romeo and Juliet of Punjab'. A story about the beautiful Heer Sayal and Didho Ranjha, the poor herdsman with whom she falls in love. A story told in words spoken and sung by the story-tellers from whom Temple and

Swynnerton collected their stories. A Muslim poet I once met told me that his illiterate grandfather used to read it every evening.

"How can you read this, grandfather?" he asked him once, seeing him sitting in his chair with the book open on his knee. "I thought you couldn't read."

"I can't read anything else," the old man said, "only this."

The Romeo and Juliet of Punjab

A long time ago, in a village called Jhang on the banks of Chenab, one of the five rivers of Punjab, there lived a beautiful girl called Heer Sayal. She was so beautiful that if a man wanted to pay his wife or daughter a compliment he would say that she was as beautiful as Heer Sayal. But if he said that she was more beautiful than Heer Sayal, they knew he was lying, because no one was more beautiful than Heer Sayal.

Her father, Chuchak Khan, was head of the Sayal clan. His herds grazed on the banks of Chenab and his crops grew in the fields. Everyone in the village depended on him and everyone respected him. They were all his kinsmen and he called them brother. If there were disputes between them, they asked him to resolve them and everyone accepted his decision, even if it went against them. There was no one in the village who resented him or bore him any grudge.

But there was one man in the village who resented his daughter. His name was Kaidon. He was born lame and his parents had never been able to arrange a marriage for him. They loved him and looked after him, but he did not love himself. Sometimes, people thought that because he was lame he must be simple-minded and treated him as if he was. Kaidon was far from simple, but he kept his thoughts to himself and let people think what they liked.

When Kaidon's parents died and he was left to fend for himself, Chuchak Khan offered to give him work to do and somewhere to live. But instead he went to live in a hut on the edge of the village and dressed like a holy man with a loin cloth around his middle and a shawl around his shoulders. He threw away the crutch that his father had made for him and carried a long wooden staff instead. No one really believed that he was a holy man, but some of the women brought him food and Chuchak Khan gave him a goat, which he kept tethered to a post outside his hut.

Most people ignored him, but the children who played in the village streets made fun of him, limping past his hut and pulling faces, and sometimes Heer Sayal and her friends joined in. He threatened them with his stick and complained to their parents but it made no difference. So he stopped complaining and pretended not to hear them.

But when Heer Sayal laughed at him he thought he could hear the whole world laughing too, enjoying a joke at his expense, the joke that had been played on him in his mother's womb. Heer's laughter hatched a maggot in his soul which grew fatter and more ugly as she grew taller and more beautiful.

Soon the time came for Heer to be married. Her mother was eager for a wedding and there was no lack of proposals, but her father brushed them all aside. Heer was his only daughter and he was in no hurry to give her away. Who else would fill his hookah for him in the evening? Who else would keep him amused with her chatter while he sat and smoked? Who else would throw her arms around him and open her eyes wide with wonder when he brought her a gift from the market?

Even so, everyone knew that there would be a wedding soon and Heer's friends teased her, pretending they knew which of her suitors she secretly hoped that her parents would choose. But when they put their arms around her shoulders and whispered a name in her ear, she just burst out laughing and said, "I'd rather marry Kaidon!"

One day, her friends came running to her and told her that the ferryman had let someone sit in her special seat on the ferry. No one knew who he was or where he came from but he was sitting in her seat and playing the flute and everyone was listening and the ferryman couldn't persuade them to get out and let him take the ferry back across the river.

Heer was furious. That seat had been hers since she was a little girl and no one else was allowed to sit on it. It was lined with silk and stuffed with down and it had been made specially for her when she complained to her father that the seats on the ferry were too hard. She rushed down to the river in a temper and her friends rushed after her, eager to see what would happen, because when Heer was in a temper there was no knowing what she would do.

But when they reached the banks of the river, they slowed down and soon they stopped. The sun was going down. The ferryman was rowing his empty boat back across the wide river and was already halfway to the other side. On this side, two little boys sat cross-legged on the river bank watching a man who stood on the edge of the jetty, playing an evening *raga* on his flute. Bare foot, silhouetted against the sky, a simple dhoti covering his lean frame, he looked like one of the long-legged river birds which dotted the shore.

When he saw Heer and her friends, he stopped playing.

"Don't stop!" said the boys.

"You'd better go home," he said. "It's nearly dark."

The boys stood up, holding hands.

"That's Heer Sayal," one of them said, pointing at her.

"I know," said the man.

"How do you know?"

The other boy laughed.

"Don't be silly," he said.

Then they turned and walked slowly back towards the village, past Heer and her friends.

"Who is he?" Heer asked them as they went past.

The boys went on walking, answering her over their shoulders.

"His name's Ranjha."

"He's been looking for you."

Heer watched them go, hand in hand, vanishing into the shadows of the village. Then she turned and looked again at the man on the jetty. He was standing with his back to her now, looking out over the river.

Dhido Ranjha had been looking for her for weeks, ever since he left Takht Hazara. His brothers and their wives had taunted him with her name when his patience finally broke and, cursing them all, he strode out of the house.

"He will come back a rich man," they jeered.

"He will come back with Heer Sayal as his bride," they mocked.

"Your room will be waiting for you when you bring her back," they called after him.

"Make sure you invite us to the wedding!"

But that was not why he left. He left because he was the youngest of eight brothers. He left because, when his father died and the land was divided up between them, his share was just a patch of dry, stony ground. He left because there was nothing left for him in Takht

Hazara. He left because of Nooran.

Nooran was the youngest of his brothers' wives. She was also the most beautiful, as beautiful, they said, as Heer Sayal, with skin so smooth and feet so small and eyes so big that he was taken by surprise each time he saw her. Every day, when the sun was at its height and he was resting in the shade of the trees, she brought him his food and when he had finished eating he played his flute for her.

"This was a cruel trick your brothers played on you," she said to him one day. "They've made you into a poor farmer."

"No girl would refuse you for a husband," she said another day, "but no father would choose you for his daughter."

"What will you do for a wife?" she asked.

One day he fell asleep under the trees and when he woke up she was leaning over him, her black hair hiding the sun. He reached out and touched her face, which was so smooth it felt like cool water on his fingers, and he looked into her eyes, which were so near he thought he might drown in them.

"Will I do?" she asked.

But the answer he gave was not the answer she wanted to hear.

When he left, Nooran's voice was the loudest of all and he could hear the sound of her laughter long after he had left the village.

He walked for weeks, playing his flute and remembering how happy he used to be when all he did every day was look after his father's herd and play his flute for the cows and the buffaloes and the

85

birds that perched on their backs. Slowly, his anger faded and he began to feel happy again. When he came to a village, people came out to hear him play and they gave him food and sometimes they invited him into their houses and let him sleep outside on the veranda.

He did not realise that he was looking for Heer Sayal until he came to a river, unwinding like a sari across the fat green fields, and saw a village on the other side and begged the ferryman to take him across. But he had no money to put in the ferryman's outstretched hand.

"Here," he said, putting his flute into his hand, "take this and give it back to me on the other side. If you won't take me, I'll swim across."

He waded into the water, the ferryman climbed into the boat and soon they were keeping pace with each other, one swimming, the other rowing, while the passengers took sides, some cheering for the ferryman, some for the stranger.

"What's your name?" one of the women called.

"Ranjha," he called back, holding his head above the water.

"Come on, Ranjha! You can do it!"

"Come on, Luddan! Pull harder!"

"I can't! You're all too heavy! You women are too fat!"

"Ranjha! Ranjha!"

"Luddan! Luddan!"

But Chenab is wide and before they were even halfway across Ranjha began to fall behind.

"Slow down, Luddan!"

"Slow down? Why should I slow down? I'm winning!"

But even Luddan's supporters could see that the race was over.

"Slow down!" they all cried. "Look at him! Do you want him to drown? If he drowns it will be your fault!"

Luddan stopped rowing and rested on his oars while the women leaned over the side of the ferry, stretching out their hands to the flagging swimmer.

"Come on! We'll save you!"

"Swim to the side of the boat!"

"Take my hand!"

"Be careful!" cried Luddan, as they hauled him out of the water, causing the boat to rock wildly from side to side. "Do you want to drown us all?"

Ranjha quickly recovered his good spirits when he found himself surrounded by fat women all convinced that they had saved him from drowning. One of them took off her woollen shawl and wrapped it round his shoulders, another took off her chunni and used it to dry his hands and arms. They sat him down on a padded seat at the back of the ferry.

"Hey!" cried Luddan. "That's Heer Sayal's seat! He can't sit there!"

But the women poured scorn on his objections.

"When does she ever sit on this seat?"

"When does she ever come on your ferry?"

"She was a little girl when this seat was made. She's a woman now, old enough to be married. Now she has padding on her behind like the rest of us."

So now Ranjha knew what had brought him to this place. He picked up his flute and started to play. The children leaned their heads on their mothers' bosoms. The women smiled and stroked their children's hair. Two boys sat in the bottom of the boat, watching Ranjha as closely as they watched the old man in the village who did magic tricks with bangles and scarves and birds. This man could do magic with a piece of wood. Luddan rested on his oars until, with a start, he realised that the boat was drifting downstream and started to row again. When he brought the boat alongside the jetty, nobody moved.

When he saw Heer Sayal, Ranjha's heart beat quickly with excitement and fear. He understood the excitement but not the fear. It was not her beauty that moved him, but something else. When he looked at her, his life went out of him and into her. He turned away and looked over the water, trying to understand.

When she saw Didho Ranjha, Heer felt a sob rise in her throat. It was a sob of joy and a sob of grief. She felt as if he had come back to her after a long absence and she was afraid that he might not recognise her. If he had not turned and walked towards her, she would have walked away.

"My name is Ranjha," he said, bowing to Heer and her friends.

Heer moved a little closer to her friend, Sajda, and held her hand.

It reminded Sajda, who was older than Heer, of the way she used to hold her hand when they were little. She looked at Heer, smiled and looked back at Ranjha.

"I tried to swim across the river but the people on the ferry had to rescue me. I'm a stranger here. Can you tell me where I am?"

The other girls glanced at Heer, wondering what she would say.

"This is Jhang," said Sajda.

"Jhang," said Ranjha, thoughtfully. "When I saw it from the other side of the river, there was something... If I could find work here... Once I was a cowherd. There must be work for a cowherd in Jhang. But I'm tired. I've been walking for a long time. I need somewhere to sleep. Do you know anyone who would give me a bed for the night?"

They took him to the home of the old barber woman and left him there.

In the evening, when she was filling her father's hookah, Heer told him about the stranger.

"He said he might stay here," she said, "if he could find work. He said he was his father's cowherd but when his father died he left his village. He's been walking from place to place, living on what people give him for playing his flute. When he came to the river he decided to swim across but he nearly drowned and the women on the ferry had to rescue him. When we met him he was playing his flute on the jetty. Will you give him a job?"

"He sounds like a fool," said Chuchak Khan.

"Please!"

Ranjha was the best herdsman Chuchak Khan had ever had. The cows and the buffaloes gave more milk than ever before. The sound of their contented lowing seemed pitched to a deeper note. The butter was whiter, the curd more glossy. When his wife, Malliki, brought him lassi to drink in the afternoon, he thought he had never tasted anything so good.

Every morning, when the sun was rising, Ranjha played his flute and led the herd out to pasture and when the sun was sinking in the west he led them back for milking. His morning raga was a sign for the women to light the fires in their kitchens, his evening raga for the birds to roost in the trees.

Every day, when the sun was up and the cattle were grazing in the fields, Heer and her friends brought him his midday meal and sat with him under the trees. They talked and laughed and sometimes the girls sang to him and sometimes he played to them. When the sun was at its height, they covered their heads and walked back to the village, leaving him alone to eat his meal.

In this way, without ever being alone together, Heer Sayal and Didho Ranjha came to know each other, Heer with her joy and her grief, Ranjha with his excitement and his fear.

One day, when the girls were singing one of their songs, Heer and Sajda came to sit beside Ranjha. Some of the girls stood up to dance and soon they were all dancing, clapping their hands and singing. One of them broke out of the circle and walked towards Heer and Sajda, reaching out her hands. Sajda took her hand and joined in the dance but Heer shook her head and stayed beside Ranjha on the grass.

"They're dancing for our wedding," said Ranjha, his fear gone.

Heer looked at him and smiled, her heart full of joy.

When the dance was over, the sun was past its height and the girls hurried away, calling goodbye to Ranjha as they went. Sajda bent down to pick up her chunni, which had fallen off in the dance. Standing up to put it on, wrapping it over her head and round her shoulders, she looked at Heer sitting at Ranjha's side. Then she turned and ran after the others.

Every day, Ranjha drove the herd past Kaidon's hut. Every day, Kaidon saw Heer and her friends walking out to the fields and every day, when the sun was at its height, he saw them walking back. When he saw them coming, he went inside and listened to their voices as they went past. Once, they stopped outside to feed his goat.

"Hello, Uncle!" they said. "You're goat is hungry. You should give her more food."

One of them knocked on his door.

"Uncle? Are you there?"

It was Heer's voice.

"Should we bring food for your goat every day? Should we bring something for you too?"

He waited until they had gone, then opened the door and looked outside. On the ground, just out of reach of the tethered goat, was an apple. He picked it up and bit into it. It was good. There was no maggot inside. But he knew they were up to something.

Every day, on their way back to the village, they fed his goat and left food for him outside the door.

"Hello, Uncle!" they called. "Kaidon Uncle? Are you there? There's food for you outside the door."

He knew they were laughing at him. If he could see them, he would be able to see through their kindness.

"They feed Kaidon like they feed his goat," he thought. "Is Kaidon a goat too?"

Once, the door opened and from the corner where he sat in the dark he saw Heer's face in a shaft of sunlight.

"Uncle?" she said. But she didn't see him sitting in the corner. She turned away and closed the door behind her. He could still see her face in the darkness.

"Why should Kaidon sit in the dark," he thought, "when Heer is in the sun? If she wants to feed me, let her put the food in my hand. Kaidon is not a goat."

The next day, when they came to Kaidon's hut and saw him standing outside, leaning on his long staff, one of Heer's friends turned to the others and said, "Look! Two goats! One tied to a little post, the other to a big one!"

Everyone laughed, but Heer said, "That's unkind. You shouldn't say such things about poor Kaidon."

The girl was about to object that Heer herself had said far worse things about 'poor Kaidon', but Sajda put a hand on her arm and she thought better of it. None of them had got used to the change in Heer, although they all knew what had caused it, and none of them quite believed it. So they went on letting her have her own way as they always had done. Some of them went to feed the goat, while Heer went up to Kaidon, stooped and touched his feet.

Kaidon took the food which she placed in his hand and wondered, as she and her friends walked away, what she was plotting.

A few days later, when the girls stopped as usual on their way back to the village, Heer was not with them. It was Sajda who touched his knee and gave him something for his midday meal before hurrying back to the village with the others. The sun was going down when, squatting outside his hut, a shawl over his head, he saw Heer walking towards him. She stopped to touch his feet and then walked on. A little later, Ranjha came past with the herd.

"Every day," Kaidon said to Chuchak Khan, "your daughter and her friends follow your herdsman out to the fields. I see them every day, going past my hut."

"And they make fun of you," said Chuchak Khan. "I know, I know. I'll talk to them about it. Take no notice of them, brother. They're only children."

Kaidon shook his head.

"No," he said. "They don't make fun of me."

"What then? I thought you'd come here to complain. That's what you usually do."

He laughed and Sultan, his eldest son, who was sitting with him, laughed too.

"I haven't come to complain," said Kaidon. "I've come to tell you about Heer and Ranjha."

He told them that he wanted to protect the honour of the Sayals, because he was a Sayal too, poor though he was. He told them that he had taken his goat to find new grazing on the edge of the forest. He told them that he had seen Heer and Ranjha sitting together under the trees. He told them that he had seen them lie down together.

He would have told them more if they had not heard someone shouting outside the gate. He would have told them more if Sajda had not seen him hurrying back from the fields with his goat. He would have told them more if she had not torn a branch from a thorn bush and scratched her face and arms with it till they bled.

"There he is!" she shouted, standing at the gate.

Her father and two of her brothers rushed towards Kaidon. Sultan stood up. Sajda's mother stood at the gate, comforting her weeping daughter.

"Take him away!" said Chuchak Khan to his son. "Put him in a room and make sure he doesn't run away."

"Kaidon can't run," said Sultan, kicking his staff away and dragging him across the courtyard.

The panchayat agreed, when Chuchak Khan called them together the next day, that Kaidon should be flogged for what he had done to Sajda and banished from the village for a year. Malliki was overjoyed when, later that same day, he told her that it was time to find a husband for their daughter.

But Sultan was unhappy. What Kaidon had said was only what other people were thinking. For the honour of the family, he said, Ranjha should go. But Ranjha was the best herdsman Chuchak Khan had ever had and he did not want to lose him.

"Let him stay," he said, "and we will find a husband for your sister. Soon she will be gone. Let me hear no more about this."

The time that Heer and Ranjha spent together was a kind of oblivion. They were like gods, for whom time and life have no meaning. They worshipped each other and the ritual of love made them immortal. Sometimes, in his ecstasy, Ranjha thought he had died and then he remembered his fear. Sometimes Heer sobbed and thought she was in paradise and then she remembered her grief.

Where now there are only shrines to holy men, then there were no shrines but only holy men. Holiest among them were five whose lives are now remembered in the shrine at Panch Peer. Their meeting with Heer and Ranjha was part of the long journey which brought them at last to that state of perfect understanding for which they are revered by those who visit their shrine.

Walking together in meditation through the forest, the five peers found Heer and Ranjha sitting together in a clearing. Hearing their footsteps on the leaves, Heer jumped to her feet and would have run away, but Ranjha had seen the blue robes of the holy men between the trees and held her wrist.

"No," he said. "Don't run away. There's nothing to be afraid of."

Heer looked round and saw the five men with their long, white beards walking towards them across the clearing.

"Who are they?" she said, looking up at Ranjha, who still held her tightly. When he told her, there was something in his voice that made her heart beat faster. Letting go of her wrist, he stepped forward and greeted the five peers. Heer stood behind him with her head bowed.

"Please," said Ranjha, stooping to touch the ground where the holy men stood, "rest here a while and sit with us. We need your blessing."

The five sages gathered their robes around them and sat down on the grass. Ranjha placed before them the food that was left from their midday meal. Heer picked up the pitcher that she brought with her every day and poured a little water on each of their hands. She gave them the end of her dupatta to dry them with, then stepped back and stood beside a tree with her head bowed.

"People say you have been walking for many years in your search for wisdom," said Ranjha, sitting on the grass in front of them.

"It takes many years to forget what you think you know and empty your mind so that it can receive the truth," one of them said.

"Often children know more than old men," said another. "You are young and already you have begun your journey towards ignorance."

"Old men learn to hide from the truth," said another.

"First we learn to lie to each other, then we learn to lie to ourselves. Soon, the truth is forgotten."

"And you?" said Ranjha, leaning forward eagerly. "Have you found what truth is?"

The five holy men took food from the thali but none of them spoke.

"Forgive me," said Ranjha. "It was stupid of me to ask such a question."

"No," said one of the men. "It was not stupid to ask the question, only to expect an answer."

"Why?" said Heer.

Everyone looked at her and for a moment she regretted giving way to the impulse that had made her speak. But only for a moment.

"Why should he not expect an answer?" she said, meeting their surprised looks with a bold stare. "Is that not what you expect? Is that not what you are searching for?"

The five old men stopped eating and looked at each other.

"Ask me the question," she went on, "and I will give you my answer."

"Very well," one of them said. "Tell us, what is truth?"

"The answer is easy," said Heer. "The truth is Ranjha. He is my truth. I love him."

Slowly, the five old men in their blue robes rose to their feet. Ranjha stood up too, afraid that Heer had offended them with her boldness.

"And Ranjha?" one of them asked. "Does he love you?"

"I know he does, but if he did not it would make no difference. It would grieve me, but I would still love him."

"And you?" said another, turning to Ranjha. "What is your answer?"

Ranjha stood beside Heer and took her hand.

"My answer is the same," he said. "Heer is my truth. I love her as she loves me. But sometimes I feel afraid. I don't know why."

"Some people say that love is the way to God," the holy man replied. "If that is true, who would not feel afraid?"

The five peers fell to disputing.

"Other people say that the only way to know God is to turn your back on human desire," said the first.

"What has the love between a man and a woman to do with the love of man for God?" said the second.

"How can the way to human happiness also be the way to the love of God?" said the third.

"How can it not be," said the fourth, "if the love of God is the way to human happiness?"

"The love between Heer and Ranjha is beyond dispute," said the fifth.

"You asked for our blessing," he said, turning to Ranjha. "You shall have it."

But Ranjha shook his head.

"How can you give us your blessing," he said, "when we are not married? Marry us first and then give us your blessing."

Heer joyfully gave her consent and knelt with Ranjha before the holy men. One of the five peers spoke the words of the nikah and the others were witnesses to the contract. So they were married.

"Now," said Ranjha, "please give us your blessing."

Heer and Ranjha bowed their heads and listened to the words of the blessing.

"There is one life and one life only."

"Though we spend a lifetime with those we love, no one goes with us when we die."

"May God give you his special blessing."

"May you be always together in life."

"May you be together too even in death."

They clung to each other and, when they looked up, the five holy men had gone.

The Khairas were a wealthy and powerful family from the village of Rangpur. Saida was the eldest son and he was a good match for Heer. The arrangements were made quickly. When Heer found out, she went to her bedroom and wept. The next day she went in search of Ranjha. But one of the other men drove the herd to the fields that day. Ranjha was missing.

"Where is he?" she asked Sajda. "Where has he gone?"

"Perhaps he has gone away to make it easier for you," said Sajda. But Heer shook her head.

"No," she said. "He would not leave me. Look for him, Sajda. Please find him for me."

Sajda spent the day searching for Ranjha, but there was no sign of him. She went down to the river to ask the ferryman whether he had crossed the river. But Luddan had not seen him. She looked across the wide river, remembering how Ranjha had tried to swim across and nearly drowned. She walked across the fields and asked the herdsman if he knew where he was. But the herdsman shrugged his shoulders.

"They told me he had gone away," he said. "That's all."

"Who told you?"

"The Khan's son," he said. "Sultan."

Sajda turned away and walked back to the village, past Kaidon's empty hut. She wondered where Kaidon was now. Perhaps it would have been better after all if she had let things take their course. Feeling helpless and foolish, she went back to Heer.

"Ranjha loves you," she said, "and that is why he has gone, because he knows he cannot be your husband and he does not want you to suffer because of him."

But Heer shook her head.

"What then?" Sajda said.

Heer looked away.

"Sultan has killed him."

Saida Khaira left the village of Rangpur before dawn on a white horse. He was dressed all in white, white turban, white sherwani, white churidar, white jutti. His mother stood outside the gate and watched until he was out of sight. In the evening he would return, proud and tall on his horse, and behind him would come his bride in her doli. There would be music and dancing and a great feast. She turned to go back inside. The servant closed the gate, yawned, sat down beside the wall, shivered and pulled his shawl around him. Slowly the sky lightened and Heer's groom galloped across the plain, like the moon in search of the sun.

In the morning, Heer was unable to speak. Her mother explained to the maulvi who had come to perform the marriage ceremony that a wasp had flown into her mouth and stung her. Her tongue was swollen and they had given her some medicine to ease the pain but it had made her drowsy. Naturally, Heer did not want the marriage to be delayed but she was worried that, when the maulvi asked her if she consented to the marriage, she would not be able to answer.

"Will she be able to give some sign?" he said. "If she can nod her head or make some other sign, I think there will be no problem."

When they told him that Ranjha had gone, Chuchak Khan wondered what he had done to lose his beautiful daughter and his wonderful herdsman both in the same week. Neither his hookah in the evening nor his lassi in the afternoon would ever taste the same again. It put him in a bad temper for the wedding and he was glad when it was over.

Heer could not understand how she came to be sitting in the doli. She had not given her consent, so how could she be sitting there? Everything was confused, as if she was dreaming. In the morning, there had been an argument with her mother. She remembered calling for her father and running to the door, but her mother caught her and slapped her face. She touched her cheek under her veil. It was still sore. She hadn't dreamed it. Her mother had caught her and slapped her face and thrown her on the floor. Perhaps she was still dreaming, still lying on her bed, dreaming she was in this doli, being carried through the village. She remembered someone picking her up. She tried to call for her father again but they covered her mouth and pushed her down onto the bed. What then? She remembered hearing horse's hooves clattering outside and music playing and drums and loud voices. She remembered Sajda painting her hands with henna, speaking gently to her, telling her that she must try to forget about Ranjha and accept her fate. She tried to speak but no words came out. All she could do was shake her head. Sajda asked her if her mouth still hurt.

"Open your mouth and let me see," she said. "Where did it sting you?"

Later, they put on her wedding clothes and took her outside. There was a white horse in the courtyard and when she came out everyone clapped and the drums started playing and the horse reared up on its hind legs. They led her to her father and he took her arm and told her to lean on him. She looked up at him and smiled, knowing he would take care of her. All she had to do was to say no when the maulvi asked if she gave her consent. But when she heard him ask and tried to speak, she found she could not. She moved her lips behind her veil, but she could make no sound. She tried to lift her veil so that they could see her mouth, see her saying no, but her hands were weak and she could not find the end of her veil.

"No!" she said. "No! No! No!"

But no one could hear her.

"It's alright," said her father, patting her hand. "It's alright."

"Is it?" she said, looking up at him through her veil, but no sound came from her lips.

"It's alright," he said. "He knows all about it."

She gave up trying to speak and bowed her head, knowing she

would be safe, because she had not said yes.

So why was she here in the doli? She reached for the door but her hands were still weak and she could not find the handle. She felt very tired. She just wanted to sleep. The doli swayed backwards and forwards. She closed her eyes and dreamed that she was sitting on a swing and Ranjha was pushing her, backwards and forwards, backwards and forwards.

"Heer!" he called, as he pushed. "Heer!"

Backwards and forwards, backwards and forwards.

"Heer! Heer!"

She opened her eyes.

"Heer!"

Ranjha was calling her.

"Heer!"

She put her face to the window.

"Heer!"

"Ranjha!" she called, but no words came out. "Ranjha! Ranjha!"

She tore off her veil so that he could see her lips saying his name.

"Ranjha! Ranjha!"

They had thrown him onto the road from the back of the cart. He rolled over two or three times and then lay still. His arms and legs were bruised and one eye was closed from the beating they had given him. Someone laughed.

"Challo!" said one of the others. "Let's go!"

Hooves scuffled in the dust, cart wheels scraped, leather strained, wood creaked. He lifted his head and saw the cart turning in the road. He struggled to his feet and stumbled out of the way. As the cart went past, someone struck him on the back of the head with a stick, then tossed it up into the air. More laughter. The stick bounced on the road and rolled towards him. It was his flute.

He sat for a few minutes at the side of the road, gathering his strength. They had told him that if he went back they would kill him, but he had no choice. He had to find Heer. He could feel his heart thumping. He could hear it in his head. It was the old excitement. The old fear. He picked up his flute and set off to walk along the road, driven on by the relentless beating of his heart. Heer. Heer. Heer. Heer. Heer. Heer.

Eventually, he came to the river. Luddan was sitting in his boat beside the jetty and, when he saw Ranjha, he came running towards him.

"What have they done to you?" he said. "Come! Let me take you across the river. Come!"

He tried to drag him into the boat but Ranjha would not go with him.

"Are you mad?" said Luddan. "They've half killed you already. Do you want them to finish the job? Get in the boat! And lie down," he added, looking round nervously. "If they see you, they'll kill me too."

But still Ranjha refused.

"I must find Heer," he said. "I must see her."

"It's too late," said Luddan. "Too late."

Luddan was right. He found her, but it was too late. He could run no further. He sank to his knees and watched in despair as they carried her away. A cloud of dust rose, as the dust rises from the plain every day to hide the setting sun, and she was gone.

He stood up and walked back to the river. There he sat through the night, watching the moon floating on the water, and in the morning Luddan took him over the river. Luddan's wife bathed his wounds and gave him some food. He stayed with them for a few days and Luddan's wife took care of him. But one morning, when she took him his food, he had gone.

"He is so sad," she said to her husband. "All day he sits by the river. I am afraid he will take his own life. You must look for him."

Luddan took his boat and rowed downstream, looking for Ranjha on the river bank or his body in the water. But he found nothing and gave up the search.

"Poor boy," said his wife, shaking her head sadly. "His parents should have found him a wife, then none of this would have happened."

At the wedding feast, Heer hid behind her veil and said nothing. Khaira told everyone about the wasp. When they offered food, she shook her head. After a while Khaira's sister, Sehti, put her arm around her and took her inside. When Khaira came to her later, he lay down beside her, but she was asleep and he was afraid to touch her. The next day, they sent for the hakim but she refused to lift her veil and let him look in her mouth. He left some medicine for her but she would not take it. At night, when Khaira lay down beside her again, he put his hand on her head and stroked her hair, but she turned away from him. On the third night, he tried to force himself on her but she pushed him away. Sometimes he pleaded with her, sometimes he ordered her, sometimes he spoke gently to her. Once, he struck her, then fell on his knees and begged her forgiveness. Often, he lay awake all night staring at the ceiling, waiting for the sun to rise so that he could get up and leave her. They had made her his bride, but he could not make her his wife. He was angry and ashamed, too ashamed to tell anyone, but his mother knew and Sehti guessed.

Sehti had her own secrets. She liked to sit with Heer and talk to her. There was nothing Sehti liked more than talking, especially if there were secrets to tell. And Heer was a good listener. She said nothing, but Sehti knew that she was listening. There was a man in the village who was dumb. Sehti liked talking to him because of the way he answered with his eyes. It was the same with Heer. She knew that she could trust her and she told her things she had never told anyone else. They had already become friends long before Heer broke her silence.

The first hint came when a smile crept across Heer's face, like the shiver that runs across frozen water at the break of day.

"What is it?" said Sehti. "Why are you smiling?"

But Heer shook her head and Sehti went on talking about her friend who was in love with Murad, the camel driver.

"Murad wants her to run away with him and go to live with his aunt in the hills. He says they will be safe there because his Baluchi kinsmen will protect them. But my friend is too scared to go with him because she knows her family will be angry and will go after them. What do you think, Heer? What should she do?"

Another day, she told Heer about the yogi who had come to live in a hut in the garden of Kalabagh on the edge of the forest. He had become a favourite with all the women in the village, brides and widows, betrothed and bereaved, blessed and barren. No one knew who he was or where he came from, but they took him food and he answered their questions and then he played beautiful music to them on his flute.

"My friend went to see him," she said. "She was going to tell him about Murad and ask him what she should do. But when she got there, she was too scared to say anything. Wasn't that silly of her?"

"Take me to him," said Heer. "I will ask him for her."

The next day, they walked to the Kalabagh garden. On the way, they passed other women walking back to the village, their faces half hidden behind the scarves that covered their heads, glancing curiously at Sehti and Heer as they went past. They stopped at the gate.

"You speak to him," whispered Sehti, pushing her forward. "I'll wait here for you."

From the gate she could see an old hut at the end of the garden, where the tall dark trees of the forest leaned over the wall. It reminded her of Kaidon's hut and she thought of Sajda. As she came closer, she saw a man sitting cross-legged on the ground. His body, smeared with ash, was the colour of clay. No, she thought, looking at him through her veil, it is not him. But then he turned his head and looked at her and she saw that it was him.

A wave of cold water slapped her face and stopped her breath. She tried to walk towards him but the water drove her back. She saw him stand up and come towards her. She reached out her arms but the water lifted her off her feet. She tried to speak but her head was under the water and all she could feel was its powerful arms wrapping themselves around her limbs. She let go and the water swept her away.

"What did he say?" asked Sehti, when Heer joined her again at the gate.

"He said it would be alright," said Heer. "He said everything would be alright. He said he would help your friend. He said she would be happy again and everything would be alright."

Sehti took her hand and they walked back to the village.

A briar thorn, a potion made with herbs, two planks removed from the back of the hut, a dark night, a friend with a horse. These were the ingredients for their escape. On the road that led from the village to the garden, Heer broke a thorn from a briar and pressed it twice into her ankle. Beads of blood sprang from the two small holes like jewels. Then she drank the potion that Ranjha had given her.

"It will make you sweat," he said. "You will feel dizzy and then you will fall asleep. You must be with me by nightfall. I will see to everything else."

People came running when Sehti called for help.

"She has been bitten by a snake," she said. "Look at her ankle. Look at the sweat on her face. Help me carry her home."

They laid her on a charpoi and sent for the hakim, but Heer's eyes were closed, her breath was faint and her face was pale. The hakim shook his head. Khaira stared at his bride's pale face and turned to his mother.

"Is this how it ends?" he said.

His mother turned to the hakim. "Is there nothing you can do?" she said.

The hakim scratched his beard. "You could ask the snake charmer to play," he said. "That sometimes helps to draw the poison."

They sent for the snake charmer and he sat on the ground in front of the charpoi and looked at the two red marks on Heer's ankle and put the gourd pipe to his mouth and blew out his cheeks and played. But it made no difference and in the end they gave him some money and he went away.

"She is dying," said Khaira. "There is nothing we can do."

"We must keep trying," said Sehti. "If the hakim can do nothing and the snake charmer can do nothing, send for the yogi and ask him to help. We can't just stand here and watch her die."

"What can he do?" said Khaira.

"I don't know," said Sehti. "But at least let's ask him."

"You are right, Sehti," said her mother. "Send someone to the Kalabagh garden and ask him to come."

"I will go," said Sehti and ran out of the courtyard before anyone could stop her.

When she came back, she was alone and out of breath. Her mother looked at her anxiously.

"He would not come?" she said.

Khaira shook his head. "There is nothing we can do," he said. "She is dying."

"No," said Sehti, panting. "He says he will help if he can. But we must take her to him and leave her there."

"Leave her?" said Khaira.

Sehti nodded and took a deep breath. "It's the only hope we have," she said. "He says there are herbs he can use and prayers he can say, but we must leave her with him and in the morning we can come for her."

Her brother looked away and shook his head. She went to him and put her hand on his arm.

"It's our only hope," she said.

They carried the charpoi to the Kalabagh garden and put it down in front of the hut, where the yogi sat beside a small fire. The air was filled with the smell of smoke and the scent of herbs. Night was falling and the garden was noisy with the sound of birds roosting in the trees beyond the wall. The yogi stood up and asked them to carry her into the hut and leave her there until morning

As they walked back towards the gate, the sun sank below the horizon and, like children whose games are over for the day, the birds fell silent. They stopped at the gate and looked back. Pale smoke from the fire drifted through the air and draped the branches of the trees like ghostly creepers.

"Stay here," said Khaira to the men who had carried the charpoi. "We will come at dawn."

As they walked back to the village, a flute began to play and they looked over their shoulders. The music seemed to be in the air, falling around them like soft evening rain. Each note sounded like a drop of water falling onto a leaf. It made them want to stop and listen, but Sehti hurried them on.

Heer opened her eyes. Ranjha took the flute from his lips and bent down to kiss her.

"Will everything be alright?" she said.

"Yes," he said. "You will feel better soon, as if nothing had happened. But we must be careful. They will have left a guard at the gate. I will leave you here and sit outside. Then if they come into the garden they will see me. Later, they will lie down to sleep and then it will be safe for us to go."

In the middle of the night he came back into the hut and closed the door behind him. She stood up when he came in and he wrapped a woollen shawl around her. Then he went to the back of the hut and carefully removed two planks from the wall. He stepped through and turned to take her hand. She followed and found herself standing in the forest.

"Come," he said, leading her through the trees.

She saw something move and held back.

"It's alright," he said. "Murad is waiting for us."

The camel driver stepped out from behind a tree and led them to the edge of the forest, where he had tethered a horse to a tree. He untied it and held the reins while Ranjha climbed into the saddle. Then he gave the reins to Ranjha and helped Heer to climb up behind him. She put her arms around his waist and rested her head on his back. Ranjha leaned down and took Murad's hand.

"Wait until they follow us," he said. "Then it will be safe for you to go."

The two men held hands for a few moments.

"You should go now," said Murad, releasing his hand. "Get as far away as you can before dawn."

Then he turned and walked back through the forest to wait for the morning and the ride he would make later, with Sehti behind him, while her family were looking the other way, busy chasing after her brother's wife and the man who had stolen her away from him by a trick. Such a clever trick, he thought, as he settled down to sleep beside his camels. Such a clever trick!

He woke, as usual, just before dawn, fed the camels and ate some breakfast in the house. Then he waited and listened. Rumour was already wide awake, flying around the village like a flock of noisy starlings.

"He was a fool to marry her."

"The Sayals kept it hushed up."

"You can't stop people talking."

"The Sayals are big people. They can do what they like."

"The Khairas are big people too."

"They will find them and bring them back."

"Do you think they will kill them?"

"They must for their honour."

Later in the morning, Murad led his horse out of the village and waited by the side of the road. When he saw a boy running down the road towards him, he climbed onto the horse and the boy jumped up behind him.

"I wouldn't have recognised you," he said, feeling Sehti's arms around his waist. "Did anyone see you?"

"No," she said. "When they found out they'd gone, all they thought about was chasing after them. It was easy for me to go without anyone noticing."

"And when they do," said Murad, "there will be no one left to come looking for you."

"Will they get away, Murad?" she said. "Will they be alright?"

Murad shrugged his shoulders and Sehti tightened her grip as their horse carried them at a gallop across the plain and up into the hills.

Heer and Ranjha rode from place to place for three days before their pursuers caught up with them. The people of Kot Kabula saw a cloud of dust and out of it came a band of horsemen riding towards the town. Children stopped and stared, then turned and ran back to their houses. Their mothers pulled them inside and closed the doors. The men saw the swords which the horsemen carried and some of them ran to fetch the thanedar, thinking the town was being attacked by bandits.

The thanedar and his men were sitting under a tree in the courtyard, drinking tea with two thieves who had, over many years, become regular inhabitants of Kot Kabula's gaol. But when they heard people banging on the gate and shouting for them to come quickly because the town was under attack, they bundled the men back into the gaol, picked up their weapons and hurried out to see what was going on.

Ranjha broke off another piece of chapatti and dipped it into the bowl of kali dhal which he was sharing with Heer at a table beside the road. Heer was tired. Her eyes were closed. She heard someone shouting and opened them. Ranjha stood up and Heer looked round. A group of men on horses were galloping along the road and people were hurrying to get out of their way. Someone stumbled and fell. One of the men jumped off his horse and ran towards them. Ranjha picked up the bowl of dahl and threw it in the man's face. The man gasped and staggered, putting his hands to his face. Heer took Ranjha's arm and tried to pull him away. The horsemen had all dismounted. Some of them held the horses, while the others ran towards them. Two of them lunged at Ranjha, another pulled Heer away from him.

"Stop them!" cried Heer. "They will kill him!"

The thanedar and his men pushed their way through the crowd and blocked the men's path as they dragged Heer and Ranjha back towards the horses. They tried to push past them, ignoring the thanedar's order to stop, until his men raised their sticks and looked as if they would be glad of an excuse to demonstrate their skill in using them.

"That's better," said the *thanedar*, when the men stopped and he stood facing them with his men behind him. "Now, tell me who you are and what your business is here."

Still holding Heer and Ranjha, the men told him in a few words about the offence they had committed and the punishment they would receive when they took them back to Rangpur. But the thanedar shook his head.

"No, no!" he said. "No, no! Not permitted. If there has been any offence, the case must be tried here in Kot Kabula."

The men held their prisoners more tightly and looked at each other.

"Why here? The offence took place in Rangpur. The case must be tried there."

"No, no!" said the thanedar. "No, no! Offence took place in Rangpur, but arrest takes place in Kot Kabula. No, no! I am thanedar in Kot Kabula. Arrest is my job. Let them go."

Reluctantly, but with little choice now but to do as they were told, their captors let them go. Ranjha took Heer's hand, then turned to their rescuers and thanked them. The thanedar turned to his men.

"Arrest them," he said.

They took them to the elders who agreed that the case should be tried in Kot Kabula where the arrest had taken place and both sides of the story could be heard without prejudice.

"The qazi of Kot Kabula is famous for his wisdom," they said. "He will conduct the trial and decide who is telling the truth and who is lying, who is in the right and who is in the wrong."

Rooms were found for the runaways and their pursuers while the qazi made his preparations. When he had spoken to them one by one and listened to their stories, he set a date for the trial and sent for witnesses from Jhang and Rangpur to give their evidence and help him decide which of the stories he should believe.

The trial was held in the courtyard of a big house belonging to one of the elders. The witnesses waited in rooms inside the house where they could neither speak to each other nor hear what was going on outside. The town was thronged with people eager to catch a glimpse of the beautiful Heer Sayal about whom they had heard so many stories. Some of them tried to climb the wall and peep over, but if the thanedar's men saw a pair of hands at the top of the wall they gave them a sharp rap with their sticks and listened with satisfaction to the cry of pain that came from behind the wall, followed a moment later by the sound of a body falling to the ground.

The qazi was an old man with a long, white beard and eyes that looked thoughtfully and dispassionately on all those who were brought before him to answer his questions and tell him their stories. He heard many stories. Malliki told him about a wasp. Sajda told him about a thorn bush. Chuchak Khan told him about his afternoon lassi and his evening hookah. Luddan told him about a seat with a silk cover. Sultan told him about a cripple. Khaira told him about a yogi. Ranjha told him about the five peers. Heer told him about a snake.

But there was one more story yet to hear. He drank some tea. He took a little food. He closed his eyes and slept for a while. Someone touched his shoulder. He opened his eyes. It was the thanedar.

"Are they here?" he said.

The thanedar nodded.

"Take me to them."

The courtyard dozed through the afternoon, sinking into the shade like a bucket lowered into a well. The thanedar's men lounged against the wall. Lizards blinked. Birds flew in and out of the shadows, splashing through the sunshine. And inside the house, they waited.

Heer was thinking about Sehti and Murad. If they made it to the hills, she thought, they will be safe. She imagined the moment when they stopped to look back across the plain and knew for the first time that they were free. All it takes to be free, she thought, is one moment. One beat of a bird's wing. One look.

Ranjha dreamed that he was back in Takht Hazara and when he went to his room he found Nooran in his bed. When he asked her why she was there, she said it was because she loved him. He objected that she was his brother's wife, but she said that she loved him, not his brother. He warned her that his brother might kill her, but she said that she did not care because she loved him. He dragged her out of the bed and threw her on the ground and when he looked down he saw that she was dead. But when he looked more closely at the body he saw that it was not Nooran, but Heer.

He was woken from his troubled sleep by a voice outside the door.

"Qazi is ready now. All come please! Qazi is waiting. Challo! Come please! Challo-ji! Qazi is waiting. Please come!"

The thanedar's summons rescued him from his dream. He jumped up and went outside, where the thanedar's men were using their sticks to show people where to stand, a display of authority which was resented by the grandees of Jhang and Rangpur almost as much as it was enjoyed by the ordinary people of Kot Kabula, some of whom had now managed to climb to the top of the wall and were waiting eagerly to hear the qazi's verdict. When everyone was assembled, the thanedar ordered his men back to their positions around the walls, the qazi stood up and everyone fell silent.

There was no doubt whose side the people of Kot Kabula were on and when the qazi delivered his judgement a great cheer went up and at least one person fell off the wall. But the thanedar's men were too busy keeping order among the people in the courtyard to notice what was happening on the wall. The thanedar had to call several times for silence, while his men threatened to enforce his request with their sticks, before order was restored and the qazi was able to speak again.

"The matter is settled," he repeated. "Ranjha and Heer are free to go."

Later, when everyone had gone, he sat with the elders in the courtyard and told them the whole story, as he had heard it from Heer and Ranjha and Chuchak Khan and Malliki and Luddan and Sajda and Sultan and the Khairas and the five peers. He shook his head sadly when he came to the end of the story.

"Thank God," he said, "we do not have such people in Kot Kabula."

The elders agreed wholeheartedly and congratulated him on the way he had got to the bottom of the whole sad business. So many lies, they said. So much unhappiness. Such beauty. Such sadness. Heer Sayal, they all agreed, was as beautiful as everyone said she was.

The qazi nodded. "Please God, she will find happiness now," he said.

The Khairas and the Sayals left quickly and had little to say to each other. In some ways, for some of them, the verdict had come as a relief. The Khairas were glad to put it all behind them and the only thing the Sayals could do was to put a brave face on it.

"The Rhanjas are a good family after all," Chuchak Khan said to his wife. "As good as the Khairas."

Life, he thought, would soon return to normal. There might even be times when Heer would fill his hookah again in the evening. And if Ranjha could not be reconciled with his brothers, why should he not stay in Jhang and look after the herd? He could give him land, build him a house. Why not?

"It will take time," said Malliki. "Feelings have been hurt. Fresh wounds need time to heal. Remember you have sons as well as a daughter."

"Come with me now to Takht Hazara," said Ranjha, as he led his horse out of Kot Kabula, with Heer at his side. "That's where we belong now. Everyone will welcome you. Come!"

He mounted the horse and held out his hand for Heer to climb up behind him. But Heer hesitated and looked back at her family, her brother on his horse, her mother sitting in the tonga, her father talking to the servants.

"They will expect me to go back with them," she said. "They will want to send me to Takht Hazara dressed as a bride, carried in a doli, not riding behind you on your horse."

She took his hand in both of hers and put it to her lips.

"I would like that too," she added, smiling up at him.

"You are my wife already," he said.

"But they are still my family. Wait a few days and then I will come to you as your bride. Then your family will be my family."

"How long must I wait?"

"Not long," she said. "A few days. Make peace with your brothers and let me make peace with mine. I will come to you in a week."

"A week is too long," he said.

She laughed.

"A week is seven days."

"A week is for ever."

She shook her head.

"Seven days. That's all. It will soon be gone and then we will be together always."

She stood by the side of the road and watched until his horse was lost in the dust and the dust had settled and all that was left was an empty road. She turned and walked towards her family, climbing into the tonga beside her mother. Sultan looked round, then dug his heels into his horse's flanks and rode off at a gallop. Her father climbed up in front, took the reins from the servant's hands, straightened his back, clicked his tongue and set off on the journey home, with as much dignity as circumstances would allow.

Ranjha stopped in the village and, letting his horse graze on a patch of grass, picked up his flute and started to play. A woman came to the door of her house to listen. She held a sleeping baby in her arms. Another child, just old enough to walk, pushed his way past her and tottered across the road, holding out his arms. Ranjha stopped playing and held out his flute. The child took it from him and stared at it with big eyes. He held out his hand and the child gave the flute back to him, then turned and rushed back to his mother, holding his arms out to her. When he reached her, he held onto her legs and looked up at her. The woman smiled shyly at Ranjha and he smiled back at her.

"Another baby," he said. "A boy?"

"A girl."

"I have a wife now," said Ranjha, imagining Heer with a baby girl in her arms and a little boy at her feet.

"What is her name?"

"Heer," said Ranjha. "Heer Sayal. She is in Jhang now with her parents, but in a few days she will be coming to Takht Hazara."

The woman stared at him with eyes as wide as those of the little boy holding onto her legs. He picked up the horse's reins and led it through the village, happy to be back home again and thinking of the day when Heer would join him. There would be a great feast, the biggest there had ever been in Takht Hazara. The whole village would be there to see Heer step out of her doli and take his hand.

Word of his return spread from house to house as he walked through the village. The women and children came to their doors to see him. People stopped to shake his hand.

"Come to my wedding!" he said to them all. "Please! Come to my wedding!"

"When will it be?" they asked.

"Seven days!"

"How long will it last?"

"Seven days!"

"Who is your bride?"

"Heer Sayal!"

Someone put a garland round his neck. Someone else took the reins of his horse and two men lifted him into the saddle. Some girls started to sing and dance. More joined in, singing and clapping. Soon, he was riding through the village at the head of a long procession and everyone was singing and dancing and clapping their hands.

It was Nooran who told him one day when she brought him his midday meal how his going had cast a shadow over their lives. The brothers had quarrelled, their wives had been sullen, people in the village had turned their backs on them. They would have sent for him, but no one knew where he was. So when they heard the noise in the village and saw him riding at the head of the procession, it was as if their prayers had been answered. It was like the rains coming to wash away their shame.

He led the herd out to pasture, just as he used to do when his father was still alive, and every day Nooran brought him food in the middle of the day and sat with him while he ate. She asked him about Heer and every day he told her a little more of their story.

"We will be good friends," she said. "It makes me happy to think that she will be my sister. I will love her too."

When the day came for them to bring Heer to Takht Hazara, Nooran waited outside the village, so that she could run and tell him when she saw them coming. She sat under a tree at the top of a low rise with her hand over her eyes and watched the road snaking across the plain until it melted into the heat where the land met the sky.

Sajda watched Heer walk across the courtyard through a blaze of petals.

For seven days she had watched her. She had even slept on the floor beside her bed. Her brothers were sullen. Her father looked sad. Her mother said nothing. After a year's banishment, Kaidon had come back to the village. She was afraid and dare not leave her.

She watched her father take her arm and lead her towards the doli. She watched a servant open the door. She watched Sultan mount his horse. She watched Kaidon walk out from behind the gate. She watched him hold out a dish. She watched Heer reach out her hand. She tried to push through the crowd, but someone held her arm and someone else blocked her way. She watched Heer take a sweet from the dish and put it in her mouth.

Ranjha turned when he heard someone come in. It was Nooran.

"Is she here?" he said.

But Nooran just looked at him and he saw that she was crying. To begin with, he did not understand. He went up to her and took her hand.

"Nooran?"

Her shoulders shook. She could not speak. All she could do was look at him and weep. Then he understood.

She kept vigil outside his door, while his brothers and their wives gathered in the courtyard. When they heard the news, the people from the village hurried to the house to see if it was true. A crowd gathered outside the gate, all dressed for a wedding, but no one in the house could bring themselves to speak to them. After a while, most of them turned away and went back to their houses. A few lingered into the night. Nooran said she would keep vigil and the others went to their beds.

"What is he doing?" they asked. "Is he weeping? What is he

doing?"

"He is praying," said Nooran. "When I left him, he was kneeling on his prayer mat. The last time I looked, he hadn't moved. He was still kneeling there. You go. I will watch him."

They left her and she stayed outside his room through the night. In the middle of the night, she saw him in the moonlight, kneeling on the floor. At daybreak, her husband came to her.

"What is he doing now?" he asked.

"Still praying," she said.

"Should we take him some food?" he said.

"No. Leave him. I will wait here."

"Should I bring you some food?"

She shook her head and he went away.

The same thing happened the next day and the next. Until one day he went in and saw his brother lying on the floor with Nooran crouched over him, her black hair hiding his face.

"Is it over?" he asked.

"Yes," she said. "It is over."

After lunch, we drive to the Rock Garden. This is a misnomer. An English visitor to Chandigarh's famous Rock Garden, expecting dwarf conifers, cascades of aubrieta and pockets of edelweiss and gentian, will be disappointed. I explain to my mother that it is not like the Rose Garden, not in fact a garden at all, more a sculpture park. But even that is misleading. In the end, I tell her just to wait and see.

The way in is through a narrow gate in a stone wall, where a small, thin woman sits on a stool and lets people in and out. She is wearing a blue cardigan for extra warmth on this warm February afternoon. She smiles when she sees my mother and invites her to sit down. She takes her hand and looks pleased when I take a photograph of them together, hand in hand, smiling at each other, white haired English woman with a string of pearls around her neck and black haired Indian with jewels in her ears and nose, both wearing cardigans.

"Who was that?" my mother asks when we walk through the gate.

"She takes the entrance money."

"She was *very* nice."

The path from the gate is just wide enough for me to walk beside her, holding her hand and helping her to keep her balance on the uneven surface. The walls on either side of the narrow path are covered with a mosaic of broken tiles set into rough concrete. The tiles are the pastel colours of bathroom ceramics. At the end of the path, we come to an open space with a broad ledge that slopes up to a wall. On the ledge are statues, small figures made of concrete decorated with more broken tiles.

I explain to my mother that everything in the Rock Garden was made from materials discarded during the building of Chandigarh fifty years ago, broken tiles, broken pipes, broken glass. An inspector of roads, a middle-aged man called Nek Chand, persuaded the lorry drivers at the depot to make a detour from the official site and tip the waste onto a patch of rough land where the ancient forest met the new city. Here he spent his evenings, sorting the debris and using it to create a mosaic fantasy in a grotto made out of cobble stones and concrete. In England he would have kept pigeons or worked on his allotment. It was twelve years before he was caught, by which time his secret obsession had become an extraordinary, extravagant work of art that covered more than an acre of land. Popular protest saved him from the sack and his work from demolition, both of which had been threatened by the offended authorities. Instead a grand opening was arranged, with a plaque honouring the politician who performed the ceremony. Nek Chand called it the Kingdom of Gods and Goddesses but the politician named it the Rock Garden. They gave him another twelve acres and told him to carry on.

We walk slowly along narrow pathways, up and down steps, over bridges, under archways (some of which are so low that everyone except my mother has to stoop) meeting gods and goddesses at every turn. Little men gods hug their knees, elephant gods wave their trunks, monkey gods sit and watch, dancing gods stand in rows waiting for the music to begin, wolf gods stand poised to leap, horse gods pause in mid-gallop, donkey gods refuse to move, music gods blow their flutes and beat their drums, bear gods dance, bird gods peck, dog gods bark. The Rock Garden is a visual tongue-twister. It has waterfalls and lakes and concrete creepers trailing over concrete walls. But it doesn't have a garden.

My mother is fascinated by it. Other visitors are fascinated by her and one of them stops to tell her how beautiful she is. There is no room to pass on some of the narrow pathways and my mother's slow pace causes some hold-ups (a snail crawling over the rocks) but nobody minds. There is much more to see, but we decide that she has had enough walking for today and retrace our steps. On the way back, we pass the little hut where Nek Chand, father of the gods, now nearly as old as my mother, can sometimes be seen drinking tea with his friends and inventing new deities to populate his kingdom. But he is not there today.

On the way back, we stop in the city centre and take my mother to be measured for a pair of trousers. Now that she can see again, buying clothes is easier than it used to be when she went to a stall in the market (run by Punjabis), asked them to choose something for her and gave them her purse to pay for it. Now at least she can choose for herself, but she still can't find trousers that don't need shortening. So when we tell her that she could have a pair of trousers made to measure in India for less than it would cost her to buy a pair off the shelf in England, she is enthusiastic and Rajpal knows just the shop to go to.

The shops are built around the four sides of a car park. It seems full, but Rajpal perseveres and at last we find a parking space. The shop has two big windows on either side of the door. In one window the mannequins wear suits with shirts and ties, in the other saris and salwar kameez. When we go in, we find more mannequins standing in a variety of poses among the display stands and cabinets. Facing them is a long counter running the whole length of the shop. Behind the counter, on shelves that cover the wall from floor to ceiling, rolls of cloth are laid end to end, like a box of crayons.

The shopkeeper, a tall man with short, grey hair, greets us and invites us to sit down in front of the counter, on chairs that are, even as he speaks, carried over by one of his assistants. Rajpal, who knows the shopkeeper, introduces us to him. He is impressed both by my mother's age, on which he congratulates her, and by the fact that I am taking care of her, on which he congratulates me. Something which would be unremarkable in an Indian is a mark of distinction in an Englishman. The Hindu shopkeeper has relatives in England and knows how old people are treated there. Old people in India live with their families, they are not put in homes. He shakes my hand.

We sit down. A boy approaches with glasses of coke on a tray. Two shop assistants behind the counter pull rolls of cloth from the shelves and unroll them on the counter for my mother's inspection. She finds a grey and a brown which she likes. Unable to choose between them, she decides to have both. Two more shop assistants arrive, one with a tape measure, the other with a notebook. I hold her walking stick while they measure her and act as go-between in the matter of pockets, fastenings and belt loops. When everything has been decided and written down in the book, we sit down again and watch as one of the shop assistants picks up a pair of scissors, cuts a length of cloth from each roll and gives them to one of the other shop assistants to be taken away for making up. The trousers, the shopkeeper says, will be ready tomorrow. Then he turns his attention to me. A nice suit for the summer? I shake my head and hope that in doing so I have not forfeited his good opinion.

On the way home, sitting in the back of the car with my mother, she tells me that the shop is just how shops used to be in England. There were always chairs for customers to sit on, the shopkeeper gave you his personal attention, there were plenty of shop assistants to help you. All shops were like this. Even in her mother's little off-licence there was a chair beside the counter. She remembers Mrs Brown who used to sit there and pass the time of day, hiding her jug of beer under her coat in case it looked as if she was drinking on the premises. Apart from the glass of coke, the shop was just like shops in England were before the war.

"Everything was so much nicer then. Why do they always have to spoil things?"

Tomorrow we will go to Patiala, where Rajpal lived when I first knew him. Patiala is not as old or as famous as Amritsar or Lahore, but it is nevertheless one of the old cities of the Punjab. The five rivers that flow from the Himalayas to Afghanistan in the west and Delhi in the east gave the region its name, punj ab. The geography hasn't changed, but the politics have. Three of the rivers, Ravi, Chenab and Jhelum, are in Pakistan. The other two, Beas and Satluj, are in India. Patiala is nearer to Beas, with Delhi to the east and Rajasthan to the south. The city is famous for turbans, shoes and maharajas.

The fame of the Maharajas of Patiala rests entirely on the exploits of one man, Bhupinder Singh. Maharaja of Patiala from 1900 to 1938, six feet six inches tall, cricketer, polo player and inventor of the Patiala peg, Bhupinder Singh had ten wives, three hundred and sixty-five concubines, eighty-eight children and a fleet of Rolls Royces. A Patiala peg is a generous measure of whisky, first served, the story goes, when the Maharaja was entertaining the Viceroy's polo players the night before a match against the Patiala team. The hung-over visitors lost the match and a large whisky became known as a Patiala peg.

The Maharaja was captain of the first Indian cricket team to tour England, playing a series of matches against county teams in 1911. He was selected for India's first Test match against England in 1932, but age and ill health forced him to drop out. The Indian team lost by 158 runs, perhaps missing the Maharaja's tactical skills.

Bhupinder Singh was a collector. As well as his collection of concubines, one for every day of the year, he also had the world's largest collection of medals, including England's Order of the Garter, Austria's Order of the Golden Fleece, Russia's Order of St Andrew, Japan's Order of the Rising Sun, China's Order of the Double Dragon and Thailand's Order of the White Elephant. Moti Bagh, the palace where he kept both his collections, is now a museum.

His grandson, Amrinder Singh, built himself a new palace some years ago, where he lives more modestly than his grandfather, in a style more suited to a modern Maharaja, with one wife and two children. Today, he is out electioneering. A member of the ruling Congress Party, he became Chief Minister of Punjab at the last elections. Tomorrow, according to The Tribune, he will be attending a rally in Patiala with the Prime Minister, Manmohan Singh. Browsing the election news as usual after breakfast, turning the pages of the paper from the stern rhetoric of the editorials to the latest news from Beas and Kashmir, I realise that my mother is trying to attract my attention.

She is standing just inside the open door to her bedroom, waving her arm above her head, as if she were standing on the shore of a desert island trying to attract the attention of passing ships. I put the newspaper down and go through to her bedroom, where she is now sitting on the edge of the bed.

"Is something wrong?"

She mouths the answer. I shake my head and bend down, putting my ear closer to her mouth. Sotto voce, she pronounces the word.

"Diarrhoea."

I give her one of the tablets from the packet I brought with me, take her out to the veranda and leave her sitting in the sun while I discuss a change of plan with Rajpal. We agree to postpone our visit to Patiala and spend the day at home. While I go back outside to sit with my mother, he talks to Kuldip and a few minutes later they both join us on the veranda, watching my mother with anxious faces for symptoms of more serious illness. Kuldip sits down beside her and holds her hand. Rajpal wants to call a doctor. My mother is grateful for the attention but insists that it is nothing serious.

"I'll be alright if I just sit here," she says. "Don't let me stop you doing anything. I'll be alright on my own."

But there is, of course, no question of leaving her on her own. The visit to Patiala will be postponed until she is well enough to travel. Meanwhile, we will all enjoy a quiet day at home. I fetch my paper and sit in the shade, while my mother continues to enjoy the sunshine on her face.

"I'll just sit still and hope for the best."

Here in India, fatalism and hope go hand in hand. Rama followed his dharma. Gandhi preached passive resistance. My mother sits still and hopes for the best. I watch her for a while, then pick up my paper and go on reading.

In the afternoon, returning to Rajpal's bookshelves, I take down a collection of essays about the troubles in Punjab. When I first came to India, the troubles, about which I knew nothing at the time, were not long over. There were military check points everywhere, jeeps on the streets and armed guards outside government buildings, banks, schools and many private houses. It seemed that everyone who could afford it paid a man with a rifle to sit outside their gate. Our plans for a school exchange began to seem imprudent. But the advice from the Foreign Office was that Punjab was now stable, so we went ahead. Not long after, Beant Singh, Chief Minister of Punjab, was killed by a suicide bomber in Chandigarh.

It was the last in a long line of killings. Three years before, Talwinder Singh Parmar, a member of the Sikh militant group, Babbar Khalsa, had been shot by police in Bombay. Six years before that, Sikh militants had shot General Arun Shridhar Vaidya, retired Chief of Staff of the Indian Army, on his way home from the market in Pune. A year before that, a bomb had blown up Air India flight 182 off the coast of Ireland, killing over three hundred passengers. Twelve years before that, three thousand Sikhs had been killed in New Delhi following the assassination of Indira Gandhi by two of her Sikh bodyguards. Five months before that, Jarnail Singh Bhindranwala and two hundred members of his Sikh separatist movement had been killed in Operation Blue Star at the Golden Temple in Amritsar. Four years before that, Jagat Narain, former freedom fighter and prominent opponent of Bhindranwala, had been shot on his way from Jalandhar to Patiala. Thirty-three years before that, Mahatma Gandhi had been shot by Nathuram Ghodse for betraying the Hindu cause. Five months before that, nearly a million Muslims and Sikhs had been slaughtered as they fled in opposite directions across the new border between India and Pakistan. Five years before that, Udham Singh had been hanged in London for the murder of Sir Michael O'Dwyer. Thirty-two years before that, Brigadier-General Reginald Dyer had ordered his troops to open fire on the protesters at Jallianwala Bagh.

We sit down to an evening meal of chicken, vegetables, rice, dhal, dahi, chapatti and, for my mother, a baked potato. Kuldip asked her earlier what her favourite food was and that was her answer. She has not eaten anything since breakfast and, as food and happiness are virtually synonymous in Punjab, concern about her welfare has been growing all day. A feeling of helplessness overcomes a Punjabi woman when she is unable to feed her guests. The baked potato saves Kuldip's honour.

When she has eaten it, my mother decides to have an early night. I help her to her room, make sure that everything she might need during the night is to hand and then leave her to get ready for bed. Her stomach seems settled now and, if she has a good night's sleep, we should all be able to go to Patiala tomorrow.

"You will see a lot of changes in Patiala," Rajpal says. "They are trying to attract more tourists. The Chief Minister has put a lot of money into it. They are widening the roads, putting in new street lighting, improving the drains. Preservation work on the fort has begun again. There is a team of people working on it now."

Qila Mubarak, the old fort in the middle of Patiala, has been neglected for years. Only the bazaar in the streets which surround it, with scores of shops clustered around the red stone walls, some of them actually built onto the walls like swallows' nests, has continued to thrive, while the paintings on the walls inside slowly fade and the stone wears away and the stories are forgotten. So the preferential treatment which the Chief Minister has given to his home town seems, in this respect at least, something to be welcomed.

I go back to my mother's room to say goodnight, as I used to do when my daughters were little girls, as she used to do when I was a little boy. It seems like a game in which we all take turns. Tonight it is my turn to be the daddy and hers to be the child. The shape of her body lying perfectly still, curled up under the sheets with her small white head resting on the pillow, is like a form carved in bas relief on a tomb. Looking down at her makes me feel fantastically tall and reminds me of one of Robert Louis Stevenson's poems about childhood.

'I was the giant great and still
That sits upon the pillow-hill
And sees before him, dale and plain,
The pleasant land of counterpane.'

She looks up at me and smiles a toothless smile which, for a moment, makes the face on the pillow look like the face of a chuckling baby.

"I've kept my knickers on," she confides in me, "just to be on the safe side."

I bend down to give her a kiss on the cheek and turn out the light.

Closing the door behind me, I return to my natural size and, seeing that someone has moved my glass to a table beside one of the armchairs, I sit down, pick up The Tribune and carry on reading where I left off in the morning. After a few minutes, Rajpal joins me and opens another bottle.

"If mom is well tomorrow," he says, "we will drive to Patiala. But first we will go to my village. It will be the first time mom has been to a village. They were expecting us today and they were very disappointed when I telephoned to say we could not come. They will be very happy if we can go tomorrow."

That settled, I take the opportunity of asking him about the fake encounters in Kashmir that I have been reading about.

"If I understand it correctly, the police shoot someone and make it look as if the person they shot was a terrorist so they can claim a reward. Is that right?"

"Everyone exploits the situation for their own ends. It has been like that ever since partition."

I ask him what he means and he gives me a history lesson. He explains that in 1947 all the princely states had to decide whether to remain independent or give up their independence within either India or Pakistan. Hyderabad held out for independence, Portugal refused to give up Goa and Maharaja Hari Singh wanted to hang onto Jammu and Kashmir. He had ruled there since 1925. He was a Sikh, most of the people were Muslims and he was very unpopular. He had already crushed one uprising in 1931 and he didn't want to let go. Then, after partition, there was an incursion by tribal people from the north-west and the Pakistani army joined forces with them. The Maharaja quickly agreed to join the Indian Union, Nehru sent in the army and that was the start of the first Indo-Pak war, which lasted more than a year. In the end, Nehru asked the UN to intervene. There was a ceasefire. Pakistan took part of the territory but most of it stayed with India. Mountbatten had demanded a plebiscite before the war and the UN repeated this demand, but it still hasn't happened.

I ask him about Hyderabad and Goa.

The Nizam of Hyderabad, he says, held out for a year and a half. Nehru imposed an economic blockade and eventually the Nizam caved in. Portugal held out until 1961. Then Nehru sent in the army and Operation Vijay put a swift end to Portuguese rule nearly five hundred years after Vasco da Gama landed on the southern tip of India.

Kuldip, as usual, has cleared the table and withdrawn to the kitchen, leaving us to talk. Now she joins us again and asks me a question.

"What is the feeling of people in England about the war in Iraq?"

I tell her about the 'Stop the War' march in London, how this march and the anti-war movement it represented were ignored by the government, how only two members of the cabinet opposed the Prime Minister and resigned, how the government's determination to control the media led to a confrontation with the BBC which the BBC lost.

"In India everyone is against it."

The conversation moves on but leaves me remembering the despair and disbelief which my mother felt when she heard news of the invasion on the wireless (as she still calls it). Born before the end of the First World War, married four years before the start of the second, she has a simple explanation for the folly of starting a third. They were too young. No one who remembers the last war, she says, could be so stupid as to think that wars solve anything.

"An older man would never have done it. He would have known better. All those people killed. And for what? What good will it do?"

She sums it all up in one word, a word which she pronounces with biblical ferocity like a character in a medieval morality play. Truth as an old woman, shaking her crooked finger at War. Wicked!

"War never solves anything. An older man would have known that."

Elizabeth I took advice from an older man on affairs of state and followed it in all but the question of marriage. When Burghley was dying, his son sent him some game broth and the queen sat by his bedside and fed him with a spoon.

"I pray you," he wrote to his son the next day, "diligently and effectually let her Majesty understand how her singular kindness doth overcome my power to acquit it, who, though she will not be a mother, yet she showed herself, by feeding me with her own princely hand, as a careful nurse; and if I may be weaned to feed myself, I shall be more ready to serve her on the Earth. If not, I hope to be, in Heaven, a servitor for her and God's Church. And so I thank you for your porridges."

A few miles from Chandigarh, on the road to Patiala, we stop to buy glasses of orange juice at a roadside stall. We stand together by the side of the road and raise our glasses.

"To mom!"

The sun is shining as it does every day from a sky like a pearl, opulent with heat and light. Standing by the side of the road, between the wide plain and the wider sky, feels like walking on water, like a water-strider on a pond. In the distance, the chimney of a roadside brickworks draws a thin black line on the edge of the sky, like a stitch in the seam that joins the sky to the plain, the infinite to the everyday. Mrs Steel (whose questioning spirit accompanies us on our travels) writes in praise of the everyday in her autobiography.

'It is these little things that make life worth living. They stay with one through thick and thin. Surely, surely they are immortal. They have been, they are.'

She quotes a line from the Bhagavad-Gita.

'"What has been, can never cease to be." It is there in the history of the world, for all time, all Eternity – though which is Time, which is Eternity, it would puzzle anyone to say.'

These things puzzle my mother too.

The road takes us past fields of green wheat and yellow mustard, past houses with flat roofs half-hidden behind gated courtyards, past rows of cow pats stacked to dry in the sun, past women carrying bundles of sugar cane on their heads, past narrow strips of land planted with onions and carrots, peas and potatoes. We drive slowly past a man sitting on a flat cart pulled by a horse. We look at him as we go past and he looks back at us. My mother tells us that her parents took to her to church on a cart like that to be christened. Other memories follow, like sheep straying through a gate left open, memories of the hard life that people in England once led. She talks about her father, around the time that Queen Victoria died, leaving his parents' home in Hull and arriving in Leeds with sixpence in his pocket.

"That was all he had. They wouldn't even give him a handkerchief to wrap his things in."

She talks about her mother, a sixteen year old girl in service, marrying an older man, a farm labourer who lived in a cottage at the top of a hill.

"After they were married, she set up a stall outside the door, selling drinks to people who needed to quench their thirst when they got to the top."

She talks about her brother and sister turning the taps on and off when the family moved to a house with running water.

"Until then they'd had to fetch water from the pump every day. Water for washing, water for cooking, water for the animals. Can you imagine it? They couldn't believe that all they had to do was just turn a tap."

She talks about the doctor taking her sister's tonsils out on the kitchen table. She talks about the day when she was a toddler playing in the farmyard and a cart horse came galloping through the gate. Everyone thought she would be killed but the horse jumped right over her.

"My mum said that my dad worshipped that horse. There was nothing he wouldn't do for it."

She remembers worshipping her father, who died when she was only two.

"I used to follow him about the farm. It must have looked comical, a little tot following him round."

She talks about his loss of an eye when he was kicked by a horse.

"He would have got compensation for that now, but there was nothing like that then."

She talks about his death in 1919 from the Spanish 'flu that killed more people than the war did. He told her mother that he was dying.

"Nay, Jack," she said, "you're not dying."

But he knew that he was.

"I haven't deceived you yet," he said, "and I'm not going to start now."

She remembers someone lifting her up so that she could see him after he had been laid out, telling her that he had gone now.

"It all happened," she says, echoing Mrs Steel. "It was all real. Where does it all go?"

The car stops and we get out.

"This is my village," says Rajpal. "But it is much changed since I was a boy."

We are standing on some open ground on the edge of the village. There are fields on one side and a cluster of buildings on the other. A low wall surrounds a green space where trees are growing. Some boys are playing cricket on the grass. Behind them is an old building, its walls crumbling and half covered with creepers, like an old engraving.

"It used to be the cremation ground," Rajpal explains, shaking his head sadly. "Look at it now."

There is in my mind a ragbag of things Rajpal has told me about his childhood in this village and how he came to leave it. One day I will ask him to tell me the story again and write it down so that I have all the facts in the right order. The story starts with the Sikh Guru who blessed one of his ancestors. I have forgotten which Guru it was, but Gobind Singh was the last of them and he died at the beginning of the eighteenth century, so it must have been at last three hundred years ago.

"Because of this," Rajpal told me once, "my family is much respected among Sikhs. I had a privileged childhood."

But he fell out with his father when he was a boy and ran away. His mother was only one of his father's wives and this, I think, had something to do with it. Rajpal has always been a free spirit. His adventures as a runaway led eventually, like Kim's, to an education in the hills, in his case a college in Mussourie where he studied English literature. *Romeo and Juliet* must have seemed very familiar to someone who had grown up with the story of Heer and Ranjha. He tells me that *King Lear* is very much like another Punjabi story.

We climb back in the car and Rajpal drives along the narrow village roads until we come to a big metal gate. He drives right up to the gate and blows his horn. The gate opens as if by magic and we drive through. The family are waiting for us outside an old house, two men and three women, all smiling and waving. One of the men points to a space under a tree, not with his finger but, as Punjabis do, with the whole of his hand, a wide, sweeping, welcoming gesture. Rajpal parks the car in the shade and turns off the engine.

The family gather round and when we climb out we are at once hemmed in by black beards, colourful turbans, pale saris, sparkling jewels, everyone smiling, bowing, shaking our hands, touching our knees and our feet, talking to us in a language we don't understand. It feels like taking part in a country dance, constantly changing partners and never knowing what to do next. When the dance is over, our host gestures with his hand again and we follow as if it were a signpost.

The room we enter is two storeys high. A gallery runs all the way round the upper floor and a chandelier hangs from the ceiling, high above our heads. The only windows are high up in one wall of the gallery. Down here we are in a cool half-light. Chairs and tables are arranged around the sides of the room, between doors that lead to other, smaller rooms, one of them a kitchen into which the women now disappear. The hand directs us towards an imposing sofa with deep red upholstery. Cushions are re-arranged for my mother and we sit down.

The conversation is all in Punjabi and we are, for a while, left to our own devices, which gives my mother the opportunity to ask me who everyone is. The age of Punjabi men is disguised by their turbans, their straight backs and their fondness for hair dye. Our hosts have the lean build of men who live in the country and lead physical lives. Neither has the embonpoint which is otherwise the trademark of a successful Punjabi, the bureaucrat or the businessman who spends most of his time in his office, with someone sitting on a chair outside the door ready to run errands or bring tea and someone else waiting in the car outside ready to drive him home when his work is done, the kind of man who enjoys the food at weddings but leaves the dancing to younger men. It is easy to imagine either of these two men dancing the bhangra without putting their own hearts or other people's feet in danger. But now they sit and talk, while the three women bring tea and cakes from the kitchen.

"I'm not really sure," I say, leaning towards my mother, "but I think that's his wife and that's his son and she's *his* wife and that's their daughter."

My mother nods. "That's what I thought too," she says.

When we have finished our tea, we go for a walk in the village. The youngest of the three women, the only one in the family to speak any English, walks by our side. During our slow walk, I find out a little about her and tell her a little about me and my mother. Her name is Ramandeep. She is, as the matrimonial adverts in The Tribune would say, a beautiful Punjabi girl, slim, 5'2", well educated, good family.

She leads us along a pathway between old stone walls and takes my mother's hand to help her down some steps under an archway into a wide courtyard with a tall tree growing in the middle and old buildings on all four sides. This is the house where Rajpal spent his childhood, before he ran away. I remember him on a previous visit pointing to one of the upper windows and telling me that was where the women lived and where he spent the first few years of his life. Whether it is the beauty of the courtyard or the beauty of our guide or just the fact that she is here and her feelings are too big for her heart, my mother starts to cry.

"She's crying because she's happy," I explain, to reassure Ramandeep.

She puts her arms around her and they stand together for a few moments, holding onto each other, while I find a tissue to dry my mother's eyes.

"I'm alright," she says. "It's just silliness. Don't worry about me."

Ramandeep takes her hand and we continue to walk around the courtyard. Rajpal is waiting for us. He opens a door and we follow him into a room furnished with tables and chairs that seem to belong to the days of the British Raj. Old paintings and black and white photographs hang on the walls. He points out a photograph of his father and a painting depicting the blessing of his ancestor by the Guru.

"It was Guru Hargobind Singh," he says, in answer to my question. "The sixth Guru."

That makes it nearly four hundred years ago. But the room we are in, he says in answer to more questions, is part of the fort that was built about a hundred years ago, along with the gurdwara and the rest of the buildings that were his home once.

"This is where Rajpal lived when he was a boy," I explain to my mother. "It was built just before you were born."

"It looks older than that," she says, looking round.

Then she remembers how old she is.

"After all," she says, shaking her head in disbelief, "I *am* ninety.

I keep forgetting."

We sit for a while around a table on the veranda, while our hosts talk to each other in Punjabi. The sun falls lower in the sky. The trees cast lengthening shadows across the courtyard. Someone brings us cold drinks and bowls of crisps and nuts. There is a crescendo of twittering as the birds start to roost in the trees. My mother looks tired.

A little later, walking back to Ramandeep's house, we pass the gurdwara. Ramandeep leaves us for a moment and steps briefly inside, pausing first to take off her shoes and touch the threshold with her hand. I ask my mother if she would like to go in, but she shakes her head.

"Not now," she says. "Another time."

Perhaps she feels as if she would be intruding on Ramandeep's devotions or perhaps she feels that it would be wrong to go inside merely out of curiosity or perhaps she is just tired.

"We'll be going to the Golden Temple when we go back to Amritsar," I say. "You can save it till then."

"There is the free kitchen here every day," Rajpal says, while we wait for Ramandeep, "the langar. When the Guru blessed my ancestor, Bhai Rup Chand, he told him to serve food every day to anyone who needed it."

Our hosts are disappointed when we say that we are unable to stay for the night. They insist on feeding us before we go. The tradition of the langar is as much a part of the home as it is of the gurdwara. We sit down to a traditional Punjabi meal of saag and makki di roti, served with generous helpings of white butter which melts into the saag like snow melting in a field. For my mother there is a baked potato.

It is a short drive to Patiala but, by the time we get there, she is already asleep. Instead of waking her and making her walk, it would have been kinder to carry her upstairs like a child and put her to bed.

Sitting in our hotel room in the morning, sipping our bed-tea, we look out of the window at the street below, where two women squat on the pavement, each holding a dish of food, dhal perhaps, which they scoop into their mouths with pieces of chapatti. They are surrounded by piles of plastic bags, the flimsy, tissue-thin bags which every little shop in India uses and which blow around the streets of every village, town and city in the sub-continent.

When they have finished eating, instead of standing up and walking away, they go on with their work. Without rising from their squatting position, they pick over the rubbish, moving it from one pile to another. In their bright but faded clothes, they are all but indistinguishable from the colourful mounds of rubbish which surround them, like painted moles among painted molehills. People walk past and no one takes any notice of them, but occasionally someone throws something onto one of the piles. Squatting on the pavement, moving with an easy, unhurried grace, as if performing some traditional task learned from their mothers, like spinning thread or making butter, the women go on sorting the bags to sell back to the shops they came from so they can blow around the streets another day.

The telephone rings. Rajpal invites us to join him in the hotel restaurant. Over breakfast (dahi and parathas for Rajpal and me, toast for my mother) we discuss our plans for today. When everything is agreed, I turn to my mother and explain.

"After breakfast, we're going to have a walk in the market. Then Rajpal's going to drive us to another village where we're going to hear some Punjabi folk music. Then, in the evening, we're going to meet some friends at the Gymkhana Club."

"Don't bother to explain," she says. "Whatever it is, I'm sure I'll enjoy it. Everyone is so kind."

The narrow streets of Patiala's bazaar were meant for people and animals to walk on, for animals to pulls carts on, for people to stand and talk on. They were not meant for the cars, vans and scooters that now elbow their way through them, honking their horns. Each sounds like a different animal. The scooters quack, the vans yelp, the cars squawk. But no one takes any notice, no one even bothers to look over their shoulder. Everyone goes on walking. Rickshaw drivers stand on their pedals. No one complains. People, animals, cars, vans, scooters, rickshaws jostle their way through the narrow streets. No one seems to be in a hurry. Crowded and noisy as it is, there is an air of tranquillity.

That, at least, is how it seems to me. From my mother's point of view, four and a half feet above ground level, the impression may be different. Even among these benevolent, unthreatening crowds, good eyesight, good hearing and a degree of agility are useful attributes, none of which she has. Walking by her side, I look down at her face but see no signs of anxiety or distress. Perhaps, I think, she has the advantage of us all. Perhaps a little blurring of the vision serves only to enhance the impression of harmony. Perhaps the cacophony of horns and hooters is muted for her to a distant hum. Perhaps, with her stick in one hand, me holding the other and no need to look where she's going, she can watch whatever she chooses, whatever catches her eye. The stall selling sugar cane juice, perhaps, the liquid poured out pale and clear, the cane discarded like a chewed up twig. Or the bangle stall like a jackdaw's nest, with armfuls of glistening bracelets piled high in jewel-studded pillars. Or the bhindi stall, draped with packets of plastic spots, red, blue, purple, green, black, white, raindrops, dewdrops, teardrops, instant stick-on peel-off beauty spots. Or the stall selling sugary, syrupy sweets deep fried in smoking hot oil, under a dense cloud of flies. Or the booths with two steps leading up to an open door, where the shopkeeper sits on a stool waiting for customers, talking to friends, guarding his treasure trove of turbans or shoes, jewellery or clocks.

Patiala is famous for turbans and shoes. The turban sellers' shelves are lined with rolls of cloth from white at one end to black at the other and every colour of the rainbow in between, ready to be cut into twenty foot turban lengths and tied Patiala-style in the fashion set by Maharaja Bhupinder Singh a hundred years ago. Curly-toed slippers, jutti, each shoe embroidered with gold and silver thread, hang from the shoe sellers' doors like pheasants outside an old-fashioned English butcher's.

We walk through an alleyway of tailors' shops, where men sit cross-legged on the floor behind old Singer sewing machines, stitching shirts and trousers and salwar kameez. One of them looks up and smiles when he sees my mother and gestures towards a chair, inviting her to sit down. Glad of the rest, she stops and I help her up the step. A boy brings water. Rajpal takes some but advises us against it. The man goes on sewing. He looks happy. He looks as if he would be happy if we stayed there all day. He looks beatific. If he is, it is a blessing conterred by his own act of hospitality, his good deed for the day. To an Englishman, the phrase recalls Baden-Powell and the Boy

Scouts. Good deeds in England are performed by small boys in short trousers. To a Hindu, it means karma. Good deeds in India are performed by good Hindus hoping to contribute to the sum of human happiness and give their own souls a better start next time round. Different religions find different ways of encouraging people to be nice to each other.

In the afternoon, we sit outside on armchairs at the end of a road on the edge of a village. The afternoon sun is falling across the fields. A group of children sit beside a wall on the other side of the road, waiting, like us, for the entertainment to begin. An hour ago, when we arrived in the village, Rajpal wound down the window and asked some men standing beside the road if they knew where the dancers were. There was a lot of shrugging of shoulders, shaking of heads, blank looks. A crowd gathered. The question was repeated and passed on. More shrugs, more head shaking, more blank looks, until a teenage boy made his way to the front of the crowd. Rajpal repeated the question and the boy nodded his head. Rajpal leaned over to open the passenger door, the boy walked round and climbed in.

"He knows where they are," Rajpal explained, looking over his shoulder. "He will show us the way."

The dancers were in the village for a wedding. We found them in a farm building by the side of a road on the edge of the village. We sat in the car while Rajpal and the boy went to talk to them. There were eight of them, all men, standing beside the road, listening to Rajpal and, by their gestures, a slight inclination of the head, a smile, agreeing to what was being proposed. Rajpal came back to the car and got in, leaving the boy with the dancers.

"They have just finished rehearsing," he explained. "They have changed out of their costumes but they say if we can wait half-an-hour they will put them on again. So we will go for a drive round the village and then come back."

Every Punjabi has a village. They may live in cities, they may live in other countries, but they all have a village which they belong to by birth, go back to for weddings and call not by its name but simply 'my village'. From time to time I look back fondly on the village where I grew up, but I don't think of it as my village. Not in the way that an Indian does. An Indian's feelings about his village are more than nostalgic. It is as if his village reminds him who he is.

Perhaps it used to be like that in England, but so long ago that we have forgotten. Perhaps it is still like that in France, where villages have been invaded, occupied, destroyed, starved to death, brought back to life, loved and fought for. In England, the battle was lost a long time ago, when the gentry stole the common land from the people.

'They stop the course of agriculture,' wrote Sir Thomas More in 1516, 'destroying houses and towns, reserving only the churches, and enclose grounds that they may lodge their sheep in them.' The villages of England are prettier to English eyes than those of Punjab, but they are not *ours*.

Our slow drive around the village took us along dusty roads between dusty brick walls where thin little hens scratched in the dust outside closed gates. Some children were playing in the road, but they ran away when they saw us coming. A cow standing beside the wall swung its head round and watched us go by. A woman carrying a baby on her hip stared as we went past, her eyes as big and round and disinterested as the cow's. What are you doing here, she thought, in my village?

The dancers are ready when we come back. Two of them are dressed as women, arranging and re-arranging their chunni around their head and shoulders. The others have pugree on their heads, turbans tied like crested birds. All are dressed in pink and yellow, saffron yellow lungi or kameez covering their legs down to their ankles, fuschia pink kurta or salwar down to their hips, strings of beads around their necks, jewels on their foreheads. The two dressed as women are barefoot, the others have plain, white sandals on their feet. One of them, a tall man, older than the rest, carries a set of bagpipes over his shoulder, with red and gold tassels hanging from the ends of the pipes and a windbag made of pink cloth that matches their shirts. The rest hold drums and other instruments whose names I don't know.

The boy who showed us the way brings a tray with glasses and bottles of Coca-Cola. A crowd gathers on the other side of the road, women carrying babies, boys lounging against the wall, little children playing in the dust. It is late afternoon and as the sun sinks lower in the sky the light grows opaque, not just something to see by, but a palpable presence.

"Ah yes!" Mrs Steel whispers in our ear. "It was always like this when something was about to happen."

The piper's cheeks swell like a gourd, his eyes bulge, his fingers flicker, the drums beat loud around him and the two men dressed as women link arms and start to spin, making circles in the dust. One of the drummers plays the dhol, using a curved stick in one hand and the fingers of the other to make a loud, insistent, unrelenting rhythm. The others beat small, round drums with drumsticks, like drummers in a regimental band, except that no regiment could march to this rhythm. Another man, older than the rest, like the piper, holds a long stick covered in silver bells, which he shakes and beats like a tambourine, dancing with his arms and shoulders, beating the ground with his feet.

But the dancers, the men-women, dance with their hands, their legs, their heads, their arms. If we had not seen them when they were men, we would think they were women. They smile like women, they use their hands like women, they hold their heads like women, they fuss with their scarves like women. Only the rules prevent them from being women. In Punjab, bhangra is the dance for men and giddha is the dance for women. When women dance together, they make a circle and clap their hands and sing and take it in turn to dance by twos in the middle of the circle. They sing about their lives as Punjabi women, making fun of the men behind their backs, getting the better of them, having the last laugh and dancing their hearts out.

But these men in women's clothing are not making fun of women or their dances. Their aim is not to parody, just to imitate. One of them, to my mother's amusement, is fighting a losing battle with his chunni, which keeps falling off his shoulders. He catches it and drapes it over his head, but soon it unwinds itself again and slips to the ground. Eventually, he abandons it. He is, after all, only a man.

Rajpal takes out a hundred rupee note and holds it out. One of the dancers dances towards him, takes the note from his hand and dances away, tucking it into the top of his fuschia pink salwar. I ask Rajpal whether I should do the same. He nods and I take some money from my pocket. The dance ends, we applaud, the music starts again. I hold out a note. One of the men dances towards me and takes it without breaking step. My mother indicates that she would like to give some money too. I give her a note and she holds it out. The dancer takes it from her, but before he dances away he waves it three times in a circle over her head.

"He is blessing her with it," Rajpal explains to me, "warding off evil spirits."

I lean towards my mother and tell her what Rajpal has said. A few moments later, when I look at her again, I see that she is crying. Nobody has ever blessed her before, not like this anyway.

The sun is sinking. The music stops. Day and night are evenly balanced, like the vegetable seller's scales. Dancers and musicians gather round and touch my mother's feet. She is, I can see, as full of emotion as the day was full of light. Both have more than they can hold and the scales are tipping now. I help her into the car. The crowd follows us as we drive slowly down the village street. The man who blessed my mother with her hundred rupee note waves goodbye. She weeps again, holding my arm, as we leave the village, driving past fields guarded by the dark silhouettes of trees. Suddenly, it is night.

When we sit down to dinner at the Gymkhana Club, somebody asks my mother to say grace.

"For what we are about to receive," she says, "may we be truly thankful," and almost at once a waiter brings her a baked potato.

We are sitting at a long table in the members' dining room. Usually, I tell her, we would eat outside, but the nights in February are too cold. The old colonial building with its domes and towers looks very elegant when it is lit up at night. In the summer, a fountain plays in the middle of the lawn. There is a cricket ground behind it with a pavilion modelled on the pavilion at Lord's.

"Next time we'll sit outside."

"Next time?"

"You'd like to come again, wouldn't you?"

"Of course I would."

"You didn't think you'd manage it this time, did you? But you have."

"Mr Neil," someone says to the table at large, seeing me cut up my mother's baked potato, "is son of Sravana."

She asks me what he means. I know Sravana is a character in the Ramayana, but there are so many characters in the Ramayana that I have to ask Rajpal to remind me who this one is.

"He is the one that Dashrat kills by accident when he is hunting in the forest. Sravana looks after his parents. That is why he compares you to Sravana. His parents are blind and when Sravana is killed, they die too. But first they put a curse on Dashrat that the same thing will happen to him. He remembers this when Kaikeyi makes him keep his promise to her by banishing Rama. Then he dies too, just like they did, because of his grief."

It is impossible to understand any one episode in the Ramayana without knowing how it fits in with all the others, so I limit myself to telling my mother that Sravana is someone in a Hindu legend who looks after his parents when they are old.

Every year, in the few days before Diwali, Hindus act out the story of Rama and Sita. Every town puts on its own Ramlila and people gather every evening to watch the story unfold. In medieval England, the guilds used to act out the bible story in the same way. Here in India, for a few nights every year, gods and humans play their parts in this long and complicated story. I was in Patiala once on Diwali and saw the last night of the Ramlila there. A giant effigy of Ravana, the ten-headed demon whose battle with Rama lasts for ten days and brings the story to its climax, swayed moodily against the night sky, as if determined to ignore the amateur theatricals going on below him. When Rama and Sita were re-united and the last words of the play had been spoken, someone struck a match. The king of the demons exploded like a torched arsenal. All hell was let loose.

It does not take long to eat a baked potato. When everybody else has finished, we take our leave. I take her hand and everyone follows us to the broad flight of stairs that she had to climb on the way in and must now, with the eyes of the audience on her, climb down again. She gives me her walking stick and holds onto the handrail. We walk down, one step at a time. Everyone applauds when we reach the bottom. She takes her walking stick again and when we get outside, keeping tight hold of my hand but playing shamelessly to the crowd, skips the first few steps down the path. To more applause we walk the rest of the way to the car.

I wake in the middle of the night to the sound of rain falling. In the distance, thunder rumbles. I get out of bed and stand at the window, watching the rain. Lightning flickers like a torch with a faulty connection. There is no wind. The heavy rain pours down like water from a watering can. It could be some old god in his dotage, watering the garden by torchlight, grumbling to himself.

In the morning, the sun is shining and the air is full of the fresh, clean smells that come only after rain. The dust has all been washed away. There are puddles along the road, with little islands in between. From the veranda, it looks like a map of the Aegean. I steer my mother out of the gate and down the road to the little park at the end, navigating a passage between the puddles.

In the park, children are playing on the grass. Mothers and grandmothers sit with their children and grandchildren like nursemaids in Kensington Gardens a hundred years ago. A dog ambles out of one of the houses and lies down beside them. Four old men are playing cards on a rug which they have spread out on the grass. We walk along the path, past the roses and the dahlias, until we come to an empty bench. The children stop and look, then go on with their game. No one else pays us any attention. We sit down. The dog closes its eyes, waiting for the dust to settle. By the time we get up to walk back along the road, the sun has already dried up the puddles and put on its dusty veil.

We have tickets booked for the afternoon coach to Amritsar. But first we have to collect my mother's trousers and Rajpal has to have the portrait wrapped for the journey back to England and Kuldip wants to buy some presents for me to take back for my daughters. The coach leaves at four o'clock, so there is plenty of time. We decide to go to the shops with Kuldip and meet Rajpal at the bus station. But first, we have lunch.

All her life, my mother has set her clocks five minutes fast so that she would never be late for anything. If she had a bus to catch, she would always be waiting at the bus stop ten minutes before the bus was due. If she had an appointment with the doctor, she would be there half-an-hour early, which usually meant that she had to wait at least an hour before she saw the doctor. But now she is an Indian and has not looked at a clock for over a week.

Rajpal asks me what time it is and, when I tell him, drops his chappati, grabs the portrait and runs out of the door. Kuldip clears the table and disappears into her bedroom to get ready. I tell myself as I always do that we will be there on time, but I still can't bring myself to believe it.

At last, Kuldip emerges from her bedroom.

"Challo!" she says, throwing a shawl over her shoulders. "Let's go!"

Gorky stands up, tosses the car keys nonchalantly into the air, catches them deftly and leads us out to the car.

The trousers need altering. The shopkeeper studies my mother when she comes out of the changing room, sends for one of his assistants and, running his finger along the waistband, explains to him what needs doing. The assistant hurries out through a door at the back of the shop and the shopkeeper turns to me.

"They will be ready in half-an-hour."

We walk slowly along one side of the plaza, looking for a shop that sells jewellery. We find one and go in. The shopkeeper greets us and we sit down in front of the counter. Helped by a young boy, his son perhaps, he lifts boxes off the shelves and displays their contents for inspection. Kuldip examines them carefully before choosing two sets of bangles, one for each of my daughters. The shopkeeper and the boy go on opening boxes regardless, like clockwork toys that won't stop until they have run down. The counter begins to look like a pirate's chest, overflowing with treasure. Kuldip opens her purse, takes out some notes and holds them out. He takes them and counts them, then shakes his head. It is not enough. Kuldip laughs. She picks up the bangles and walks out of the shop. The shopkeeper shrugs his shoulders and the boy stows the treasure back in the boxes.

The trousers are nearly ready.

"Five minutes only. Please sit down."

We sit down. One of the shop assistants brings glasses of water on a tray. I try not to look at my watch. There is no need, I tell myself. In India, they do things differently. Things happen. Time is irrelevant. In ten minutes, the assistant returns with the trousers. I am ready to pay for them but the shopkeeper insists that my mother should try them on first. She does. They fit. The shopkeeper puts them in a bag. I give him the money. We say our goodbyes and go back to the car. The time is ten to four.

Gorky finesses his way through the traffic like a footballer dribbling the ball past the opposition. A feint, a swerve, a sudden burst of speed and the other car is left standing. Young men in India don't learn to drive, they pick it up, the way boys in England learn to ride a bike. You go out with a friend in his car, he lets you have a go, you soon get the hang of it and the driving test is more or less a formality.

My mother reminds me that this, like so many other things in India, is how it used to be in England. Her brother, learning to drive in the first few years of the last century, never took a driving test. When I was a boy, playing on streets where games of cricket were only occasionally interrupted by passing cars, L-plates and driving tests were a novelty. They were introduced before the war, then dropped again until the war was over.

Perhaps in those days time was less important too, but now it's five past four, which in England would mean that we had missed the four o'clock coach to Amritsar. Rajpal looks relaxed when we see him outside the bus station, chatting with Rahi and Sangeeta. They wave and come to meet us. Rahi gives me the portrait, well wrapped in brown paper and bubble-wrap. Sangeeta and my mother embrace. My mother won't let go. Rahi joins in. My mother is crying. Rajpal takes our luggage to the coach, then comes back for the portrait. We say goodbye to Kuldip and Gorky. Sangeeta walks with my mother to the coach, holding her hand, and helps her up the steps. We sit down near the front and Rajpal talks to the driver. No one is in a hurry. Rahi, Sangeeta, Kuldip and Gorky look up at the window, smiling and laughing. My mother wipes her eyes with a tissue. The driver's assistant switches on the DVD player and fiddles with the controls. Rajpal goes to his seat. The driver starts the engine. Someone else gets on. The door closes. The time is nearly half-past-four. The video screen flickers. The coach starts to move.

"Give them a wave!" I say. "We're off!"

She waves, but she can't see through her tears.

The journey to Amritsar, on the same road we travelled ten days ago, takes nearly four hours. The video lasts nearly as long, on and off. It is a Bollywood movie of no more than average length but the DVD is faulty and the driver's assistant is kept busy most of the way to Jalandhar trying to get it to play properly. He makes one final attempt when we get back on the coach after the halfway stop, but the picture on the screen looks more like a flicker-book than a video and when, flickering ever more slowly, it stops at a single, blurred image, he abandons it altogether.

"Has it finished?" says my mother, who has been able to ignore the pictures but not the soundtrack, which has played intermittently since we left Chandigarh.

"I think so."

"Thank goodness! What was it?"

I try to explain about Bollywood. The genre seems to me to owe more to Pinewood than Hollywood. The film stars of Bombay might have the glamour and wealth of Hollywood in its heyday, but the films they make are more like *Summer Holiday* than *High Society*. The heroes all look like Cliff Richard and the heroines are English roses, with the fashionably pale skins that Punjabi mothers look for when choosing a bride for their sons. The video we have been forced to watch in fits and starts has all the usual ingredients, including a comic character played by an actor who looks like Melvyn Hayes. It is, I think, rather sad that India is famous now for making poor imitations of American musicals, when it used to be famous for Satyajit Ray.

A minibus takes us from the bus station to the hotel. It belongs to Pingalwara, a home for the destitute and disabled just outside Amritsar. Rajpal is a friend of the doctor in charge of the home and she has sent the minibus to pick us up. The literal meaning of Pingalwara is cripple home. The first time I went there, with one of our exchange groups, a banner had been hung over the entrance which read:

PINGALWARA
HOME FOR THE INSANE AND RETARDED
WELCOMES SHROPSHIRE COUNCIL.

The home was founded in the year I was born by a man called Bhagat Puran Singh. Bhagat means saint. For years he carried a disabled boy, Piara Singh, on his back. It is said that he saw him at some festival, picked him up so that he could see what was happening and never put him down. When he got too old to carry him, he pulled him on a cart behind his bicycle. He looked like a holy man, tall and thin. The paintings I've seen make him look like Jesus, but in photographs he looks like a down-and-out, disreputable, even dangerous. Paintings of Jesus are probably just as misleading. He was an environmentalist as well as a saint, a prolific writer and publisher of pamphlets, with his own printing press and a stall outside the Golden Temple. He was nearly as old as my mother when he died. Rajpal knew him but my first visit to Pingalwara happened just too late for me to meet him.

When Bhagat Puran Singh was dying, he told a woman who had been helping at the home that he wanted her to take charge. Inderjit Kaur was a doctor, busy with her own medical practice, but when a saint appoints you as his successor I don't suppose you have much choice. When I visited Pingalwara for the first time, she had only just taken over. Conditions were still quite primitive and the visit was a moving but harrowing experience. There were lots of children wanting to be carried, lots of old women who had been abandoned by their families and lots of very disturbed men and women of all ages, some of them tied to their beds.

I haven't been back for several years and Rajpal tells me that Dr Inderjit Kaur has made a lot of improvements. One of the first things she did was to raise money to open a primary school, so that the children could be educated as well as fed. She has opened a secondary school now and started an organic farm on a few acres of land outside the city. Rajpal would like to take my mother to visit Pingalwara tomorrow but he will be busy in the morning and, with the Golden Temple to visit in the afternoon and the evening to be spent with some friends at the university, we decide we can't fit it in.

The lift man at the hotel welcomes my mother back, the porter carries our cases and, back in our old room, which it no longer seems unusual to be sharing with her, the day that began with the sound of falling rain comes to a quiet end.

We have the morning to ourselves and, while we are discussing how to spend it, there is a knock at the door. Two men, wearing the hotel uniform of grey trousers, short-sleeved grey jumper and shirt from which the colour has been washed out long ago, stand outside with a trolley between them.

"Breakfast please?"

"Breakfast?"

"Breakfast two peoples. Indian breakfast. English breakfast. Come in please?"

I hold the door open and make way for the trolley, which is pushed by the smaller and darker skinned of the two men. He stops nervously just inside the door. The first man says something to him in Punjabi, then turns back to me and points out the various contents of the trolley, lifting the corners of the white cloths draped over them.

"Hot water in flask for making tea please. This is milk in jug also for tea. Paratha here. This is made with potato. This is curd. Very nice. Also we have toast with butter and jam. This is omelette made with eggs. Very nice for memsahib please. I should tell him to put on table? Thank you please."

Courtesy in England is normally expressed in words. We are brought up to mind our p's and q's. In India a please or a thank you is conveyed by a look, a gesture, a tilt of the head. The everyday language of courtesy, the small change of verbal intercourse in England, has no equivalent in India. The consequence is that it is frequently misused by Indians whose command of English is less than perfect. They say thank you when they should say please and please when they should say thank you. They say both either too often or not at all, giving rise to two common and contradictory stereotypes: Indians are ingratiating and Indians are rude. A conversation in England ends with a coda. In India it just stops. The polite circumlocutions which postpone the end of a telephone call in England, sometimes almost indefinitely, are replaced in India by a single, terse and, ironically, English phrase.

"OK bye."

When breakfast has been laid out on the table in front of the window, I give each of the men a tip. They take the money and wheel out the trolley without another word.

"Rajpal must have ordered breakfast for us. Tea for the memsahib?"

"Yes, please."

After breakfast, we decide to go shopping. Through the glass wall of the lift, we watch the people outside on Lawrence Road. We must look to them like specimens in a test tube, volunteers in a futuristic experiment. The glass door slides open and we step out into a strange

141

world, time-travellers from the twenty-first century.

The lift goes only as far as the first storey. When developers can't find empty land to build on in Indian cities, they build on top of the buildings that are already there. This hotel and the buildings on either side of it stand on top of a row of shops. The lift opens onto a walkway, with steps that lead down to the pavement. Next door to the hotel is a bank. Two guards sit outside the door, one leg stretched out across the walkway, a machine gun resting on the other. They draw in their legs and push their chairs back against the wall to make room for my mother when we go past.

I help her down the steps and we walk down the road in search of a shop where she can buy a box of chocolates for Rajpal to take back to Kuldip. As we make our way slowly along the uneven pavement, attracting the usual curious glances, a rickshaw wallah pedals slowly alongside us.

"Ricksha? Golden Temple?"

I consider briefly asking him to take us to a shop that sells chocolates, but quickly dismiss the idea.

"Ricksha?"

I shake my head and try to ignore him. But he follows us like a stray dog. We walk very slowly, picking our way round the potholes. Sometimes he goes on ahead, but he always stops after a few yards and waits for us to catch up.

"Ricksha? Ricksha? Golden Temple?"

I see a shop at the other side of the road that looks as if it might sell cakes and sweets. We stop and wait for a gap in the traffic. The rickshaw wallah stops too and looks at me. I watch the traffic and try not to catch his eye. The road is like a river in flood, wide, deep and impassable.

"Let's walk back and see if we can see anything the other way."

The rickshaw wallah watches us go, then stands on his pedals and joins the flow, in search of other customers.

Near the hotel, we find a gift shop and in the window I see what we are looking for.

"Ferrero Rocher!"

"What?"

"Chocolates!"

The women in the shop make a fuss of my mother and gift-wrap the chocolates for her. They hold the door open for us and we make our way back to the hotel, up the steps, along the walkway, past the armed guards, to the lift. I press the button and wait. Nothing happens. I press the button again. Perhaps the lift man is busy. One of the guards comes across and leans on the button.

"It will be down soon," he says.

The other guard brings a chair for my mother. She thanks him and sits down. When the glass door slides open and the lift man looks out, he sees her sitting on a chair with me by her side and an armed guard behind her. One of them helps her out of the chair and the lift man stands by the door. She waves to the guards as the door closes. They smile and put their hands together.

We eat lunch in the hotel restaurant, where the music playing in the background sounds like an Indian version of English pop music circa 1959 and starts me wondering again about the surprisingly pervasive influence that Cliff Richard and, in this case, the Shadows seem to have had on Indian culture. Cliff was, I remember, born in Bombay, so perhaps that has something to do with it.

After lunch, we take the lift to the hotel car park, where the Pingalwara minibus is waiting to take us to the Golden Temple. Once there, we follow the crowds past shops selling books about the Golden Temple, plastic models of the Golden Temple, Golden Temple place mats and Golden Temple key rings, past the stall collecting money for Pingalwara, past the Golden Temple information centre, past the kiosk selling headscarves and the shoe depository (heads must be covered and feet bare inside the Golden Temple). We find a bench and sit down. I take off my shoes and socks. Rajpal ties a headscarf round my head. My mother puts a shawl over hers. I kneel down and take off her shoes. Rajpal takes our shoes to the man at the desk and hands them in. When he comes back, he is looking pensive. He sits down beside me.

"Mom is still wearing tights," he says, looking at her feet. "I am afraid they will not let her in without bare feet."

It is a situation we should have anticipated.

"When the Queen visited Golden Temple," he says, "she would not go barefoot. They thought about it for a long time and in the end they made a special pair of white socks for her to wear. But I don't think they will do the same for mom."

"I don't suppose so."

"But why not? After all, they should. She is old lady. They should make exception for her. Let me go and ask."

While he is away, I explain the problem to my mother.

"I'm not taking my tights off," she says, firmly. "I'm not even sure if I'll be able to walk without my shoes on."

When we see Rajpal walking back towards us through the crowds, his step is less jaunty than usual. He sits down beside me and puts a hand on my arm.

"How can we manage this?" he says, squeezing my arm as he struggles to find a solution to the problem. "Will she let me cut off the toes of her tights and roll them back over her feet up to her ankles?"

"You'd better ask her."

"They should change the rules," he says, thinking better of it. "No one should be turned away from gurdwara. Golden Temple has four gates and this is meant to show that everyone is welcome. But first you have to cover your head and take off your shoes and walk through water. Why should you have to do this? I think it should be changed. Let me go and talk to someone about it."

Giving my arm a final squeeze, he jumps up and walks away again through the crowds. A few minutes later he comes back carrying our shoes in one hand and a book in the other. He kneels down in front of my mother and helps her to put her shoes on. Then he gives her the book.

"Mom," he says, "if you can't go in, you can at least read about it and look at the pictures."

"Oh, that's lovely! That's even better. I'll be able to look at it any time I want now."

"Come!" he says, taking her hand and helping her to her feet. "You can see Golden Temple through the gate, even if they won't let you in."

He leads her to the gate and points through the archway, but she is so small and there are so many people going in and out that she can't see over their heads. She can't see the golden building in the middle of the lake, with its golden walls, golden turrets and golden dome. She can't see the people bathing in the lake. She can't walk across the causeway to the gurdwara, which sits like a precious box in the middle of the lake. She can't go inside to see the priests fanning the holy book, the Guru Granth Sahib. As she can't see any of this, we turn and walk away.

"How about a rickshaw ride? We're going back tomorrow and we still haven't been in a rickshaw."

Rajpal turns this over in his mind.

"Mom will like this?" he says, as if he doesn't think she will.

"Just a short ride. Just for the experience."

After giving the idea further thought, he agrees.

"But not here. Here the streets are too crowded. It will be better if we go now to the university. Then you and mom can take a tour of the grounds in a ricksha before we pay our visit. I think she will like that."

As we drive away from the Golden Temple, leaving the old city streets for the quieter suburbs, I wonder how and why ricksha became rickshaw. What made the English prefer one vowel to the other when they brought the word back from India? Does rickshaw sound more English than ricksha? Is it because we never feel quite comfortable with a foreign word until we have turned it into an English one? Or did we just think the native pronunciation was wrong and it was our duty to correct it? Noblesse oblige.

I mention it to Rajpal and he gives me another example. Delhi, he tells me, is really Dilli.

"And Bombay is really Mumbai?"

He shakes his head. This, he explains, is not a matter of pronunciation. The similarity between the two words is coincidental. Bombay was given its name by the Portuguese about five hundred years ago, Bom Bahia, Good Bay. When Charles II of England married Catherine de Braganza of Portugal, Bombay was part of her dowry. Six years later, it was handed over to the East India Company who made it their head office. But many languages were spoken in the city and some of them kept the old name. In Gujerat, Bombay has always been Mumbai.

Giving cities new names is an old game. Sometimes the old names just disappear. Sometimes, as in Mumbai, they survive through the confusion of language until someone in power seizes the chance to make a winning move. Madras used to be two places, Chennapatnam and Madraspatnam. The two places got bigger and turned into one city, which became known as Madras. But the people who lived in old Chennapatnam went on calling it Chennai and now, on the wheel of fortune, they have risen to the top.

Some of the new names correct the English pronunciation. Pune, Bengaluru, Kolkata. Some replace an English name with an Indian one. Bombay's old Victoria railway station is now Mumbai's Chatrapati Shivaji, the nineteenth century Queen of England usurped by a seventeenth century Indian Emperor. The name game goes on. Ahmedabad, Lucknow, Patna and Delhi are all on the list. Dilli will be easy to remember, but Karnavati, Lakshmanpuri and Pataliputra will take a bit more effort.

Even without the road signs pointing to Guru Nanak Dev University, we might guess that we were approaching academia. Signs of another kind are everywhere. Quiet, tree-lined roads, houses with well-kept gardens, young people in ones and twos walking along the pavement. We turn off the main road and stop at a barrier. The security guards look curiously at the white faces in the back of the minibus, then let us through. We could be on the campus of any English university built in the 1960s, except that the red brick and concrete buildings are hidden behind taller trees with greener leaves and the shrubs beside the roads bloom with bigger and brighter flowers.

The minibus pulls off the road and parks in a lay-by, where two ricksha wallahs are waiting for customers. Rajpal jumps out and talks to them. One of them, a young man, perhaps no more than nineteen or twenty, turns his rickshaw round and follows him.

"He will take you round the grounds. It will be very nice for mom. The grounds are very beautiful. Very quiet. Very peaceful. I have told him to go very slowly, take his time, so that you can see everything."

"I'm not sure if I can get in," my mother says, looking doubtfully at the leather bench perched over the back wheels of the rickshaw.

But we show her where to put her foot and, one either side of her, help her up onto the seat.

"I've done it!"

Rajpal stands back and applauds as the ricksha wallah looks over his shoulder, leans forward and pedals slowly out of the lay-by onto the empty road. I sit with my arm along the back of the seat, enjoying the slightly eerie sensation of travelling in almost total silence. The streets of Venice have the same quality, silence felt first as the absence of noise, then as the presence of sound, small, individual sounds, the sound of a gondola or the sound of a rickshaw, the sound of water lapping against a bridge or the sound of bicycle tyres on a dusty road.

It is very easy to get lost in the streets of Venice and it would be just as easy to get lost in the grounds of Guru Nanak Dev University, though for different reasons. In Venice, the streets and bridges and squares are as bewildering as a kaleidoscope. At every turn, the pattern changes. Here, at GND, everything looks the same. Roads, trees, buildings glimpsed between the trees, more roads, more trees, more buildings. Or perhaps the same ones we saw five minutes ago from the other side.

Two young women are walking towards us, hand in hand. When they see us, they stop and stare. Their faces light up with excited smiles. One of them steps out into the road and holds up her hand. The ricksha wallah slows down and stops, putting one foot down on the ground. The two students stand beside the rickshaw and put their hands together. My mother and I do the same.

"Hello!" say the students, grinning.

"Hello!" we reply.

"We saw you a few minutes ago and you looked so sweet with your white hair and all and when we saw you again just now we just wanted to stop and say hello."

"We hope you don't mind."

"Are you staying here?"

"Are you from England?"

"You look so sweet together."

"Thank you for stopping."

"It's so nice to talk to you."

"Thank you!"

"Thank you!"

"Goodbye!"

"Goodbye!"

The students step back onto the pavement. The ricksha wallah stands on the pedals, the students stand and wave, we sit on our leather bench and wave back. We come to a crossroads and turn into a road that looks exactly like the last one.

"This seat's a bit hard," my mother says.

The seat on a rickshaw always has a slight tilt to the front, so you have to sit up straight to stop yourself from sliding forward. My mother would be more comfortable if she had claws at the end of her legs instead of feet, then she could perch instead of sitting. Perhaps she will come back as a bird.

"Look! There's Rajpal."

He is standing at the end of the road, talking to someone, and I give him a wave. We think we have come to the end of our journey, but halfway down the road, the ricksha wallah takes a right turn and we continue our leisurely tour of Amritsar's academic hinterland. More trees, more roads, more students walking hand in hand smiling shyly as we drive slowly past. My mother shuffles on her seat.

"It's been very nice, but I think I've had enough now. Can't you tell him to go back?"

"I don't suppose he speaks English."

In India, time is nought. Better sit still and hope for the best.

The house where we spend the evening is more English than any house we have visited since we arrived in India nearly two weeks ago. When we sit round the dining table to eat birthday cake, we could be the guests of middle-aged academics in Sussex or Keele or Warwick or any other modern English university. But perhaps this is true of universities everywhere, not that they all look English, but that they all resemble each other. They all, in one way or another, hold themselves aloof from their surroundings. Whether you're in Cambridge or Keele or GND, you know you're not in the real world.

The birthday cake, which the professor's wife has baked, is a very good Victoria sponge. She asks whether we like it and glows with pride when we say without hesitation that we do.

"She is very good cook," says Rajpal.

The professor agrees and his wife does not disagree. False modesty is common in England, rare in the Punjab. The professor's wife knows she is a good cook and does not try to pretend otherwise. When we leave the kitchen to sit in the living room, there is a plate of little pastries on the table.

"Did you make these as well?"

"Please try," she says.

I take two and give one to my mother.

"You like them?"

"Delicious!"

She goes back to the kitchen and returns with a plate of sweets.

"You made these too?"

Her response is a slight inclination of the head, a gesture which can easily be mistaken for no but which means yes.

"Please try."

The professor's wife is also a professor, but at home she is the professor's wife. The English house is no more than a shell, the kernel is all Indian. The professor opens a bottle of whisky, his wife brings more snacks. Their son joins us, a boy of about fifteen, not yet old enough to sit with the men, still young enough to help his mother serve the guests. He is very quiet, very polite, but not shy. He speaks when spoken to and is not embarrassed when spoken about. He reminds me of the two girls we met on our first day in Amritsar.

His parents tell us a story about him. When he was a little boy, some other English people came with Rajpal to visit them. His mother went up to his bedroom to bring him downstairs and found him hiding under the bed.

"Don't make me go down!" he pleaded.

"Why not?"

"They might kill me!"

"Don't be silly! They won't kill you."

"Yes, they will! They're English! We've been learning about them at school. They made us their slaves and they used to kill people. Why did you let them in? Please send them away!"

We all laugh.

Later, we are joined by two more guests, one a retired civil servant whom I know from previous visits, the other a businessman and property developer, the hotel where we are staying being one of his properties. The professor pours more whisky, his wife and son bring more plates. Conversation shifts from English to Punjabi and back again. In the Punjabi interludes, I talk to my mother and sip my whisky and help myself to whatever the professor's son brings from the kitchen.

Punjabi is a melodious language which seems always on the brink of song. Being in a room full of Punjabis feels like being trapped inside an aviary. The retired civil servant is a cheerful little man, a willow warbler perhaps, with a laughing, chirping voice. I met him first a few years ago, when he was something important in the government of Punjab, with an office in one of the Secretariat buildings in Chandigarh, where we drank tea and he told me about living in digs when he was a student in Birmingham. Switching from Punjabi to English, he talks about it again now, setting English words to a Punjabi tune.

"It was so cold!" he says, his eyes wide with astonishment, one hand open, its fingers like a row of exclamation marks. "On my first day I stood at the bus stop at eight o'clock in the morning with my coat buttoned up and my scarf wrapped around my neck thinking, 'My God! It's so cold!' And that was in September before winter had even begun!"

The conversation changes key, back from English to Punjabi. I imagine a row of little birds in turbans perched on the telephone wires ready to fly south for the winter. Back home now, they chirp and twitter contentedly, pecking at the food the professor's wife has put out for them.

My mother reaches out for a glass of water but, before she can take it, the retired civil servant snatches it away.

"That's not for you!" he says.

It sounds like an alarm call and my mother, alarmed, looks to me for an explanation.

"It must be tap water. Not safe for us to drink."

Someone says something to the professor's son and he takes the glass away. The professor's wife brings a glass of bottled water for my mother. The business man says something in Punjabi. She sends her son out and he returns with toothpicks and a plate of samosas. He gives the toothpicks to the businessman and the samosas to his mother. She goes round with the plate. My mother refuses but I take one and so does everyone else. I thank her, as I have been brought up to do. They ignore her, as they have been brought up to do. The business man picks his teeth. They help themselves from the plate and the woman holding it makes herself invisible.

It reminds me of the stories my mother tells about her father, stories told to her by her mother. She was lying in bed, having just given birth, and he was sitting beside her.

"I'd give anything for a cup of tea, Jack," she said.

"Your mother will be here soon," he said. "She'll make you one."

If she sat knitting or doing needlework in the evening, he would say, "If you've got time to do that, we could get another cow."

Her advice to other women was never to learn how to milk.

"If you do," she said, "you'll never get another day's rest."

She did what she had been brought up to do and so did he. So did my own mother and father, who each had their own allotted tasks. He lit the fire, drove the car and went to work every day. She stayed at home and did the housework. He joined the army when he was called up. She stayed at home with the baby. He came back five years later and went back to work. She stayed at home and had me.

The business man goes on picking his teeth. He does it with a degree of enthusiasm I have never seen anyone apply to the picking of teeth before. It is auto-dentistry. No part of his mouth is left unexplored. His jaw slides first one way, then another. He opens his mouth wide enough to admit his whole hand. It is difficult not to stare at this public display of an activity which is normally carried out, if not in private, at least discreetly. But he is so absorbed in it that if we all stood round him in a circle watching, like students observing an operation, I doubt whether he would even notice. Some of the other men take toothpicks too, but they are amateurs compared to him. Toothpick dilettantes. He is an artist.

When everyone stands up and the professor's wife crosses the room and takes my mother's arm, she asks her for her coat. The professor's wife looks at me.

"She is feeling cold?"

"I don't know. Are you feeling cold, mum?"

The professor's wife goes out to fetch her coat.

"Isn't it time to go?"

"No, not until we've had dinner."

"Not more food! I thought that was it!"

When the professor's wife comes back with her coat, I explain the misunderstanding.

"When she saw everyone standing up, she thought it was time to go."

She laughs and takes my mother's arm.

"Come! I have prepared your favourite dish for you."

After dinner and another baked potato, we stand outside the door where the businessman's car is waiting. His driver stands beside the car, ready to open the doors for him and the retired civil servant, who is going with him. The expense of running a car includes, for many middle class Indians, the employment of a driver, just as the expense of running a house used to include, for middle class families in England, the employment of domestics. Even my mother, living in an off-licence in Leeds with her brother and sister and their widowed mother, was looked after by Mary during the down times at the mill.

"Where did we all sleep?" she sometimes says. "It was only a small house. I can't remember where Mary slept."

Perhaps there was an attic as well as a cellar, where she remembers seeing the beer barrels bobbing about one morning after a night of heavy rain. She often talks about Mary and her contrary way of putting things.

"As one door opens, another shuts."

The driver closes the doors, gets in and drives away, leaving us standing outside enjoying the cool night air. The professor's wife brings my mother her coat. The professor gets into his car and starts the engine. I help my mother into the back seat. The professor's wife and son stand by the side of the road and put their hands together as we drive away, along the quiet, moonlit roads, back to the noise and lights of the city.

"He's got a very nice hotel," my mother says, when we are back in our room, "but I didn't like the way he sat picking his teeth."

In the bathroom, her own teeth smile at me from a glass on the shelf above the sink. They remind me of Yorick. A surreal disembodiment of humour. I imagine Hamlet performing the famous speech holding Yorick's dentures instead of his skull. Has it ever been done? Probably. I brush my teeth and try to concentrate on my own reflection in the mirror, but my eyes keep straying to the memento mori on the shelf.

Our clothes are still in the suitcases, lying open on the bedroom floor. I put my dressing gown on top, get into bed and turn out the light.

"Have you set the alarm?"

"Yes."

"What time for?"
"Six o'clock."
I lie on my back, looking at the ceiling fan slowly turning.
"There's someone looking after me," she says. "I know there is."
A toothless voice, fluttering in the dark like a moth.
"There must be something, some meaning to it all."
A moth on the windowpane, trying to get in or out.
"Even if this is all there is, it can't be just chance."
Silence now, as if the moth has settled somewhere.
"Which is very hard to say without your teeth in."
The moth folds its wings.

"It's your turn now," she said one day, not long after we had returned to England. "Where shall we go for *your* birthday?"

We went to Uzès in the south of France, where we sat every day at one of the cafés in the Place aux Herbes, watching children playing in the fountain, looking at the medieval arcades around the square, enjoying the shade cast by the old, gnarled plane trees and talking about India.

We left Amritsar on a foggy morning and, as the world turned obligingly to meet us halfway, arrived in the evening to find that it had been snowing all day in England.

"The airport staff are trying to clear the runway," the pilot announced as we flew over the channel. "If they can't get it cleared in time, we may have to divert."

I was just about to explain what the pilot had said, when he went on.

"I'm going to fly as slowly as I can to give them plenty of time. I'll keep you informed."

I decided to wait for further announcements before saying anything, a decision that was justified when we landed safely an hour later at the right airport. The only diversion we encountered was on the motorway, reduced to one lane because of the snow which, we later found out, had been falling heavily for the last twenty-four hours. Like the pilot, I was obliged to drive slowly and it was late when we got home. But when we caught up with the news we realised that things would have been much worse if we had flown back the day before, when all the airports were closed and a lot of the roads were impassable.

"Someone was looking after us."

"Ganesh, perhaps."

"There's a pattern behind everything. I know there is. There must be."

The little glass elephant god sits on the dresser in her room, transparent and inscrutable. One day, seeing him on the shelf behind her, I remembered that Ganesh is often depicted holding his broken tusk in one hand and a bowl of sweets in the other, riding proudly and cheerfully, if a little improbably, on the back of a mouse. The metamorphosis I sometimes imagine for her seemed suddenly more plausible.

She did not bring Ganesh to France with her, but wore her pearls every day. She has worn them every day since her birthday, proud and cheerful as Ganesh, he with his broken tusk and bowl of sweets, she with her string of pearls. Ganesh broke off his tusk and used it as a pen to write the story of India. She wears her pearls to remind her of it. Every day she re-lives her two weeks in India. Like *Margot's Secret* when she was a girl, it is a story she never tires of reading. She has read it so many times now, she knows it off by heart.

"It's all so plain," she says, "just as if I was still there."

So we sat in the shade of the plane trees and talked about India, about the children who wanted to be photographed with us, the vegetable seller on his bicycle, the baby asleep on the bed, the rickshaw ride at the university, the girls who stopped us to say hello, the birthday cake and the roses, Ratty and Señorita, the dancers in the village, the gate-keeper at the Rock Garden, the grey-haired woman with the kind face, the girl who wanted to talk to us in the Rose Garden, the armed guard who brought her a chair to sit on, the beautiful girl who walked beside her and held her hand when she cried.

"France is nice," she said, "but I prefer India."

"When we got back you said you wanted to go and live there."

"Did I?"

"You said you'd rather live in India than England."

"England isn't nice anymore. I'm still in India. I go there every day."

She finds it easier now to talk about things that for years she kept to herself, crying, if she ever did, only when nobody could see her. She talks about my sister more than she has ever done before. We have sat together and cried for her since we came back. The tears of joy that she cried in India started it. Tears flowing like the spring that Manon set flowing again in Pagnol's story. The wrong that was done when Manon was a little girl put right again, as wrongs are in stories.

When her bones ache, she still says that God is cruel to keep her alive. He should let her die, she says. Until He does and her story is finished, the pattern cannot be made out. As in the Ramayana, it is impossible to make sense of anything until everything has happened.

But one day, sooner or later, everything that is going to happen will have happened and the pattern that she believes in, because she cannot understand how there could not be one, will be revealed at last.

POSTSCRIPT

All that was a long time ago, seven years ago to be precise.

She is still alive, still remembering her birthday in India, still accusing God of being cruel, still trying to fathom His intentions.

The only way to bring this story to an end, in the absence of the ending she looks forward to, is to tell a story that does have an end, a story that explains it all, the story of Rama and Sita, the Ramayana.

Here it is then, with an ending that will serve for hers and mine and, I hope, yours.

RAMAYANA

Prologue

Rama's rule in Ayodhya, Ram-raj, was a time of peace, a golden age. This was partly because Rama was a good king and partly because all the tangled threads of the years that had gone before had finally been untangled. It is not often that the knots in people's lives are untied and not long before they become knotted up again, which is why most people wish they could return to the uncomplicated lives they led when they were children and why every year in India people celebrate the return of Rama to Ayodhya by lighting candles to show him the way.

Every year, in the few days before Diwali, people act out the story of Rama's life. Every town puts on its own Ramlila and people gather every evening to watch the story unfold. In medieval England, in York and Chester and Wakefield, they used to act out the bible story in much the same way. The Mystery Plays had their day a long time ago but in India still, for a few nights every year, gods and humans play their parts in the long and complicated story of Rama and his brothers, where every action has a consequence and every event has a cause and nothing is as simple as it looks.

So, in a story of unintended consequences, where to begin? There is no one beginning, but there are some things that you need to know before we start.

You need to know that the sage Valmiki was told by the god Brahma to tell the story of Rama. Valmiki, it is said, saw the whole story in his mind, as if he held it in the palm of his hand like an orange, but when he put it into words it turned into a poem with twenty-four thousand verses.

You need to know that Dashrat, king of Kosala, had three wives. Their names were Kausalya, Sumitra and Kaikeyi. But none of them had given him a son. Wanting an heir for his kingdom, he made a sacrifice to the gods. A spirit appeared, holding a golden cup, and told him that, if his wives drank from the cup, they would each bear him a son. Dashrat took the cup to his wives and told them to drink half each. Kausalya drank half and gave the cup to Sumitra. Sumitra drank half and gave the cup to Kaikeyi. Kaikeyi drank half and gave the cup back to Dashrat. Seeing that the cup was still not empty, Dashrat gave it back to Sumitra and she finished it.

You need to know that King Dashrat had four sons, Rama, Bharat, Lakshman and Shatrugna. Rama's mother was Kausalya. Bharat's mother was Kaikeyi. Lakshman and Shatrugna were twins. Their mother was Sumitra.

You need to know that Janak, another king, found a baby girl one day in a ploughed field. She was lying in a furrow, so he named her Sita, which means furrow, and he brought her up as his daughter.

You need to know that rakshasas are demons and that the king of the rakshasas was ten-headed Ravana.

You need to know that the story is told in six books: Bala Kanda, Ayodhya Kanda, Aranya Kanda, Kishkindha Kanda, Sundara Kanda and Yuddha Kanda.

Book 1

Vishvamitra knew all this. He knew much more than King Dashrat or anyone else. He was very old and very wise and he knew that Rama alone was capable of defeating Ravana. When Dashrat's servants saw Vishvamitra coming, they ran to tell him and a welcome was prepared. Vishvamitra was ushered in and Dashrat bowed down before him.

"Oh, great sage!" he said. "You are most welcome. Your visit is like a gift of nectar, like rain in a drought, like the birth of a son to a man without an heir, like wealth restored which was lost forever! I am truly blessed by your visit! The purpose of my birth is fulfilled at last, for today I behold with my own eyes verily the supreme Brahman, the best of the rishis! Today I have been purged of all my sins! Great is my fortune and complete my bliss! Tell me what service I can render your honour! With what desire have you come, O glorious one?"

Dashrat's speech pleased Vishvamitra and he made a speech of his own in return. But his was shorter.

"I have come to ask you a favour," he said. "These days I am engaged in a holy rite, but two rakshasas who can change their shapes at will are bent upon frustrating my efforts. They pollute and spoil my rites by throwing bones, marrow and bleeding flesh on the sacred altar. Their names are Maricha and Subahu. Like all rakshasas, they do the will of Ravana, son of Vishravas, whose evil threatens the whole world. O king, it is your duty to protect your friend and guest from such fiends."

Dashrat nodded and promised to raise an army to defeat the rakshasas, but Vishvamitra shook his head.

"I don't want your army," he said. "I want your son. I want Rama."

With a heavy heart, Dashrat agreed to send Rama with Vishvamitra. At first he had tried to persuade him that Rama was too young to fight the demons, but the sage insisted and the king could not go back on his word, for his word was his dharma. Lakshman went with them, because he and Rama went everywhere together.

They stopped twice on the journey, first to sip the water of the river Sarayu and then at the edge of a forest to kill the first of the rakshasas, Maricha's mother, Tadaka. Sitting on the riverbank, Vishvamitra taught Rama about bala and ati-bala.

"When you have mastered these," he said, "neither fatigue nor age nor disease will ever touch you. No one will be your equal in strength, beauty and knowledge. Hunger and thirst will not affect you and, when you have learned these spells, great fame and power will be yours."

They walked on and climbed into a boat to cross Ganga, the sacred river, before they came to the forest.

"This is Tadaka's forest," Vishvamitra told them. "If she hears us, she will try to scare us away. If we stay, she will try to kill us."

"Who is she?" Rama asked him.

"She is a rakshasa. Her husband was Sunda. Maricha is their son. She lives in this forest and has the strength of a thousand elephants. Only you can destroy her and you must not shrink from doing so just because she is a woman. Unrighteous women have been killed before for the good of mankind. Indra himself killed Manthara, the daughter of Virochana, who was bent upon destroying the whole world, and lord Vishnu slew Brighu's wife, the mother of Shukra, because she would have made the world without Indra. Do not hesitate out of pity to kill this rakshasa by my command."

Rama lifted his bow and plucked the string. A deep note sounded, threading its way through the trees like a leopard, and Tadaka, deep in the forest, heard it and sprang to her feet. With a shout of anger, she swept through the forest like a wind. She came howling and shrieking towards them, but Rama stood his ground, waiting until he saw her shape like a dark shadow among the trees.

"I will not kill her," he said to Lakshman, who stood at his side. "She is a woman after all. It will be enough to wound her."

Out of the trees she came, a dark shape in a swirl of dust, rushing towards them with her arms in the air, her face distorted with anger. The stones on the ground were caught up like leaves in the wind, flying up into the air and falling down onto their heads. Rama lifted his bow and fired an arrow into the middle of the storm. Tadaka screamed and clutched her shoulder, feeling the arrow slice through her arm. Rama fired another arrow. They heard another scream echoing endlessly round about them, as if the world was a cave and the sky was its roof. Now she rushed towards them like a wounded tiger and drops of her blood were mixed with the dust that still swirled around their heads. But Lakshman drew his sword as she threw herself at Rama and, with three swift strokes, he sliced off her ears and her nose.

At once, the rakshasa disappeared, leaving behind only the dark cloud from which rocks and stones went on falling around them. Vishvamitra saw what was happening and shouted a warning to Rama.

"Do not be deceived, Rama. Tadaka can turn herself into whatever shape she chooses. She cannot be defeated, only destroyed. You must kill her."

Rama fitted another arrow to his bow, raised it above his head and fired into the stones that fell from the sky. As his arrow bounced and clanged among the stones, making a noise like swords clashing in battle, the rakshasa appeared again, shrouded in darkness, her disfigured face twisted into a snarl of fury, her wounded arms raised high above her head. Rama felt the darkness fold itself around him like the wings of a giant bird. But already another arrow had fitted itself to his bow. He bent the bow with all his strength and, even as he felt the demon's hand pressing on his mouth, stifling his breath, his arrow found its way to her heart and she fell to the ground, where she lay at his feet, dying.

The sky cleared and, when he looked down, all he saw was a heap of bones covered with rags of skin.

Vishvamitra took Rama and Lakshman to his hermitage and resumed his ritual, while the two brothers stood guard. The ritual lasted for six days. The fire blazed on the altar and the hermits sat beside it on the grass, surrounded by mounds of flowers, reciting the holy words and reading from the holy books.

On the sixth day, the sky turned dark and the birds stopped singing, as if a storm was brewing. Rama picked up his bow. The only sound was the murmuring of the hermits, the only light the flickering of the fire. Lakshman looked up at the sky and then at his brother. In the distance they heard a sound like whispering. Rama drew an arrow from his quiver, placed it in his bow and drew back the string. The whispering turned into a hissing and then into a howling and over the trees came a black cloud and out of the cloud came a storm of rakshasas swooping over their heads.

"Maricha!"

"Subahu!"

Maricha came first, falling from the sky like an eagle to catch and kill the man who had killed his mother.

"Rama!"

Lakshman tried to pull his brother to safety but Rama's arrow had already pierced Maricha's breast and went on flying through the air, taking Maricha with it, over the trees and the hills and the rivers, until it fell at last into the sea, where the rakshasa floated on the surface of the water like a drowned man.

"Rama!"

Lakshman's warning would have been too late, but Rama had already seen the danger and Subahu hung over their heads, his eyes wide, like the eyes of a hanged man, clutching with his hand Rama's arrow in his chest, before he fell to the ground and lay dead at their feet.

The story was unfolding as Vishvamitra knew it would and now it was time for the next chapter.

"Come," he said. "We must go to Mithila."

The brothers went with him, though they did not know why, and on the way they came to a deserted ashram. It was a beautiful place and they wondered why no one lived there. Vishvamitra explained.

"This ashram," he said, "belonged to Gautama. Here the great sage lived with Ahalya, his wife, that most beautiful of all Brahma's creations. Early one morning, when Gautama was bathing, the god Indra came to the ashram, disguised as a man, determined to make love to Ahalya. When she saw him, Ahalya knew at once that he was thousand-eyed Indra, but she could not resist the god's persuasions and she lay down with him and their desires were fulfilled. Ahalya then urged him to leave before Gautama returned and, suddenly afraid, Indra hurried to get away. But he was too late. Gautama came back, the drops of water on his skin glistening in the sunlight. He saw Indra creeping out of the ashram and cursed him. 'You made yourself look like a man,' he said, 'and now you will pay for it with the loss of your own manhood.' At once, Indra's testicles withered and fell to the ground. Gautama then turned to Ahalya and cursed her too. 'You shall live here alone,' he said, 'lying on a bed of ashes, burning in shame until Rama comes to release you from your penance. Honour him when he comes and then, only then, will you be cleansed of your sins. Your beauty will be restored and I will return to you.'"

Vishvamitra took them into the ashram and there they saw Ahalya lying on a bed of ashes. When she stood up to greet them, she was so beautiful that Rama thought she looked like the moon seen through mist or like a bright flame hidden in smoke or like the sun reflected in water. He greeted her and she, remembering Gautama's words, received him with great honour and suddenly the ashram was filled with flowers, falling from the sky like rain, and they were surrounded by beautiful apsarases and other spirits, dancing to the music of the ghandarvas, servants of Indra, and then Gautama himself appeared and was reunited with his wife.

When they came to Mithila, king Janak welcomed them and they sat down to talk. Janak asked Vishvamitra what he could do to please him and Vishvamitra asked him to show them Shiva's bow. Janak gave orders for the bow to be brought to them and, while they were waiting, he told them how the god Shiva had given the bow to his ancestor. He told them too about Sita, the baby girl sprung, not from a womb, but from the earth itself, and about his promise to give her in marriage to the man who could string and bend great Shiva's bow. He told them how many kings and princes had tried and failed even to lift it.

"Let Rama try," said Vishvamitra.

The chest containing the giant bow was brought in on a carriage pulled, not by bullocks, but by a hundred strong men with broad shoulders. Their skin gleamed with sweat as they strained to pull the carriage before the king and his guests.

"He can try if he wants," said Janak, who thought he had seen it all before.

Rama climbed onto the carriage and opened the chest. Inside lay Shiva's bow, the biggest and the heaviest he had ever seen. Janak turned away and spoke to Vishvamitra about other things. Only when he heard the crack did he look back. He had not seen Rama take the bow out of the case and place it carefully on the floor of the carriage. He had not seen him fasten the string to the bow and tighten it. He had not seen him grasp the bow in his hand. He had not heard the gasps of the people watching when they saw Rama lift the bow, straighten his arm and slowly pull back the string. He only heard the crack when the bow broke.

Messengers were sent to Ayodhya with the news that Rama and Sita were to marry. King Dashrat came to Mithila, with his wives and sons and ministers and officials, riding in carriages or seated in palanquins, and the palace guard rode beside them on horses and elephants, pulling carts piled high with gifts, and hundreds of attendants walked behind them in a cloud of dust.

In the morning, Dashrat entered the wedding pavilion which had been erected in the grounds of the palace, and took his seat. Then Janak came in with Sita and she sat at the altar, facing Rama.

"Here is my daughter," said Janak, "who will be your partner in life. Receive her by the hand as your bride, join hand to hand and she will follow you like your shadow."

Then he poured water into Rama's hand and the gods, looking down on them, showed their approval, raining flowers down from the sky. Janak then turned to Lakshman and Bharat and Shatrugna.

"Come!" he said. "The hour is auspicious. Lakshman, take Urmila from me. Bharat, take Mandavi by the hand. Shatrugna, take Shrutakirti. She is yours."

Taking Janak's daughters by the hand, the brothers joined Rama and Sita by the altar, where the sacred fire burned. Each walked three times round the fire, before leading his bride to the rooms which had been prepared for them in the palace.

Book 2

They went back to Ayodhya, where the people greeted them with music and dancing. The streets were washed clean and there were flowers everywhere. As they rode towards the palace, it seemed to rise up before them like a mountain in the Himalayas. Everyone was happy.

But Dashrat felt that he was growing old and, as the days passed, he began to feel troubled. There had been strange portents. Birds were heard screaming in the sky. In the forest, wild beasts cried out as if they were afraid. No one knew what it meant. Some said one thing, some another. Dashrat thought he saw his own death coming.

When the brother of Kaikeyi, Yudhajita, came to visit Ayodhya, he asked Dashrat to let Bharat and his brothers go back with him to Kekaya. Dashrat was happy for Bharat to go with him, but he had other plans for Rama. So Yudhajita took Bharat and Shatrugna, but Rama and Lakshman stayed in Ayodhya.

One day, Dashrat called an assembly of all his priests and ministers.

"I have ruled in Kosala for many years," he said, "following in the footsteps of my ancestors and trying always to think first of the happiness of my subjects and always to follow my dharma. But my body grows weak and every day I feel less able to carry this burden. Tomorrow, with the approval of all you wise men gathered here, I will lay down my kingship and Rama will rule in my place as regent."

It was quickly agreed that Rama's coronation would take place on the next day and, as the news spread, there was great excitement in Ayodhya. Dashrat knew that if he could see Rama enthroned before he died, he would be able to face death without fear or sorrow.

Kaikeyi, Bharat's mother, had a maid called Manthara. Manthara was a hunchback. She had served Kaikeyi all her life. No servant in the palace was more loyal than Manthara. When she heard that Rama was to become king, she saw at once what lay behind it and rushed to her mistress to warn her. At first, Kaikeyi did not believe what Manthara told her, but Manthara soon convinced her that she was right.

Why did the king send Bharat away, she asked. The answer was obvious. Who had persuaded him to do it? Who stood to gain? Who will look down on the other queens when her own son becomes king? Who will be queen now? Whose children will become kings?

Kaikeyi's mind was in a whirl, her heart was torn.

"Oh, lady," said Manthara. "Why don't you understand the simple facts? Rama is Bharat's enemy. Kausalya is a threat to you and your son. Kausalya hates you because the king loves you the most. Act now, before it is too late. Speak to the king. Make him send Rama into exile and put Bharat on the throne instead."

"But how?" asked Kaikeyi, her anger growing against those who had plotted against her. "How can I make him change his mind?"

Then Manthara reminded her of the time long ago when Dashrat granted her two boons.

"He was wounded in battle," sighed Kaikeyi, "and I nursed him back to health. When he was well again, he granted me two boons."

"Which you kept but never used."

"I said I wanted nothing from him, but he told me that, when I did, he would grant me whatever I asked."

"Ask him now. Ask him to banish Rama and put Bharat on the throne. He cannot refuse."

Nor could he. He was like a sparrow caught on the wing by a hawk. He had given his word and there was no way out. He pleaded with her but she would not relent.

"Yesterday, I told Rama that he would become king in my place," he said, distraught. "Today I must tell him that he is to be banished instead. Tomorrow, everyone will come to the palace for his coronation. Kaikeyi, wife, don't make me do this."

"You gave me your word," she said. "Truth is the highest dharma. Promises should be kept."

"What will Rama say? What will he do?"

"He will do whatever you tell him. He knows dharma too. He will not question your decision."

"I can't tell him."

"Send for him. I will tell him."

When Rama came to them and saw his father in distress, he turned to Kaikeyi.

"Something is wrong," he said. "What is it? Is it Bharat? Has something happened?"

"Yes," she said, "something has happened. But the king is afraid to tell you. He made me a promise and now he repents of it, not like a king, but like an ordinary man. He is like a man who would build a dam when the river is dry. Rama, the world is rooted in dharma. Let him not violate the truth for your sake. You should do whatever he asks. That is your dharma too."

"Lady," said Rama, "it grieves me that anyone should think that I would not obey my father. I would jump into the fire if he told me to. Tell me what is his desire and I will do it. Rama need not promise twice."

So Kaikeyi, now in no doubt that Bharat would be king, told him plainly what had been agreed.

"The king has granted me two boons," she said. "The first is that Bharat should be made king. The second is that you should be banished from Kosala for..."

Manthara had told her how long. Long enough for Rama to be forgotten. Long enough for Bharat to be king and his sons to become kings after him.

"... fourteen years."

She turned to Dashrat.

"He made his promise, but now he dare not look into your face. Will you help him keep his promise or allow him to break it?"

Rama saw the agony on his father's down-turned face and gave Kaikeyi his answer.

"Let it be as you please," he said. "I shall go into exile to honour my father's word. Neither you nor my father nor anyone else should doubt it. Send horses for Bharat and bring him back for his coronation. I will take off my royal clothes and put on the clothes of a hermit and go to the Dandaka forest to begin my exile."

When Rama went to his mother to tell her, she wept and insisted on coming with him.

"A cow stays with its calf," she said, "and I must stay with you."

But he would not allow her.

"You must stay here," he said. "Your duty is to my father, to stay with him, not with me."

When Lakshman heard what had happened, he argued with Rama and tried to make him change his mind.

"This is not dharma," he said. "It is a trick. It is the work of a jealous woman. If this is destiny, we should fight against it, not give in. That is the coward's way."

He drew his sword, but Rama made him put it away.

"I am resolved to obey my father's word," he said. "That is the path of dharma."

Then he went to Sita and told her that she should stay in Ayodhya and look after his mother.

"She is your mother too," he said, "and Bharat and Shatrugna and Lakshman are your brothers."

But Sita wanted to go with him to the forest.

"Father, mother, brother, son and daughter-in-law," she said, "reap what they have sown in their past life, but a wife alone shares her husband's lot. Therefore, take me with you into exile. I shall live with you in the forest, happy as I was in my father's palace."

Rama told her about the dangers of the forest – the lions, the bears, the crocodiles – but Sita still begged him to take her with him. Still he refused and then she wept and when he saw her tears, falling like water from a lotus flower, he relented.

"Come," he said. "We will go to the forest together. But first, take all our possessions, everything we have, and give some to our servants and the rest to the Brahmans to do with as they think fit."

Lakshman came then and touched Rama's feet and said, "Since you have made up your mind to go into exile, I will come with you and go in front with my sword, showing the path and collecting food to eat and keeping watch when you are asleep."

Rama took his hand and told him to say farewell to his friends and give away all his possessions, as he had told Sita.

Then they left Ayodhya to begin their exile.

Wearied by his grief, restless, tormented by the knowledge of what he had done or what he had been forced to do, Dashrat slept uneasily that night and, when he woke, he remembered, as if remembering a dream, something he had long forgotten.

He was young again and he was out hunting. In those days, he could kill an animal without even seeing it. The sound was enough to tell him where it was and where to aim his arrow. One night in the rainy season, on the banks of the Sarayu, he heard a sound like an elephant drinking from the river and, without hesitation, lifted his bow and fired his arrow. But then came another sound, not the sound of an elephant falling to the ground or splashing in the river or running away through the jungle, but the sound of a man in pain.

He ran towards the sound and saw a hermit lying in the shallow water at the edge of the river. Beside the hermit was a pitcher of water lying on its side. The water trickled from the pitcher, back into the river, and the blood from the wound in the hermit's side flowed into the water too. The hermit looked up at him with pain and bewilderment in his eyes.

"Why have you done this?" he said. "What have I done?"

"I thought I heard an elephant drinking from the river," said Dashrat.

"You heard me filling my pitcher," said the hermit, reaching for it, but he was too weak and it was out of reach.

Dashrat picked it up.

"I was fetching water for my parents," said the hermit, his voice faint, the words coming slowly to his lips, as his life drained slowly into the river. "They are old and blind. They have no one else to look after them. Please, fill the pitcher, take it to them and ask their forgiveness for me and for you."

Then he died.

Dashrat filled the pitcher and followed the path to the hermit's hut. Hearing his footsteps, the old people came to the door and called to him, thinking he was their son. Seeing the smiles on their faces, the king began to weep. He knelt and touched their feet and told them what had happened. He put down the pitcher and led them to the river and the old man and his wife sat down on the bank and laid their hands on their son's body where it lay in the shallow water and spoke his name quietly, over and over.

"Sravana. Sravana. Sravana."

Dashrat stood beside them, with tears in his eyes, until at last the old man stood up and faced him.

"You have killed my innocent son," said the old man, "leaving us with no one to care for us and only grief in our hearts."

His wife sat on the bank with her feet in the water, touching her son's face and saying his name over and over. Dashrat opened his mouth to speak, but could find no words.

"For what you have done," the old man went on, "I lay on you this curse, that you too will die of grief for the loss of a son, as we do now."

Dashrat looked away, unable to bear the sight of the old man's blind eyes, which seemed to see into the depths of his soul. When he looked back, the old people were walking away from him, back towards their hut in the forest.

The memory filled Dashrat with horror and he went in search of Kausalya and told her the story. Kausalya tried to comfort him, but that night Dashrat died, just as Sravana's father had said he would.

They sent for Bharat and, when he came, he heard for the first time everything that had happened. Kaikeyi told him proudly that it was all her doing and expected him to be pleased. But he was angry and went to Kausalya to ask her forgiveness. He told her that he would bring Rama back, so that he could be king, as his father had promised.

Some of the palace servants brought Manthara to Shatrugna and he ordered them to punish her. He struck her but Bharat told him to let her go, because she was a woman and should be forgiven.

When Dashrat's funeral rites were complete, Bharat kept his promise to Kausalya and went in search of Rama, taking an army with him. He rode ahead in his chariot and behind him came a long, winding procession of horses, elephants, camels and men, raising a cloud of dust that could be seen for miles.

Rama, Sita and Lakshman had reached the mountains and stopped at a place called Chitrakut and here, in a clearing, Lakshman had built them a cottage out of logs. One morning, they heard what sounded like thunder rumbling in the distance and saw a great cloud of dust in the sky. The birds flew up from the trees when they heard the noise and the animals fled in panic.

Lakshman climbed to the top of a tall tree and saw Bharat leading the army in his chariot. He thought Bharat must have come to kill Rama. Scrambling down from the tree as fast as he could, he jumped to the ground and ran to warn him.

"Quick, Rama!" he shouted, drawing his sword. "We must fight for our lives!"

But Rama made him put down his sword.

"I'm sure there is no danger," he said. "Perhaps our father has changed his mind and sent Bharat to bring us back."

So they waited, listening to the sound of the army coming closer and seeing the dust cloud gathering in the sky.

Bharat ordered the army to stop, while he went ahead on foot to look for Rama. When he saw smoke rising above the trees, he hurried towards it and soon he saw the cottage and Rama sitting on the grass with Sita and Lakshman behind him. Rama stood up when he saw him and embraced him.

"Why have you come here?" he asked. "Your place is in Ayodhya."

Then Bharat told him about their father's death and the brothers wept and Sita wept too.

"I have come to bring you back," said Bharat. "Your place is in Ayodhya now. Your exile is ended. The kingdom was given to me and now I give it freely to you."

But Rama shook his head.

"We must both follow our father's command," he said. "He is in heaven, honoured by the gods. There is no cause to mourn him. Go back to Ayodhya and leave me here to live out my exile, as he commanded."

Bharat tried to persuade him.

"This happened because of my mother," he said. "My father kept his promise to her, in spite of her wickedness, and you obeyed him. But now you can go back and put everything right again."

Again Rama shook his head. But Bharat went on.

"The people want you as their king," he said, "not me."

Still Rama shook his head and still Bharat tried to make him change his mind.

"Let us change places," he said. "Let me stay here in exile instead of you, so that you can take your place on the throne."

But Rama would not change his mind.

"I cannot disobey my father," he said.

Bharat turned to the others for help.

"I will stay here and fast," he said, "until Rama takes pity on me and agrees to return."

He sat down on the grass and folded his arms. Lakshman and Sita looked helplessly at each other, knowing there was nothing they could do.

"What wrong have I done you," said Rama, "that you should try to force me to do something against my will?"

He took Bharat's hand and lifted him to his feet and at last Bharat saw that there was nothing he could do.

"Then I will go back to Ayodhya," he said, "and rule in your name during your exile. I will live as a hermit in the palace, eating only fruit and roots, until you return. And if you do not return at the end of fourteen years, I will build a pyre and die in the flames."

Then he asked Rama to take off his sandals and give them to him. Rama did so and Bharat took them and raised them above his head.

"I will go back to Ayodhya," he said, "and place these sandals on the throne, so that when the people look at them they will know who is their king."

Holding the sandals above his head, he turned and walked away.

Book 3

They left Chitrakut and went to the Dandaka forest and there they met good people and bad people and sometimes the good turned out to be bad and the bad turned out to be good and sometimes they mistook the one for the other.

One day, they met a holy man called Agastya. They stayed at his ashram in the forest and he gave Rama a bow made of gold and two magic quivers that were always full of arrows. The bow had been given to him by lord Vishnu and the quivers by Indra, the king of the gods.

He told Rama to make sure that Sita did not suffer hardship in the forest.

"Most women," he said, "are fickle. They give their love to the man on whom fortune shines, then leave him when he falls on hard times. But Sita is not like other women. She is like divine Arundhati, without blemish. Even so, you should keep her from danger. Take her to Panchavati and build your ashram there. It is a beautiful place, with fruit and flowers in abundance and clear streams where the deer come to drink and deep pools where the lotus grows. It will be a good place for you to live. Sita will like it there."

On the way to Panchavati, they saw a vulture high in the sky above the trees. It flew down towards them and as it came lower they saw that it was bigger than any vulture they had ever seen before. Thinking it might be a rakshasa, Rama reached for one of his arrows and Lakshman drew his sword. The vulture landed in front of them and folded its wings.

"Who are you?" said Rama, standing in front of Sita, with Lakshman at his side.

"I am Jatayu," said the vulture, bowing, "your father's friend. We fought together in many battles, years ago. I will stay near you and keep watch and make sure that Sita is safe."

Rama thanked him and they walked on to Panchavati, while Jatayu flew overhead, watching them. Lakshman built them a cottage in a clearing in the forest. Every morning, they bathed in the waters of the Godavari. They lived on fruit from the trees and roots from the earth. Sita watched the deer drinking from the stream in the evening and listened to the peacocks in the hills. Autumn passed and winter came.

Early one morning, when Rama and Lakshman were bathing in the river, someone hid in the trees, watching them. Her name was Surpanaka and she had fallen in love with Rama. She had been following him for days. Sometimes she was a bird, sometimes she was a mouse, sometimes she was a bat hanging from a tree. She could be anything she chose, because she was a rakshasa. Earlier that morning, she had been a lizard on the wall of the house. Now she was herself, hiding behind a tree, watching. When they came out of the river and walked along the path through the trees, she turned herself into a bird again and flew after them, flying from branch to branch. When they came to the cottage, she turned herself into a beautiful woman and stepped out in front of them.

"I am Surpanaka," she said, looking passionately into Rama's eyes and swaying gently from side to side, like a cobra. For a moment, Rama and Lakshman thought she was a cobra, but only for a moment.

"What is your name?" she went on, standing so close to Rama that she was nearly touching him.

"My name is Rama," he said.

"Rama," said Surpanaka, with a smile. The way she said it, she sounded like a cat purring. For a moment, Rama and Lakshman thought she was a cat.

"Come," she went on, looking into his eyes hungrily, as a bee in search of nectar crawls into a sweet smelling flower. "Come with me."

"Be careful, Rama!" said Lakshman, putting a hand on his arm.

Surpanaka turned her head slowly and stared coldly at Lakshman, as a hawk hovering in the sky watches an unwary mouse.

"If you don't shut up," she said, "I'll tear you to pieces and eat you."

It is, after all, easier for a rakshasa to change her shape than it is for her to change her ways.

Lakshman drew his sword.

"Who are you?" he said.

"I've told you who I am," said Surpanaka. "I'm Surpanaka. My brother is Ravana. Rama is going to be my husband, you're going to be my breakfast and that woman standing outside the door will make a tasty snack for later."

She was herself now, no longer a beautiful woman, but a rakshasa, sister of Ravana, most evil and powerful of all the rakshasas. Lakshman stood in front of Rama. Surpanaka pushed him out of the way. His sword fell to the ground. Sita ran towards them. Surpanaka lunged at her, but Rama caught her and held her back. Lakshman picked up his sword. Surpanaka pushed Rama away.

"Save him, Lakshman!" Sita cried.

"No!" said Rama. "Don't kill her!"

Lakshman hesitated. Surpanaka flung herself at him. He lifted his sword and slashed once, twice, three times. Surpanaka staggered back, clutching her face.

"My nose!" she screamed. "My ears! What have you done? What have you done?"

And she fled through the forest, squealing like a wild boar injured in the hunt.

"My nose! My ears! My beautiful face! What have you done? What have you done?"

Peaceful Panchavati soon became the scene of two great battles. While Lakshman protected Sita inside the cottage, Rama stood outside, watching the sky.

First, Surpanaka returned with fourteen rakshasas, sent to avenge her by one of her brothers, a rakshasa called Khara, who was almost as powerful as Ravana himself. The rakshasas came like a dark cloud over the forest and swarmed over Rama's head like angry hornets, each armed with swords and clubs and spears and darts. But Rama first destroyed their weapons and then destroyed them, killing each of them in turn with one of Indra's arrows.

Surpanaka fled again to Khara and told him what had happened.

"He is too strong for us," she said. "Even you could not defeat him. He is more powerful than you or any of us."

Khara needed no more urging. In a fury, he jumped into his chariot and marched on Panchavati with a thousand times as many rakshasas as he had sent with Surpanaka. Like a thunder cloud, they marched on Panchavati. Flashes of lightning seemed to cut through the trees like swords. The sound of their marching was like rain drumming on the leaves. Water dripped from the trees, as if the whole forest was in a sweat.

Rama sent Lakshman to hide Sita in a cave, while he looked up at the sky, armed with Vishnu's bow and Indra's arrows, and waited. When the storm broke, he was like a mountain struck by lightning. Khara circled overhead in his chariot, while his army of rakshasas attacked Rama on every side. They swung at his head with their clubs, they lunged at his body with their spears, they threw iron chains around his legs and aimed blows at his arms with their swords.

But Rama dodged every blow. He slipped the chains from his legs and wrapped them around their necks. He broke their spears in half and flung them in their faces. He wrenched the clubs from their hands and threw them high into the air like a juggler. Then he reached for his arrows and soon the rakshasas were falling through the trees, crashing through the branches, thudding to the ground. The pile of bodies grew so big, it made a deep hole in the ground and water seeped up into it and it became a lake, red with the blood of the rakshasas.

Khara watched the battle from his chariot and, with a shout of fury, picked up his bow and fired a volley of arrows at Rama, now standing alone on the battle field below. Rama heard the sound of the arrows, looked up and quickly raised his shield. Khara reached for his bow again, but Rama's bow was already in his hand and twenty arrows flew up into the sky, with hardly a blink of an eye between them. The first hit Khara's head, two struck his arms, three pierced his chest, three more cut through the chariot's shaft, four slew the horses, four more broke the axles, one cut off the charioteer's head, another knocked Khara's bow from his hand and the last one pierced his heart.

But the rakshasa still clung to life, standing amid the wreckage of his chariot, hovering like an eagle over the field of death below. Rama reached for another of Indra's arrows. As he placed it in his bow, the arrow head burst into flames. He lifted the bow, took aim and slowly drew back the string.

Only one rakshasa escaped the slaughter to bring the news of Khara's death to Surpanaka. His name was Akampana. Surpanaka took a deep breath.

"Go to Lanka," she said, "and tell Ravana what has happened."

"Who is this wretch?" said Ravana, when Akampana had finished telling him the story.

"His name is Rama," said Akampana. "He is the son of King Dashrat and he is living in exile with his wife, Sita, and his brother, Lakshman."

"Rama must be very foolish," said Ravana, "to make an enemy of me. Does he not love life?"

"Life loves him," said Akampana.

"What do you mean?" said Ravana, looking sharply at Akampana

"I mean he is beloved by all the gods and cannot be defeated."

"The gods?" sneered Ravana. "Who are they? They cannot harm me. I can consume fire, I can travel faster than the wind, I can reduce the sun and the moon to ashes. I can even destroy death, if I choose."

Akampana shook his head.

"All this is true," he said. "But Rama has no equal among mortals. He cannot be destroyed. Even you cannot defeat him in battle. See what happened to Khara and his army of fourteen thousand rakshasas."

Ravana's frown deepened and the rakshasa went on quickly.

"But there is another way," he said.

Ravana looked up. "What do you mean?"

"His wife," said the rakshasa, smiling. "Sita. She is beautiful. A jewel among women. Take her from him and Rama will die."

Ravana sent Akampana away and soon a plan took shape in his mind. The next day, he rode off in his chariot, across the sea, over the mountains and the valleys, until, below him, outside a hut in a clearing in a forest, he saw the person he was looking for.

"Maricha," he said, climbing out of his chariot. "I need your help."

But when Maricha heard what Ravana was planning to do, he was horrified. He told him about his own encounter with Rama, how his brother, Subahu, had been killed and how he too had nearly died.

"Since then," he said, "I have been living here like a hermit. I never want to see Rama again and neither should you. Whoever told you that the way to destroy him was to steal his wife is a fool. There could be no better way to provoke his anger and bring certain death to you, me and all of us."

Ravana frowned. It was not in his nature to admit defeat. But he knew that Maricha's advice was worth more than Akampana's.

"You have lots of wives," said Maricha, anxious to persuade Ravana of the folly of his plan and even more anxious to avoid getting involved in it himself. "You can have as many wives as you like. Go back to Lanka now and enjoy them. You don't need Sita."

Reluctantly, Ravana took Maricha's advice and went back to Lanka. But when he got there, Surpanaka was waiting for him.

"Khara," she said, sitting down beside him, "took an army of fourteen thousand rakshasas to avenge his sister. He wasn't afraid to die."

Ravana looked angrily at her but she put her arms around his shoulders and put her fingers on his lips and spoke softly to him.

"Rama," she said, "is not worth dying for. But Sita is. Let me tell you how you can take her from him and make her your own."

Then she pulled him closer to her and whispered in his ear.

When Maricha saw Ravana returning in his chariot, his heart sank. Now there was nothing he could do to make him change his mind. He listened carefully to his instructions and did as he was told.

When Sita saw the golden deer outside the door, she was entranced. It seemed tame, but when she went towards it and stretched out her hand to stroke its neck, it turned and skipped away to the edge of the clearing. There it stopped and turned again, looking at her with big eyes.

She spoke to it and Rama, hearing her voice, came outside and stood beside her.

"Look!" she said. "Look! Isn't it beautiful! Please catch it for me so that I can keep it as a pet."

Lakshman came outside too and stood beside Rama.

"Be careful, Rama," he murmured. "There's something strange about it. It may be a rakshasa."

But Rama was as entranced by the deer as Sita and he made fun of

Lakshman.

"Everything looks like a rakshasa to you," he said. "Stay here and look after Sita. I'll go and catch the deer for her."

When he walked towards it, the deer skipped away and he followed it into the forest. Sita waited and watched, expecting him at any moment to come back, leading the deer behind him. She squeezed Lakshman's arm in her excitement, looking first at him and then at the forest. Then she heard Rama's voice calling her name and she looked up at Lakshman.

"Do you think he's caught it?" she said.

They heard his voice again and this time he was calling for Lakshman.

"Lakshman! Help me!"

"Quick!" said Sita, pushing him away from her. "He's calling for you! Hurry, Lakshman."

But Lakshman hesitated.

"It might be a trick," he said.

They heard Rama calling again and this time his voice sounded even more desperate.

"Go quickly!" said Sita, pushing him harder.

"He told me to stay with you."

The voice came again, a little fainter now. But the voice in Lakshman's head said, "It's a trick! Don't go!"

"If you won't go, I will!" said Sita.

Lakshman caught her arm as she tried to run past him.

"Wait here," he said. "I'll go."

Sita waited to hear Rama's voice again, her eyes fixed on the edge of the clearing. But the birds had stopped singing and everything was quiet. All she could hear was the sound of her own heart beating, rapid and soft, like an animal scampering across the grass. She didn't hear the sound of Lakshman's arrow flying through the trees or the sound of the deer as it fell to the ground. She didn't hear Maricha's groans as he tried to pluck the arrow from his breast or the death rattle in his throat. She didn't hear what Rama and Lakshman said to each other when they saw the rakshasa lying dead at their feet where the deer had fallen. She didn't hear the footsteps creeping up behind her.

All the birds were singing now and the sound disturbed Jatayu in his nest at the top of a tall tree. He looked down at the empty clearing and then he looked round at the birds twittering in the branches and then he looked up and saw Ravana in his gold chariot, flying through the sky, with Sita struggling on his lap.

The giant vulture spread his wings and launched himself into the sky. His powerful wings carried him up towards the chariot and soon he was flying over Ravana's head. He reached down with his claws and nearly managed to pluck Sita away, but Ravana saw him and swerved. Sita called out to Jatayu, begging him to save her, and Jatayu called out to her.

"Don't be afraid!" he said. "If you fall, I'll catch you."

Then he flew underneath the chariot so that Ravana couldn't see him and struck the chariot with his wings. The axles broke and the shafts snapped and the horses broke loose and the chariot tumbled from the sky.

"Jump!" Jatayu shouted to Sita. "Jump! I'll catch you!"

But Ravana held her tight and carried her down to the ground. Jatayu flew down and stood in front of them.

"Give Sita to me," he said, "and go back to Lanka. Otherwise, fight!"

Ravana flung Sita aside and she fell senseless onto the grass. Jatayu flew towards her but Ravana stood between them.

"Sita is mine!" he said. "If you try to take her from me, you will die."

Now Ravana threw off his human shape and Jatayu faced a rakshasa as big as himself, with ten heads and twenty arms. The vulture spread his wings and flew towards him. The wind they made hit Ravana like a blow in the chest and he fell back. Jatayu landed on top of him and, holding the rakshasa in his huge talons, used his beak like a sword to cut off his arms.

Sita opened her eyes and closed them again in horror. As she did, Ravana roared with anger and, twenty more arms growing at once to replace those he had lost, flung the bird aside. Jatayu stumbled back and then Ravana lunged at him with swords and daggers, cutting off the vulture's wings. Hearing his groans and Ravana's shout of triumph, Sita opened her eyes again and saw Jatayu lying helpless on the ground. She ran towards him and flung herself on top of him, weeping and trying to comfort him. But Ravana dragged her away.

Jatayu watched as Ravana flew away over the mountains, with Sita in his arms. He could see Sita looking back and he knew that she was looking for him, hoping that he would rescue her. But he had no wings and he was dying and there was nothing he could do. As they climbed higher into the sky, up to the top of the mountain, he watched them with his far-seeing eyes. He saw something fall and, as it fell through the air, glistening in the sun, he saw that it was one of Sita's silver anklets. He watched it bounce on the rocks and roll down the mountainside. A bracelet fell too and then a necklace, like stars falling from the sky. He saw some monkeys run and pick them up and look up at the sky. He sighed and turned his head away and closed his eyes, because there was nothing else he could do.

Lakshman pulled his arrow from Maricha's dead body.

"I should have listened to you," said Rama. "You knew it was a rakshasa."

"When we heard you calling," said Lakshman, "I thought it might still be a trick. Sita made me come."

"I didn't call," said Rama.

They ran back to the house but Sita had gone. They searched for her in the forest, by the lotus pools where she liked to sit, on the banks of the Godavari where the fish swam to her and let her touch them, but there was no sign of her.

"I should have stayed with her," said Lakshman.

"We must keep looking," said Rama.

Jatayu heard them coming and opened his eyes. He told them what had happened.

"I understand now," said Lakshman, turning to Rama. "The deer, your voice, everything. It was all a trick."

Rama knelt beside Jatayu.

"Tell me about Sita," he said. "Is she still alive? Where has he taken her? What can we do to bring her back?"

But Jatayu had closed his eyes again and Rama lay down beside him, weeping. Lakshman built a funeral pyre and together they lifted Jatayu onto it. Rama lit the pyre, as he would for a dead kinsman, and offered him libations from the waters of Godavari.

Rama and Lakshman then set off again, walking through the forest towards the mountain, in search of Sita. The forest grew dark and they heard a sound like trees being felled. Rama drew his sword. Through the trees, they saw a dark shape ahead of them. Suddenly, the shape came towards them and they saw that it was a monstrous being with no head and no neck, just a vast, shapeless body, covered in bristles, like a pig. Its mouth was in its stomach and one eye blinked in the middle of its chest. Its voice was like rocks falling down the mountain and when it moved it made a sound like trees falling.

"I am Kabandha," said the monster, seizing them by the arm, "and this is my forest."

Rama swung his sword with all his strength. First he cut off the arm that held him and the monster let him fall. Then he raised his sword again and cut off the arm that held Lakshman. The monster howled with pain and Lakshman fell to the ground. The monster staggered and sank to his knees.

"Who are you?" he said, looking from one to the other.

"He is Rama," said Lakshman, "son of king Dashrat, and I am his brother."

"Rama!" said the monster. "Best of men! You have freed me from my curse! Oh Rama! Rama! It was pride that made me as I am now. Once I was lovely as the moon but I offended Indra in my pride and he thrust my neck and head down into my body and cursed me. 'Only when Rama cuts off both your arms and cremates you will you regain your true form.' That's what he said and now you are here and you have cut off my arms. Oh Rama! All that remains now is for you to cremate me and then I shall be free from this curse!"

They dug a pit and filled it with brushwood and Kabandha crawled into it. Rama set light to the wood and they watched as the monster's body was consumed by the flames. Then, through the smoke, they saw a different body rise out of the pit and stand before them, dressed in golden robes and smiling at them. He walked towards Rama and stood in front of him.

"Let me tell you," he said, "how you can find Sita and bring her back. You need a friend to help you. Go to Sugriva on the mountain. Sugriva is a vanara and was once king of the monkeys. He needs your help too. Like you, he is an exile. Make him your friend and you will help each other."

Rama thanked him and set off to walk to the mountain, with Lakshman by his side.

Book 4

When Sugriva saw two men walking up the mountain track, he became very agitated. He jumped up and down and his teeth chattered. Hanuman and the other vanaras who had come with him in his exile did their best to calm him down.

"They must be spies," said Sugriva. "Vali must have sent them. Who else could they be? Why else would they be coming up the mountain?"

"Calm down," said Hanuman. "Don't jump to conclusions. There's no need to panic. They're probably just innocent travellers."

"Go and find out," said Sugriva, biting his nails. "Then come back and tell me. And be quick!"

Hanuman bowed, thinking to himself that Sugriva was behaving more like an ordinary monkey than a king in exile. Then he jumped onto a rock and leaped off the side of the mountain, landing a few seconds later on the track where Rama and Lakshman were walking. Hanuman was the son of the Wind God. One leap could carry him across wide mountain valleys or even from the top of one mountain to another. He could do other surprising things too.

When Rama and Lakshman came round a bend in the track, they saw a hermit walking towards them and stopped.

"You are dressed like me," said the hermit, "but you don't look like hermits. You look more like kings or warriors. Who are you?"

Rama and Lakshman told him who they were and who they were looking for and why. Then the hermit told them who he was and turned back into a monkey.

"I saw them," he said, "flying through the sky."

Rama and Lakshman stared at him in amazement.

"I didn't know who she was. Some jewellery fell to the ground. Or perhaps she threw them. I picked them up. An anklet, a bracelet, a necklace. Come with me. I'll take you to Sugriva."

As they walked, they told him about Rama's exile and he told them about Sugriva's.

"To begin with," he said, "it was all a misunderstanding. Vali is Sugriva's older brother. When their father died, Vali became king in

Kishkindha. But then he got into an argument over a woman with one of the asuras, a demon called Mayavi. Mayavi challenged him to a fight on the mountain and he accepted the challenge but he took Sugriva with him. So when Mayavi saw there were two of them he ran away and hid in a cave. They went after him but Vali thought that two against one wasn't fair, so he told Sugriva to wait outside. There was a lot of noise from the cave and it sounded as if more asuras were in there. Everyone knows that asuras never play fair. Sugriva could hear lots of voices but none of them was Vali's. So in the end he decided that the asuras must have killed him. So he did what anyone would do to avenge his brother's death. He rolled a big rock in front of the cave and trapped them all inside."

Rama and Lakshman nodded their heads in approval of Sugriva's actions. They were enjoying the story and urged Hanuman to go on.

"Well, when he got back, they made him king instead of Vali and he ruled justly and everyone was happy. But then, one day, Vali came back. He hadn't been killed at all. The fight had gone on for a long time but at last he had managed to kill them all. Then he found that he was trapped in the cave and thought that Sugriva had played a trick on him. So when he finally managed to get out and come back and he found that Sugriva had been made king, that seemed to prove it. So he banished him and the only place Sugriva feels safe now is here on this mountain."

Rama asked why and Hanuman explained that Vali didn't dare to come here because of a curse that had been put on him years ago.

"Even so," he went on, "he's always nervous in case Vali comes anyway or sends someone else. He lives every day in fear of his life and sometimes he forgets who he is and behaves just like an ordinary monkey."

He shook his head sadly.

"All because of a misunderstanding and people being too proud to admit they've made a mistake."

Now Rama understood what Kabandha meant when he said that Sugriva and he could help each other.

When they met, the bargain was quickly struck and the next day Rama went with him to Kishkindha. Sugriva stood outside the walls and gave his battle cry. At once, Vali rushed out and the two brothers faced each other. Rama stood by with his bow in his hand, ready to come to Sugriva's aid, and the two vanaras joined battle. They had no weapons, but fought with their hands and their feet and their knees, hitting, slapping, thumping, kicking. Sometimes one would jump on top of the other and wrestle him to the ground, where they rolled over and over, throwing up clouds of dust. Sometimes they picked up boulders and flung them at each other. Sometimes they pulled up trees by the roots and used them as staves or clubs.

The fight was evenly matched and the time soon came for Rama to keep his promise. He fitted an arrow to his bow and took aim. But then he hesitated. He lowered his bow and looked again. Which was which? Rolling on the ground, covered in dust, both monkeys looked the same.

"Why didn't you kill him?" said Sugriva later, nursing his wounds. "You promised to help me."

"I couldn't tell you apart," said Rama. "I didn't dare to use my bow in case I killed you instead of Vali. Challenge him again tomorrow, but wear this on your head so that I can see who you are."

He gave him a garland of flowers and the next day, when they fought again, his arrow found Vali's heart and Sugriva became king again in Kishkindha.

Hanuman asked Rama and Lakshman to go to Kishkindha for Sugriva's coronation.

"After the celebrations," he said, "we will help you to find Sita."

But Rama shook his head.

"During my exile," he said, "I may not enter any city or town or village, but must always live in wild places, in the forest or on the mountain."

So Rama and Lakshman found a cave to live in, drinking water from the mountain streams and eating whatever they could find growing wild on the slopes, while they waited for Sugriva to keep his promise.

Every day, Rama thought about Sita. It was the rainy season and he watched the rain falling like tears outside the cave. There was no end to the rain and no end to his grief. Lakshman tried to comfort him.

"Soon the autumn will come," he said, "and then with Sugriva's help we will find Sita and you will kill Ravana and bring her home."

So they waited for the rains to stop and watched the streams tumbling down the mountain side and heard the elephants trumpeting in the valleys and at last autumn came. But still they waited and now Lakshman grew angry.

"He has forgotten his promise," he said. "I will go to Kishkindha and kill him. We will find Sita and bring her back without him."

Rama put a hand on his brother's arm and spoke to him gently.

"Go to Sugriva," he said, "and remind him of his promise. But you should not give way to your anger. If he won't keep his word, leave him and we two will go in search of Sita. Come what may, I must find her. I can't wait here any longer. I can't bear to think that, while I am here, she is with Ravana. Go now, Lakshman, and hurry back."

Hanuman met him on the mountain track and walked with him.

"Don't be angry with him, Lakshman," he said. "When Vali was dying, he asked Sugriva to forgive him and the two of them were reconciled before he died. That made Sugriva very happy and then there was the coronation and then he was reunited with his wife and then he decided to take another wife and then they all drank a lot of wine and then, well, you know how it is. Sometimes it's hard not to behave like an ordinary monkey, instead of a king. Don't be too hard on him."

But when they found Sugriva, sitting like a god on his throne, drinking wine from a golden goblet and enjoying the caresses of his wives, Lakshman thought of Rama and could not control his anger.

"There is no sin like ingratitude," he said, standing in front of Sugriva, with his bow in his hand, "and no salvation for an ungrateful man. Sunk in vulgar pleasures, you have broken your word of honour. If you forget what virtuous Rama did for you, you will soon follow the path of Vali. The path Vali took is not barred."

Sugriva was drunk and he just smiled, but the others, seeing Lakshman's hand tightening on his bow, did their best to placate him and begged him to forgive the monkey king. Remembering what Rama had told him, he turned to go, but Hanuman and Sugriva's wife, Tara, begged him to stay.

"He hasn't forgotten his promise," said Tara, weeping. "Please forgive him. He has been so happy since he became king again and every day he talks about Rama. He has already sent out orders for the monkey army to assemble here at Kishkinda. He hasn't forgotten."

Lakshman looked at Hanuman, whom he felt he could trust, and Hanuman nodded.

"It's true," he said. "I sent the order myself. The army will be here soon."

So Lakshman stayed and the next day he was carried on a palanquin, with Sugriva on one side and Hanuman on the other, to the cave in the mountains where Rama was waiting. When he saw Rama, Sugriva jumped out of the palanquin and threw himself on the ground.

"You gave me back my kingdom," he said, touching Rama's feet. "Now make my happiness complete by giving me your forgiveness."

Rama invited them into the cave, where they sat and talked, until they heard a noise like the rumble of distant thunder. At first they took no notice, but then they heard it again and this time it sounded closer.

"Is that thunder," said Lakshman, "or an avalanche?"

"Neither," said Hanuman. "It's the monkey army. Come and look."

They went outside and looked out across the valley.

"Surely it's an earthquake," said Lakshman.

Everything seemed to be moving, the trees in the valley and the rocks on the mountain. The air was full of birds and a cloud of dust was rolling down the mountain side.

"Go and meet them, Hanuman," said Sugriva, jumping up and down in excitement.

Hanuman jumped up onto a rock. Sugriva turned to Rama and Lakshman.

"You can inspect the army," he said. "Look at them all!"

They turned back again, just in time to see Hanuman leap off the rock and go swinging across the valley as if he was hanging onto an invisible rope. The birds in the sky flew this way and that to avoid him and the dust swirled around him until he was so far away on the other side of the valley that he became like a speck of dust himself and they could no longer see him.

"Come!" said Sugriva. "Let's follow him!"

They went back down the mountain in the palanquin and, as they came down into the valley, they saw for themselves that the shaking of the trees and the trembling of the ground was caused by thousands and thousands of monkeys swinging through the branches and rolling down the mountain side, big monkeys and little monkeys, vanaras, like Sugriva and Hanuman, half man, half monkey, and bears too, huge bears, brown and black and yellow and gold and white, loping down the hillside. And there, standing on the wall outside the palace, was Hanuman, smiling proudly, arms folded across his chest, surveying his army.

When he saw them climb out of the palanquin, Hanuman jumped down from the wall and landed in front of them.

"Everyone is here," he said. "What are your orders?"

Sugriva spoke to him. Hanuman listened carefully, then turned and ran off. A few minutes later, he returned with four vanaras, each tall and handsome as Hanuman himself. Sugriva gave each of them their orders.

"Vanita," he said, "you will search for Sita in the east. Angad, you will search in the south. Sushena, take the west. Satavali, the north. Assemble your search parties now and share out the land between them, the forests and the fields and the mountains and the valleys and the great cities and the little villages. Everywhere must be searched, every house, every cave. Everywhere! Don't fail me. Don't fail Rama. I have given him my word. You have one month to find Sita."

He gave each of them detailed instructions, naming all the places where Ravana might have hidden Sita. Then he turned to Hanuman.

"Hanuman," he said, "your orders are to search everywhere. If anyone can find Sita, you can. Go wherever you choose and bring her back."

Hanuman leaped at once up onto the wall, but Rama called to him and held up a ring.

"Sita will recognise this ring," he said. "Take it with you and show it to her when you find her. Then she will know that you have come from me."

Hanuman jumped down and took the ring. Then he jumped back up again and watched as the great army began to move, some going east, some west, some north, some south, and when they had all gone, he held Rama's ring up high, so that it caught the sun, and then he leaped up into the sky and was gone.

Angad led his search-party to the south and Hanuman followed them. They searched the mountains and the jungles and the river valleys but found no trace of Sita. The month that Sugriva had given them to find her was nearly over.

"It's no good," Angad said, shaking his head in despair. "We can't find her. Perhaps she has already been found."

"If she had," said one of the other vanaras, "we would have heard. Sugriva would have sent one of his messengers to tell us."

"That's true," said another. "We should go on searching."

"The month is nearly up," said another. "If we don't go back, Sugriva might be angry."

"Perhaps you're right," said another. "His orders were to go back in a month. I think we should go back."

"I agree," said another. "Let Sugriva decide what to do next."

"But what about Rama?" said another. "We promised to find Sita for him. We should keep our promise and go on searching until we find her."

"Look!" said another. "Who's that?"

Everyone looked round and saw an old vulture limping towards them.

"At last!" said the vulture. "I thought I'd never catch up with you. You monkeys move so fast! You never stop long enough in one place for an old bird like me to get close enough to talk to you."

"Can't you fly?" said one of the monkeys.

"Course he can't," said another. "Look at his wings!"

The old vulture's wings hung uselessly at his side. When he walked, they dragged on the ground beside him.

"I lost the use of my wings a long time ago," said the vulture.

The monkeys gathered round. Some of them sat down with their arms around each other's shoulders, some lay on the grass with their chins in their hands, looking up at him, like children listening to a story.

"My name," he said, "is Sampati. One day my young brother dared me to race him. Of course I agreed, but when he said he would race me to the sun and back I changed my mind. So then he made fun of me and said he would go without me. He flew off at once and I watched him fly up into the sky. But then I thought I'd better go after him to make sure he was alright. The closer he got to the sun, the slower he went and I began to catch up with him. I could see that he was getting tired and the heat from the sun was getting too much for him, so I flew beside him and protected him with my wings. He quickly recovered his strength, but I could feel the sun burning my wings and it soon became too much for me and I fell to the ground. That's how I lost the use of my wings."

"What happened to your brother?"

"I went everywhere looking for him but, without my wings, it took me a long time. I walked from place to place, asking if anyone had seen him. But no one had. Then one day I saw a vulture fighting with a rakshasa high in the sky. The rakshasa was Ravana and the vulture was my brother, Jatayu. This time there was nothing I could do to help him."

He stopped speaking for a moment and the monkeys all stared at him open-mouthed.

"Now listen," he said at last, "and I'll tell you where to look for Sita."

Sampati stood on the sea-shore between Angad and Hanuman. Behind them stood thousands of monkeys. Or rather, behind them thousands of monkeys ran up and down on the sand, laughing and shouting, throwing seaweed at each other and running races with the waves that broke like strings of pearls on the shore.

"I can see it," he said, looking out across the ocean. "I can't fly any more but I can still see further than any of you."

"What can you see?" asked Hanuman.

"I can see Lanka. I can see Ravana's palace. I can see Sita."

"How far is it?" asked Hanuman.

"Once," said Sampati, looking down at his wings that trailed in the sand, "I could have been there before nightfall."

"How far?" asked Hanuman again.

"Twenty yojanas."

Angad looked at Hanuman.

"Can you do it?" he said.

"Watch me!" said Hanuman.

Book 5

Hanuman landed on a hilltop and, a stone's throw away across the water, he saw the island of Lanka, like a jewel dropped into the sea. A city of gleaming white buildings covered the island and right in the middle, at the top of a high hill, stood a golden palace. The city was surrounded by a moat, where lilies and lotus flowers shone like pale moons. Inside the moat, on the city walls, rakshasas with lanterns patrolled like fireflies.

Night fell and the island seemed to float on the water, as if someone had knelt on the shore and pushed it gently away like an offering to the gods. Floating in the darkness, a thousand candles lit up the sky and a thousand more glistened like fish flickering in the moonlit sea. Hanuman felt as if he could reach out and pick it up in his hand. Perhaps he could, because he had made himself into a giant for his leap across the ocean and he was nearly as big as the hill he was sitting on.

But first he had to find Sita and that would need cunning as well as strength. So, hoping that no one had seen him sitting on the hilltop, he made himself small again. Then he leaped across the water, slipped in through the city gate and disappeared into the shadows. The rakshasas guarding the gate took no notice of the little monkey running up the street and, a few moments later, he heard the clang and scrape and thud of the gates being closed for the night. Quietly, cautiously, keeping in the shadows, he began his search of the city.

The street wound its way up the hillside towards the palace at the top. From the buildings on either side came the sounds of laughter and music. He heard the tinkling of anklets and the jangle of bracelets and hands clapping and bare feet slapping on the floor and women's voices singing. He peeped in through the windows and saw the rakshasas in their armour and the beautiful dancing girls dressed in silk, which seemed to change colour as they moved.

At last he came to the palace and climbed in through an open window and wandered through the courtyards and corridors, looking into all the rooms. He saw many wonderful sights, rich embroidery, polished wooden floors scattered with petals, golden cups studded with jewels, and, as the night wore on, he saw beautiful women, lying with their heads in the laps of the rakshasas, and others lying alone with their heads on their arms. But none of them was Sita.

In the middle of the night, he climbed a marble staircase and found himself in a huge courtyard, where elephants and horses were tethered, and there in the middle of the courtyard he saw a huge carriage. It must be Ravana's carriage, he thought, Pushpaka. It was decorated with jewels that gleamed in the moonlight and pictures of birds and beasts and Lakshmi seated on a lotus with another lotus in her hand. Creeping past the chariot, peeping through the archways that lined the sides of the courtyard, he saw many beautiful women lying asleep with their heads on velvet cushions, arms like honey, mouths like berries and hair as black as night. But none of them was Sita.

He jumped up onto the wall that surrounded the courtyard and saw, on the other side of the hill, a grove of ashoka trees. The warm night air was heavy with the scent of their blossom. He jumped off the wall and walked down the hill to the ashoka grove. The birds roosting in the trees heard him and flew up from the branches with a flapping of wings and a rustling of leaves. He stopped and looked up as a shower of red and yellow petals fell all around him. Some of them settled on his head and shoulders like a silk shawl. He brushed them off and walked on.

Then, through the trees, he saw a woman sitting on the grass, and stopped again. She was wearing a plain white robe, but she was beautiful and her face was wet with tears. Three rakshasis sat nearby, watching her. They turned when they heard him and he quickly jumped up into the branches of a tree.

"It's her!" he thought. "It's Sita! I've found her!"

Hanuman hid in the tree and watched the sun come up over the hill. The golden palace at the top of the hill shone like the sun in the first light of dawn and then the real sun came up behind it and lit up the whole island. He watched as one of the rakshasis guarding Sita brought her water to drink. Sita, sitting with her legs drawn up and her head resting on her knees, looked up.

"Drink!" said the rakshasi.

But Sita shook her head and lay down on the grass, covering her face with her arm.

"Look!" said one of the other rakshasis, pointing through the trees. "Ravana is coming!"

Sita stood up and looked round for somewhere to hide. But there was nowhere to hide and she stood under the trees like a wild animal, frozen with terror. Down the hill towards the ashoka grove came a procession of rakshasas, with Ravana at its head, like a hunter leading a pack of dogs. He was surrounded by beautiful women, with pearls around their necks and silver bangles on their arms and feet that glistened with jewels like the dew on the grass.

Sita stood with her back to a tree and, as Ravana walked towards her, she sank to the ground, clutching her knees in her arms, as if trying to hide herself from him in the only way she could. The three rakshasis bowed low as he went past. He waved them away and they stood together underneath Hanuman's tree, watching.

"She'll give in to him soon," said one.

"They all do," said another.

"If she doesn't, he'll kill her."

Hanuman saw Ravana reach out and lift Sita's heavy, black hair in his hand. He let it fall gently through his fingers, then he put his hand under her chin and lifted her face. He spoke softly to her. She pulled her face away and he smiled. She looked up at him and said something. Ravana frowned. Sita looked away again, putting her hand to her neck and pulling her robe more tightly around her. The rakshasis laughed.

"Poor little thing!"

"Don't you feel sorry for her?"

"She's making him angry! Look!"

Ravana looked down at Sita, crouched at his feet, trembling, looking down at the ground. Hanuman gripped the branch, ready to leap. Ravana put out a hand and stroked her hair, then forced her once again to look up at him. He said something to her, then let go and turned to the three rakshasis.

"Guard her well," he said. "She's like a wild animal. A beautiful, wild animal. She needs taming. Do what you like to make her tame and bend her to my will. In two months, she will either come to me willingly or be slaughtered and served up to me in a dish."

He turned quickly and walked away, leading the procession out of the ashoka grove and back up the hill to the palace. The rakshasis watched him go, then looked back at Sita.

"Why wait?" said one. "Why not kill her now?"

"Look at her! In two months, there'll be nothing left to eat!"

"We should feed her up so that she's nice and fat when Ravana's ready for her."

"Or when she's ready for Ravana. Whichever comes first."

"Let's go to the palace and get her some food."

"Good idea! If she won't eat it, I will! I'm starving!"

They tied Sita's legs together so that she couldn't escape, then walked away through the ashoka grove and up the hill. When they were out of sight, Hanuman swung from branch to branch through the trees until Sita was just below him. Hearing a noise above her head, she looked up and watched the petals falling around her. She saw something else fall and land on the grass in front of her. She reached out and picked it up. It was Rama's ring.

Sita laughed when Hanuman said that he would carry her back to Rama on his back. How could a little monkey do that? That made Hanuman laugh too.

"I forgot," he said. "I'm not really this small. Watch!"

And he made himself as big as he had been when he made his leap across the sea.

"Be careful!" said Sita. "Someone might see you."

"Sorry!" said Hanuman, returning to his proper size again. "Are you ready now? Let's go!"

But Sita shook her head.

"Rama sent you to find me," she said. "Go back and tell him where I am. Then let him come with Lakshman to destroy Lanka and kill Ravana. It must be Rama who saves me. Only Rama."

Hanuman said nothing. It would have been so easy for him to take her back. But he knew she was right. She untied a corner of her dress and took out a jewel she had hidden there, the jewel King Janak gave her to wear on her forehead when she was married to Rama.

"Tell Rama that I have only two more months to live," she said.

"Give him this jewel and tell him that in two months I will take my own life."

Hanuman took the jewel and left her sitting alone in the ashoka grove.

It would have been easy for him to slip out of Lanka then without anyone seeing him, to leave as unobtrusively as he had arrived. But that was not Hanuman's way. He could tell Rama where Sita was, he thought, but what else could he tell him? Nothing! So before he left he decided to test the mettle of the enemy and in that way take information back to Rama that would help him prepare for the battle.

If Hanuman comes to Lanka, he said to himself, the Lankans should know about it! And, with that, he made himself three times as big, gave a mighty roar, beat his chest and set about destroying the ashoka grove, pulling up all the trees, tearing down the creepers and throwing them into the pools.

The three rakshasis had just left the palace and, when they saw a wild ape leaping about among the trees, waving branches in the air, they dropped the food they were carrying and ran down the hill as fast as they could. To their relief, Sita was still sitting where they had left her.

"What's going on?" they said. "What's that ape doing? Is this anything to do with you?"

Sita denied all knowledge of it.

"It must be a rakshasa," she said. "How do I know?"

The rakshasis hurried back up the hill to the palace to raise the alarm. But news of the commotion in the ashoka grove had already reached Ravana and, as they came to the top of the hill, the palace gates opened and an army of rakshasas flowed out like water from a burst dam. Hanuman, beating his chest, lashing the ground with his tail, leaped to the top of a pile of uprooted trees and roared his challenge to the Lankan army.

"Victory to Rama!" he thundered. "I am Hanuman, son of the Wind God! Tell Ravana to be prepared to do battle with Rama and die at his hands! But first Rama's slave will kill you and destroy Lanka!"

For a moment, the rakshasas held back, but then, urged on by their commanders, they raised their weapons and rushed down the hill towards Hanuman.

"Rama! Rama! Rama!" shouted Hanuman, holding a tree trunk in his hand and waving it over his head. "Victory to Rama!"

One by one, the rakshasas fell and soon their bodies were scattered down the hillside like the uprooted trees that littered the ashoka grove. The survivors fled to the safety of the palace and told Ravana what Hanuman had said and done. Ravana sent for one of his warriors, Jambumali, and ordered him to fight Hanuman and kill or capture him. Jambumali picked up his weapons and ran up onto the palace walls.

From there, he saw a temple in flames and Hanuman outside using one of the stone pillars to beat off his attackers. The clash of stone on metal had made a spark and the spark had caused the temple to catch fire and now the fire was spreading down the hill and up to the walls of the palace. Jambumali raised his bow and a shower of arrows fell on Hanuman. Brushing the arrows aside with his mighty tail, Hanuman flung the stone pillar at Jambumali. But the rakshasa avoided it and sent another shower of arrows up into the sky. Hanuman uprooted another tree and hurled it at him like a javelin. Jambumali quickly fired again and the arrows cut the tree into little pieces that bounced harmlessly off the palace walls and rolled on the ground. But Hanuman then pulled up another tree, leapt onto the wall and struck Jambumali such a blow that he fell to the ground.

More rakshasas rushed up then but Hanuman slapped them aside with his great hands and struck them with his fists and tore them with his nails and kicked them with his feet and lashed them with his tail and tossed them one by one over the walls. When he looked down, he saw them far below, some of them lying still, others scurrying about like ants on an ant hill.

For a moment, Hanuman stood alone on the palace walls and everything was still and silent. Then he heard a noise and looked up and saw another rakshasa flying through the sky in a chariot and arrows falling towards him. One struck him on the head, two more hit his shoulders. With a roar, he sprang up into the air, dragged the rakshasa from his chariot, struck him with his fist and flung him to the ground.

The rakshasa was Akshaya, one of Ravana's sons. When they told

Ravana he was dead, he sent for Akshaya's brother, Indrajit, and soon Hanuman saw another chariot flying through the sky and another bow pointing at him. He picked up the pillar, which still lay on the palace walls, and held it over his head, but the arrow swerved around it and turned itself into a rope and wound itself around his body.

Indrajit jumped down from his chariot and led Hanuman in triumph to his father.

"Who are you?" said Ravana.

Hanuman looked at him, sitting on his golden throne, robed in silks, surrounded by beautiful women, and thought he could have been a god.

"I am Hanuman," he said, "son of Vayu. Sugriva, my king, sent me in search of Sita, wife of Rama, and I found her here, a prisoner in your garden. You are a king too. You know about dharma. You know you should not keep another man's wife against her will. If you are wise, you will let me take her back to Rama. No one, no god, no rakshasa, can withstand Rama's fury."

Ravana laughed, but Hanuman went on.

"By a boon of Brahma, no weapon can kill me. I could, if I chose, destroy Lanka and take Sita back with me. But Rama would not approve. He has vowed to destroy himself the one who took Sita from him. Keep her here and you keep a noose around your neck. That's all I have to say."

He listened then while Ravana and his sons and counsellors argued about what to do. Ravana wanted to kill him. Indrajit wanted to be the executioner. But one of his counsellors, Vibishanha, advise caution.

"It is wrong to kill an envoy," he said. "Better to find some other punishment and then let him go."

"Death is the only punishment," said Ravana.

"Vibishanha is right," said Dashanana, one of the other counsellors. "It is against dharma to kill a messenger."

"What do I care about dharma?" said Ravana.

"People will laugh when they hear that Ravana has killed a monkey," said Vibishanha. "Find another punishment, one more suitable for a monkey to suffer and a king to inflict."

"Such as?" said Ravana.

"I know," said Dashanana. "Set fire to his tail and parade him through the streets."

"Make a monkey of him?" said Ravana.

Vibishanha nodded. "Let everyone laugh at him, then let him go. That will hurt your enemies more than it would if you killed him. Mocking him, you will mock them too."

Hanuman was led out of the palace into the streets of the city. They wrapped cotton round his tail and soaked it with oil. Then they set fire to it and marched him through the streets. Everyone came out to enjoy the spectacle, pointing at the monkey and laughing at him.

But then they saw the monkey shrink and slip out of his ropes and run between the legs of his guards and jump up onto the palace gates, where he sat looking down at them, holding his tail in his hand, like a torch.

"Catch him!" they all shouted. "Catch the monkey!"

But before they could, they saw him grow again until he was as big as the gates he sat on.

"Look out!" they shouted.

But it was too late. Hanuman was already off, leaping through the streets and over the rooftops, setting fire to everything in his path. Soon the whole city was ablaze. Lanka was burning and there was nothing the Lankans could do but watch it burn.

"Blow, wind!" Hanuman shouted, and the wind caught the flames from his tail and flung them all over the city, like a dog shaking water off its back.

"Here!" Hanuman shouted to the wind, waving his tail in the air. "Have some more! Take them to the palace!"

Then he remembered Sita.

"What have I done?" he said.

He leaped over burning buildings, lighting new fires that burned in his wake wherever he went. He raced through the ruins of the ashoka grove, past heaps of smouldering branches with shrivelled leaves and blackened flowers.

"What have I done? he cried. "What have I done?"

But then he saw her, sitting in a clearing, just where he had left her. All around her the fire burned, but she seemed not to feel its heat.

The flames ran up to the edge of the clearing, peeped at her through the trees, then turned and ran away. He watched her pick up a handful of ashoka flowers from the grass and let them fall through her fingers. The red and yellow petals looked like fire in her hand.

Even fire cannot harm her, he thought.

So he left her there and ran down the hill to the sea. When he came to the shore, he dipped his tail in the water and put out the flames. Behind him, Lanka burned. But Sita was safe.

Book 6

Ravana couldn't believe what had happened. Looking down at the city from his palace, all he could see was devastation. He sent for his brothers, Vibhishana and Kumbhakarna, Indrajit, his son, Prahasta, his army chief, and one of his ministers, Mahaparshava.

"Tell me what to do," he said.

"Just give the order," said Prahasta, "and I will personally see to it that Hanuman is killed and the rest of the vanaras are wiped off the face of the earth."

"Hanuman cannot be killed," said Vibhishana, "and neither can Rama. Make peace. Send Sita back."

"Why should you send her back?" said Mahaparshava. "Why do you wait? If she won't come to you willingly, take her by force, take her as a cock takes a hen in the farmyard."

"I would," said Ravana, "and I would do it with as much pleasure as any farmyard cock. I did as much once in my youth when I saw a lovely apsaras going to Brahma's house. I followed her and took her and Brahma cursed me for it. Now, because of that curse, if I take Sita by force, or any other woman, my head will split at once into a hundred pieces. If Sita will not come to me willingly, my pleasure will come instead from her death."

"And the death of Rama," said Indrajit, clenching his fist.

"Brother," said Kumbhakarna, bluntly, "you should have asked our advice before you took Sita from her husband. I would have told you not to. It was a mistake and now you're going to have to fight to keep her. But I'm your brother and I'll fight by your side. It's my duty. Leave Rama to me. The first arrow he fires will be his last."

"He won't even have time to pick up his bow," said Indrajit.

"This is folly," said Vibhishana.

"This is war," said Ravana.

That night, Vibhishana left the island.

Rama, Lakshman, Hanuman and Sugriva stood on the shore, looking across the sea. Rama looked at the jewel Hanuman had given him.

"She wore it on her forehead every day," he said.

"Soon," said Sugriva, "she'll be wearing it again."

Rama smiled and clasped the jewel tightly in his hand.

Behind them, stretching far inland, like another sea, was Sugriva's army, thousands upon thousands of monkeys, apes and bears, ready to follow them to Lanka to do battle with Ravana and bring Sita back.

"But how can we get there?" said Rama. "How can this great army cross the sea?"

Sugriva thought for a moment and then said, "We'll build a bridge!"

Everyone turned and looked at him.

"A bridge? Across the sea? How can we do that?"

Just then, they heard a disturbance behind them and, looking round, saw someone being led down to the shore. Two enormous, brown bears held him by the arms, two huge, black apes walked behind and Angad led the way. Lakshman drew his sword.

"Who is this?" said Sugriva, when they stopped in front of him.

"He says his name is Vibhishana," said Angad, "Ravana's brother. He says he has come to join us."

It was Vibhishana who, when he had persuaded them that he was not a spy and had come to help them, solved the problem of the bridge. He said that if Rama asked the God of the Sea to help them, he would not refuse.

"Spread darbha grass on the shore," he said to Rama, "prostrate yourself on it to propitiate the god and he will come to you."

Rama did as he said but for three days nothing happened and he grew angry. He grasped his bow and threatened to fire his arrows into the water and drain the ocean to its bed. He fixed an arrow to his bow. The sky grew dark. The earth trembled. Lightning flashed and thunder rumbled. The monkeys hid their heads.

Then the God of the Sea rose up from the waves and spoke to Rama.

"It is of no use to be angry," he said. "Earth, wind, sky, water and fire all follow their own nature. I am the sea and what I am cannot be changed. My waters are deep and no one can walk across them."

Rama remained silent and the God spoke again.

"Your anger is wasted," he said, "and your threats are empty. But your cause is just and I will help you. Among the vanara host is an ape called Nala. He is a great craftsman. Let him build a bridge across my waters and I will hold it up for you so that your army can march across."

Sugriva sent for Nala and Nala gave his orders. Trees were uprooted from the forests and carried down to the shore. Rocks and boulders were pulled out of the ground and rolled down to the water's edge. Apes and monkeys and bears toiled all day, bringing whatever Nala needed to build the bridge. They worked on into the night and soon the bridge stretched far out across the sea, shining in the moonlight like the parting in a woman's hair.

"There!" said Sugriva at daybreak, when the work was finished. "I told you we could build a bridge!"

When Ravana looked out from his palace in the morning, he could not believe what he saw. Already others had seen it and were rushing to his door to tell him. They were afraid now and some of them begged him to let Sita go and save Lanka from destruction. But Ravana refused.

"Send Vidyudjiva to me," he said. "I have a job for him."

When Sita looked out from the ashoka grove and saw the monkey army marching across the sea, her heart beat fast.

"Oh Hanuman!" she said. "Is he here? Have you brought him with you?"

Her rakshasi guards saw Ravana coming and clapped their hands.

"Your husband is here!" they said.

"He's come to take you away!"

They pulled her to her feet and pushed her towards him. But when she saw who it was, she held out her hands and backed away.

"Rama is dead," he said.

Sita shook her head.

"No!" she said.

"He came with an army, but my general, Prahasta, quickly defeated them and captured Rama. Indrajit, my son, cut off his head and brought it to me."

"No!"

"He's dead. Forget him. Take me."

"You're lying! He's not dead!"

Then Ravana lifted up Rama's head and held it out in front of her. Sita looked at Rama's face and could not speak. She felt herself swaying. She heard someone calling for Ravana. She saw Ravana look behind him. Rama's head fell on the grass at her feet. She stared at it. She heard Ravana say something to her guards. More people running towards them. More voices.

"Come quickly! Prahasta sends for you! Kumbhakarna is waiting for you! Come!"

"Keep her safe!"

She could not take her eyes off the dreadful thing at her feet. One of the rakshasis put her hand on her arm. She looked up and found that everyone else had gone. When she looked down again, the head on the ground looked like mist. Then it vanished.

"It was a trick," said the rakshasi. "One of his magicians, Vidyudjiva, made this maya-head. Now that Ravana has gone, the magic has faded."

"Is Rama alive then?"

The rakshasi nodded.

"Ravana has been called away to a war council. There will be a battle soon. Come with me. I will keep you safe until the battle is over. It won't be long now."

Rama and Sugriva held their own war council. They sat on a hill near the shore with Lakshman, Hanuman and Vibhishana, making their plans and sending orders down to the army below.

From the hill, which Vibhishana told them was called Suvela, they could see Ravana's palace.

"Look!" said Vibhishana. "There's my brother! There on the terrace! Can you see?"

While the others were still looking, Sugriva leapt from the hill and landed on the terrace where Ravana sat on a golden chair, facing the morning sun. Sugriva's shadow fell across him and he jumped up.

Sugriva snatched the crown from his head and threw it over the edge of the terrace. They heard it bouncing down the hillside. In a rage, Ravana leapt at Sugriva and soon the king of the rakshasas and the king of the vanaras were locked together, rolling across the terrace, kicking and biting and scratching. They rolled right off the terrace and landed, where Ravana's crown had landed a few seconds before, in the moat that surrounded the palace. There they fought like sea-monsters, sending waves crashing over the palace walls. Sugriva managed to loosen Ravana's grip, jumped up onto the wall and from there leapt across to Suvela hill to rejoin his companions.

Hanuman and Lakshman slapped him on the back. Vibhishana looked at him in awe. Sugriva turned to Rama.

"I know," he said. "It was a foolish thing to do. But something inside told me to do it. From now on, I'll follow orders."

Rama embraced him, then turned and led them down from the heights of Suvela to begin the siege of Lanka.

The walls were encircled by the monkey army. They filled the moat with rocks and trees and stood in their thousands outside each of the four gates. Angad led the troops at the south gate, Hanuman at the north, Nila at the west and Lakshman at the east. Inside the city, Ravana gave his orders. Indrajit stood ready at the south gate, Jambumali at the north, Nikumbha at the west and Virupaksha at the east. Then the gates were thrown open and the first terrible battle began.

Through the day and into the night, rakshasas and vanaras fought like wild animals outside the city walls and their blood flowed down the hillside, into the streams and down to the sea, and Lanka became like a slaughterhouse. The clash of weapons and the banging of drums, the groans of the dying and the shouts of their killers, filled the air. The birds hid in the trees, the animals hid in their burrows and vultures circled in the sky.

The sun went down and still the battle went on. Hanuman fought with Jambumali on a hilltop under the stars. Nila fought with Nikumbha on the shore beside the moonlit sea. Lakshman and Virupaksha fought among the trees in the dark woods. Indrajit's chariot flew over the city walls like a vampire bat. Angad watched it circling overhead and raised his bow. First the charioteer fell, then the horses. Indrajit disappeared.

Invisible in the darkness, Indrajit walked unchallenged, killing wherever he went. Angad warned Sugriva that Indrajit had made himself invisible. Sugriva sent a warning for everyone to be on their guard. Lakshman stayed with Rama, watching him. But Ravana's son was watching him too. He raised his bow. The arrows came from nowhere. Rama and Lakshman staggered and fell.

Ravana clapped his hands and embraced his son. He sent for the rakshasis guarding Sita in the ashoka grove and told them that Rama was dead.

"Tell Sita," he said. "She won't believe you, so take her in the Pushpaka chariot and show her his body, where it lies with Lakshman's. When she sees them, she will change her mind and come to me."

Beautiful Sita, he thought, watching them go. Beautiful, wild eyed Sita. She will come to me and she will be mine.

When the rakshasis told her, she knew it could not be true. Her faith in Rama, in dharma, in everything she had ever been told, was too strong. Wise men had told her that she would never know widowhood, that she would be a proud mother, that she would be the blessed wife of the crowned king. There had been so many auspicious signs over the years. It could not be true. But when they took her in Pushpaka out of the city and flew over the battlefield and showed her Rama and Lakshman lying dead on the ground and Hanuman weeping and all the monkey army standing dejected on the shore, she knew it was true.

They took her back to the ashoka grove and left her there, weeping. But a little later, one of the rakshasis came back. She sat down on the grass beside her and told her, quietly, that it was not true.

Sita looked at her and saw that it was Trijata, the rakshasi who had told her before that Rama was still alive, that he could never be killed. But this time, she had seen for herself, seen him lying there with Lakshman, seen them all grieving. It must be true. She hid her face again and went on weeping.

Sugriva stood beside the bodies with Hanuman and Vibhishana. He had sent for Sushena, a vanara who was expert in medicine.

"Can't you see?" said Vibhishana. "They're not dead. Indrajit's arrows didn't kill them. They bound them with nagapasha, wrapped around them like a snake so that they can't move. But Rama and Lakshman are too strong, too firm in dharma, for this magic to work for long. Soon you will see them stirring from their sleep."

Sushena had joined them and was listening to Vibhishana.

"Once," he said, "a long time ago, there was a battle between the gods and the Asuras. Many gods were left dying but Brihaspati revived them with herbs that grow in the mountains. If we could fetch these herbs now, they would help Rama and Lakshman to escape from the nagapasha."

"How do I find them?" said Hanuman, bracing himself for a leap into the mountains. "Tell me what they look like."

Sushena began to describe them, but before he had got very far, a wind started to blow, sending clouds racing across the sky, bending the trees on the hilltops, whipping up waves on the sea. Cowering down, holding onto each other to stop themselves from being blown away, they looked up and saw a dark shape in the sky.

"Look!" said Hanuman, pointing excitedly. "It's Garuda! The eagle! The one who carries Vishnu on his back."

As it came closer, the eagle stopped beating its wings. The wind dropped and the gigantic bird glided down towards them. They watched with open mouths as it settled on the grass and folded its wings. Its bronze beak was like a scimitar, its golden eyes like jewels, its green and red feathers like dyed silk. Walking slowly around the bodies on the ground, Garuda lifted his wings and trailed them, gently as a woman's fingers, over their arms and legs and faces, caressing them, healing their wounds, slowly waking them, releasing them from the spell of the nagapasha.

Rama and Lakshman stood up and smiled, their faces glowing, their arms and legs stronger than before. Garuda lowered his head and touched the ground in front of them. Then he turned and, with a few strokes of his powerful wings, disappeared into the sky. A few minutes later, Ravana heard the drums of the monkey army beating again outside the city walls.

One by one, he sent his warriors out of the city gates to lead the rakshasas in battle. One by one, the warriors fell and the rakshasas fled back behind the city walls. First, Dhumkarna, crushed to death by a rock thrown by Hanuman. Then Vajradamashtra, his head cut off by Angad. Then Akampana, another of Hanuman's victims, felled like a tree by the tree in Hanuman's hand. Then Prahasta, the fierce general of the rakshasa army, exchanging blows with Nila outside the west gate, falling at last under a rock thrown by the vanara, his head split into a thousand pieces. Then Kumbhakarna, Ravana's brother, strongest and fiercest of all the rakshasas.

But first they had to wake him. Sometimes Kumbhakarna slept for seven or eight months at a time. When he woke, he gorged himself on whole pigs and drank gallons of liquor. Then he slept again. That was how he lived. In spite of his reputation as a ferocious warrior, he preferred sleeping and eating to fighting.

"Go and wake him," said Ravana.

The rakshasas went to Kumbhakarna's house and stood outside, banging drums and blowing conch shells. Then they went in and stood outside Kumbhakarna's bedroom and banged their drums and blew their conch shells again. Then they went into the bedroom and banged their drums and blew their conch shells and shook Kumbharkana and beat him with their fists and shouted in his ear and threw things at him and, at last, he woke up.

"Food!" he said, sitting up and stretching. "Bring me food! I'm hungry! I haven't eaten for months!"

They brought him a pig and a barrel full of apples and a bucket of blood and jars of liquor and, while he was eating, they told him that Rama was outside the city walls with an army of monkeys.

"He should have sent her back," said Kumbhakarna. "I knew this would happen."

Then he wiped his enormous mouth with the back of his enormous hand and climbed up to the city walls. When the monkeys saw him looking down at them, they thought it was Yama, the Lord of Death. Their teeth chattered and they ran to Sugriva to tell him that Ravana had sent Death himself to fight them.

"Death!" shouted Kumbhakarna, in a voice that sounded like thunder breaking over the city. "Death! Death to the monkey that dared to disturb my sleep! Death! Death to you all!"

Angad led the apes and bears in a charge, hurling rocks and trees at Kumbhakarna. But they just bounced off him and he picked them up and threw them back, crushing the vanaras and sending them running for cover. The rakshasa seemed to be made of stone himself, as if the walls had become a living thing. When they saw him climb down the wall and come lumbering towards them, as big as an elephant, it looked as if the city itself was moving. The monkeys lost their nerve and started to run away.

"Why do you run?" Angad shouted to them. "He is one and we are many. Will you run away and make yourselves a laughing stock? Dishonour is worse than death! Turn and fight! Fight and die fighting, like heroes! Fight for Rama!"

His words gave them back their courage and they took them up as their battle cry, turning and marching back to face Kumbhakarna.

"Rama! Rama! Rama!" they chanted. "Rama! Rama! Rama!"

Many of them fell, but they managed to check his advance and now Hanuman joined them. Holding a huge boulder over his head, he charged at Kumbhakarna and hurled the boulder at him. Kumbhakarna staggered back, then drove his spear into Hanuman's chest. Hanuman fell to his knees, roaring with pain and anger, clutching the spear. He pulled it out and blood poured from his wound.

Some of the monkeys thought all was lost again and started to run away, but Nila came running down the hill and drove them back. He too picked up a massive rock and threw it with all his strength. Kumbhakarna knocked it out of the way with his fist and it shattered into fragments. Angad attacked again, hitting him first with a rock and then with his open hand, knocking him sideways. The monkeys jumped up and down, baring their teeth and cheering. Hanuman was on his feet again now, but so was Kumbhakarna and he ran towards Hanuman and struck him such a blow on his head with his fist that Hanuman fell to the ground again.

Kumbhakarna rushed on, like a mad bull, and Sugriva now joined the battle from his vantage point on the hill, driving Kumbhakarna back with a hail of stones and tree trunks. Enraged, Kumbhakarna took aim with his spear, drew back his arm and threw it like a dart. But Hanuman had seen him and, leaping through the air as fast as a blink of the eye, caught the spear in his hand and snapped it in two over his knee. The monkeys jumped about and cheered. But Kumbhakarna now showed that, big as he was, he could run as fast as any monkey. Up the hill he ran, fast and dangerous as a boulder rolling downhill, knocked Sugriva to the ground, picked him up and ran with him down to the walls, though the gate and into the city.

The gate clanged shut and the monkeys just stared. None of them spoke. None of them moved. Angad looked at Hanuman. Hanuman looked at Angad. Everyone looked at the gate.

Then they looked up and saw Sugriva standing on the wall. In his mouth was Kumbhakarna's nose. In each hand, he held one of his ears. A great cheer went up from the monkeys, when their king jumped down from the walls. Angad and Hanuman ran towards him.

"What happened?" they said.

"I made him drop me," said Angada, letting the nose fall from his mouth and dropping the ears. "Then I ran for it."

A roar came from behind the walls and the gate was thrown open. The monkeys jumped up and down, laughing and pointing, when they saw Kumbhakarna without his nose and ears. But then, when he rushed out of the gate, they ran in all directions to try to escape. Some were luckier than others when Kumbhakarna ran amongst them, trampling them underfoot and knocking them down with a mace in one hand and a club in the other. The vanaras ran to Rama for protection and Lakshman came out to challenge Kumbhakarna.

The monkeys watched as they fought and gasped when Kumbhakarna ran past Lakshman towards Rama. He stumbled when Lakshman threw a spear at his legs, but got to his feet again and went on running. An arrow from Rama's bow hit his arm and his mace went flying through the air. Now, snorting like a goaded bull, he lashed out with his club, cutting a swathe through the monkeys who stood bravely between him and Rama. Both Lakshman and Rama fired arrows at him, but his club swirled so swiftly in the air that the arrows were swatted away like flies. Closer he came and closer.

Lakshman stood in front of Rama and drew his sword. Rama fitted another arrow to his bow, stepped out from behind Lakshman and let fly the arrow. Blessed by the Wind-god, the arrow sliced through Kumbhakarna's shoulder and cut off the arm that held the club. Both fell to the ground. Kumbhakarna kicked them away and, with his other arm, pulled up a tree by the roots. Holding it up like a javelin, he drew back his arm, ready to throw. But another arrow, blessed by Indra, found him first and his arm fell to the ground. Even so, he went on running towards Rama. Two more arrows cut off his legs but his body, like a sea monster driven onto the shore by the tide, its mouth gaping, came closer and closer to Rama, threatening to devour him, until a volley of arrows fell into his mouth and he fell, choking, at Rama's feet. Lakshman gave Rama his sword and, with one stroke, Rama cut of Kumbhakarna's head.

When news of his brother's death was brought to Ravana, he sank to his knees, howling with grief and despair. His sons stood by his side. None of them knew what to say. No one had ever seen Ravana like this before. One by one, they asked his permission to go out onto the battlefield and avenge their uncle's death. One by one, like a man releasing birds from a cage, he let them go. One by one, they met their deaths. Narantaka fought Angad and died fighting. Hanuman killed Devantaka and Trisaras with his bare hands. Lakshman and Atikaya fought a long battle until one of Laskhman's arrows cut off the rakshasa's head.

Indrajit was the last of Ravana's sons to leave the city. He rode out on a chariot, leading an army of rakshasas. Outside the city walls, he jumped down from his chariot and, with the rakshasas standing in a circle around him, performed a ritual of fire, a homa, chanting spells to give him power over his enemies and protection from them. When the ritual was finished, he jumped into his chariot, gave the order to his charioteer, rose into the air and vanished.

While the rakshasas did battle on the ground, Indrajit did battle in the air. His arrows came over the horizon like flocks of birds, darkening the sky, falling like a huntsman's net on his prey. The charioteer's whip cracked like lightning, the horses snorted like thunder, their hooves thudded like rain. Looking down from his chariot, Indrajit saw his father's enemies fall, saw the mounds of bodies grow, saw the ground turn red with their blood, saw at last Rama and Lakshman stagger and fall and lie motionless on the ground.

Hanuman saw them and ran towards them. He bent over them, called their names, touched them, looked into their eyes.

"Hanuman! Quick!"

He looked up and saw Vibhishana.

"It's alright, Hanuman," he said. "He hasn't killed them. But we must revive them quickly before the battle is lost. Indrajit has gone back to the city to tell Ravana that Rama has fallen, but he will be back to finish the job."

"What can we do?" said Hanuman. "Tell me what to do!"

"The herbs," said Vibhishana. "You must fetch the herbs."

"What herbs?"

"The herbs that Sushena told you to get before the eagle came. Do you remember?"

"I do!" said Hanuman. "I do! But I've forgotten where they grow."

"They grow in the Himalayas," said Vibhishana. "On a mountain peak called Rishabha. Quick!"

Suddenly, Hanuman became as big as a tree. He bent his legs, raised his arms, took a deep breath and leapt. All that was left where Hanuman had been was a deep hole in the ground.

The monkeys on the mountain jumped into the trees when they saw Hanuman coming. The sound of their chattering filled the air, but when Hanuman landed they fell silent. He looked on the grass under the trees and saw that it was covered with herbs. There were herbs with small flowers and herbs with big flowers, herbs that smelt sweet and herbs that smelt bitter, red herbs, pink herbs, yellow herbs, white herbs, blue herbs, herbs of every colour.

"I thought there were only three," he said to himself, scratching his head. "Now what shall I do?"

Vibishanha looked up when a shadow passed over the island. At first, he thought it was Indrajit returning in his chariot. But the shadow was too big for that. The sky grew dark and he saw Hanuman coming over the horizon, carrying a mountain in his arms.

"I didn't know which herbs to bring," he said, landing beside Vibhishana. "So I brought the whole mountain. Can you see the ones you need?"

Vibhishana reached up and picked three bunches of herbs from the mountain.

"Have you got them?" said Hanuman.

Vibhishana nodded, kneeling beside Rama and Lakshman with the herbs in his hand.

"Are you sure?"

"I'm sure," said Vibhishana, rubbing the herbs to release their scent.

"I'll take it back then," said Hanuman, leaping back up into the sky.

When Hanuman got back, having put the mountain back where he found it and said goodbye to the monkeys, Rama and Lakshman were on their feet and he embraced them both. But at once the sky turned dark again.

"It's Indrajit," said Vibhishana. "He's back."

Out of the dark sky, Indrajit's arrows sped towards them. Rama and Lakshman raised their bows and fired their arrows, not at invisible Indrajit, but at the arrows which they saw speeding towards them. It sounded as if an army was fighting by night as arrow clashed against arrow and sparks flashed in the dark. Sometimes, as if to taunt them, Indrajit made himself visible and they turned to face him, but then he made himself invisible again and all they could do was stand back to back, wondering where the next arrows would come from. Indrajit was like a cat playing with a mouse and every moment they waited for him to pounce.

"He knows he can't kill you," Vibhishana warned them. "He's playing for time."

A mist seemed to rise up out of the ground and swirl around them. Though Rama and Lakshman stood back to back and Vibhishana stood beside them, they were all hidden in the mist. Even their voices seemed to come from far away.

"Where is he?" said Lakshman. "Where has he gone?"

"He has gone back into the city," said Vibhishana. "His only chance is to increase his strength by performing the sacred rites. That's why he needs time."

They heard a shout in the distance, then footsteps running towards them. Lakshman drew his sword. A dark shape in the mist, footsteps, a voice calling.

"Who is it?"

"It sounds like Hanuman."

"Be careful! Remember rakshasas can change their shape."

"Rama! Rama!"

"It is Hanuman!"

"Rama! She's dead! Sita's dead!"

Rama stared at him. Tears rolled down Hanuman's face.

"She's dead! She's dead! He came in his chariot, out of the city. He had her with him. I jumped onto the chariot to save her, but he was too quick. He had a sword in his hand. He killed her. She's dead. Sita's dead."

Rama took hold of Lakshman's hand and slowly sank to his knees. Lakshman knelt on the ground beside him and spoke to him. His voice was low and full of bitterness.

"There is no dharma!" he said. "It's all false. Everything that's happened, your exile, Sita's death, everything. None of this would have happened. It's all a lie! All that's left is revenge!"

He got to his feet, leaving Rama lying on the ground, and his bitterness turned to rage.

"Revenge!" he shouted. "Death is all that's left, now that Sita is dead."

"She's not dead," said Vibhishana, quietly.

They all looked at him.

"I saw him kill her," said Hanuman.

Vibhishana shook his head.

"Believe me," he said. "She's not dead. Indrajit would not dare to kill her. Ravana would not allow it. This was his magic, a maya-Sita, to make you think she was dead, so that you would tell Rama. A trick."

"Are you sure?"

"I'm sure. Sita is in the ashoka grove where you left her."

He turned to Rama and gave him his hand.

"Come," he said. "The battle is not over yet, but we must be quick. Indrajit has bought too much time already. His strength is growing. Hanuman, send your apes and bears to the west gate. Tell them to make as much noise as they can. Make him leave his homa before it is finished, before he becomes invincible. Quick!"

Hanuman besieged the west gate with screaming monkeys, roaring bears and bellowing apes. They beat their chests and stamped their feet. They flung rocks and trees over the walls.

"Rama!" they chanted. "Rama! Rama! Rama!"

Over the walls came the rakshasas, like a cauldron of milk boiling over and spitting on the fire beneath. Under the gate they came, like snakes. Out of the walls they came, like bats. Out of the sky, like wasps. Out of the earth, like rats. But Hanuman wasn't interested in snakes or bats or rats or wasps. All he wanted was Indrajit. He had seen him cut Sita's throat with his sword and he couldn't forget it. Trick or no trick, magic or no magic, he couldn't get it out of his mind.

Losing patience, he jumped up onto the gate and swung it back against the wall with a crash.

"Rama!" he shouted. "Rama! Victory to Rama!"

Then he jumped onto the wall and stood there, as big as the wall, as wide as the gate, beating his chest.

"Rama! Rama! Victory to Rama!"

Then he reached down, tore the gate from its hinges and threw it over the rooftops.

"Victory to Rama!" he shouted, as the gate crashed through the palace walls.

Then he heard someone shout a warning.

"Hanuman! Look out!"

He looked round and saw Indrajit, with drawn sword, standing behind him.

"Death to Rama!"

Two arrows flashed through the air, two beats of a wing. The first took Indrajit's sword from his hand, the second took his head from his body. The sword clattered to the ground. The head bounced off the wall, scattering drops of blood like the rubies that hung from its ears, and came to rest at Lakshman's feet. Hanuman picked up the body in one hand, drew back his arm and flung it over the rooftops.

When they brought the headless body of the best and bravest of his sons and laid it down before him, Ravana's grief was too hot for tears. While his wives lay weeping on the floor, cast down like flowers in a windswept garden, their stems broken, their petals torn, Ravana raced like a lit fuse, his sword a flame, to the ashoka grove.

The three rakshasis jumped up when they saw him coming. He saw Sita under the trees, rushed forward, raised his sword to strike, to cut her into pieces and send them to Rama. The bright flame of his sword flashed in the air. Sita sat on the grass in front of him, still as a pool, her legs drawn up, her hair falling like water over her shoulders. The flame flickered.

"Kill Rama," said Trijata. "She will be yours yet. Kill Rama, not her. She will be here when you come back."

An army of giants marched out of the city, trampling on the monkeys, picking up the apes and the bears, crushing them in their hands, throwing them into the sea. Ravana flew over the walls in his chariot, Pushpaka. The sun saw him coming and hid behind a cloud. The earth saw him coming and shook with fear. The sea saw him coming and the tide turned. The gods saw him coming and looked down from the heavens. Sugriva saw him and shouted a challenge. But Ravana was looking for Rama.

At last, he saw him. Pushpaka flew near. Ravana raised his bow and plucked the string. Rama heard the sound and looked up. The gods heard the sound and looked down. Sita in the ashoka grove heard the sound and wondered what it was. Lakshman in the thick of the battle heard the sound and went on fighting. Vibhishana heard the sound and thought, "The battle is about to begin."

Rama looked up at the chariot, circling over him like an eagle over a rabbit. He too raised his bow and plucked the string. The eagle swooped. The battle began.

When a storm breaks, people run for shelter. When a ship is tossed on the waves, everyone rushes to watch. When Rama fought Ravana, the monkeys hid in the trees, the rakshasas hid behind the walls and the gods sat down to watch. Sita looked up at Trijata.

"Is this the end?" she said.

Trijata nodded.

Vibhishana held Lakshman's arm.

"There's nothing you can do," he said.

They stood like men turned to stone, waiting for the battle to end. Ravana's arrows poured down from Pushpaka like an avalanche from a mountain. Rama's arrows swarmed around the chariot like locusts.

"Rama should have a chariot too," said Indra. The other gods agreed and sent for Matali, the charioteer.

The monkeys swung from the branches when they saw Rama in his chariot with Matali holding the reins. The rakshasas crouched behind the walls and hid their heads.

"Look!" said Trijata to Sita, pointing at the two chariots circling overhead. "It will be over soon."

Ravana's arrows turned into serpents, their tongues flickering like fire. Rama's arrows turned into eagles that caught the serpents in their talons and ripped them with their beaks. Pushpaka swooped and Ravana's spear cut through Matali's reins. The horses reared and plunged. Rama drove Pushpaka away with a volley of arrows. Matali steered the chariot down to the ground.

The rakshasas jumped up onto the walls, watching Pushpaka in the sky, thinking the battle was won. The monkeys climbed up to the tops of the trees, looking for Rama on the ground, thinking the battle was lost. Lakshman drew his sword, but Vibhishana held him back.

"Wait!" he said.

"Look!" said Indra, pointing to the ground. "Agastya, the sage, has come. Listen!"

The gods leaned closer. They heard Agastya speaking to Rama. They saw Rama looking up at the sun. They heard him reciting a sacred mantra.

"Ah yes!" said Indra, nodding. "A prayer to the sun. Agastya has taught him this."

Rama climbed back into the chariot and Matali drove the horses back up into the sky. Rama drew back his bow and loosed an arrow like a shaft of sunlight breaking through the clouds. The monkeys swung from branch to branch when they saw Ravana's jewelled head go spinning through the air.

"He's cut off his head!" they shouted. "He's cut off his head."

Then one of them gave a shout and they all turned round.

"Look!" he cried. "He's grown another one!"

The monkeys sat on the branches and stared. Rama loosed another arrow and, like the first, it found its target. Ravana's head went tumbling through the air. At once, another one grew in its place.

"He's done it again," said the monkeys.

Rama fired a hundred arrows and a hundred heads grew on Ravana's shoulders. Each gave a shout of triumph, each louder than the one before. Each brought an echo from the rakshasas on the walls, each sent the monkeys hiding among the branches.

"Now!" said Matali, pulling on the reins. "Now! The arrow Agastya gave you, the one he had from Indra, the one forged by Brahma! Use it now!"

The wind in its feathers, the moon in its shaft, the sun in its head, Rama's arrow struck like lightning. Pushpaka went spinning through the air. The horses broke loose from the shafts and galloped away. Like wounded birds they fluttered and flapped as they raced through the sky, dragging the charioteer behind them.

For a moment, Ravana seemed to hang in the air. Then, as if the thread that held him suddenly snapped, he fell. His body, impaled on Rama's arrow, rolled over and over, like an animal turning on a spit, until it hit the ground and stopped turning.

"Sita!"

When she opened her eyes, she saw a monkey standing in front of her.

"Hanuman?"

He smiled.

"Rama is waiting for you," he said. "You wouldn't let me rescue you. But now Ravana is dead and Rama is ready to take you back."

"I knew he would come," said Sita.

"We all helped," said Hanuman. "We built a bridge across the sea. There was a big battle. A really big battle."

"I know," said Sita. "I heard it. I saw it. They made me think Rama and Lakshman were dead."

She looked round and Hanuman saw that the three rakshasis were hiding behind the trees.

"They took me in Ravana's chariot," she said, "and showed me their bodies lying on the battlefield. It looked as if they had been killed. But they can't have been."

Hanuman shook his head.

"The gods sent help," he explained. "And I went to the Himalayas to fetch some herbs."

He looked again at the rakshasis.

"Did they mistreat you?" he asked, frowning. "If they did..."

"No," said Sita, putting a hand on Hanuman's arm. "They did what they could. Let them go."

Trijata put her hands together and bowed her head. Then she and the other two rakshasis turned and ran away through the trees.

She watched them go, then turned back to Hanuman.

"Take me to Rama," she said.

"Yes," said Hanuman, smiling. "He has a palanquin ready for you. I will bring it here and take you to the palace. Rama has made Vibhishana king of Lanka. He helped us in the battle. You will be able to bathe and change your clothes. Everything is ready for you. Then the palanquin will carry you to Rama."

Sita would have walked to Rama dressed as she was but she followed Hanuman out of the ashoka grove to where the palanquin was waiting. She bathed in the palace and put on the silk clothes that had been laid out for her, wondering why Rama had not come to her himself.

There were crowds outside the chamber where Rama waited, all eager to catch a glimpse of her. The bearers stopped in the midst of the crowd. She pulled the curtain aside and saw the faces of vanaras and rakshasas pressed against the window. Quickly, she let the curtain fall. Outside, the excited chatter grew louder. There was shouting. Then a sudden hush. The door opened.

"It is Rama," she thought, "come to meet me!"

But it was not. Someone she had not seen before leaned into the palanquin and held out his hand.

"Who are you?" she said, shrinking back into her seat.

"My name is Vibhishana. Rama has sent me to escort you through these crowds. Please, follow me."

The crowds fell back when she climbed out of the palanquin, but she felt all their eyes on her and looked only at the ground as she walked beside Vibhishana. She heard a door close behind her. Suddenly, it was so quiet all she could hear was the sound of her own soft footsteps on the marble floor. For a moment, she thought

Vibhishana must have led her into an empty room and left her there. She stopped and listened, her eyes still fixed on the ground. But what she heard was not the silence of an empty room. There were eyes everywhere, she could feel them looking at her. What were they waiting for? Why did no one speak? Where was Rama? Had they lied to her? Was Rama dead? When she looked up, would it be Ravana she saw? Like someone breaking loose from the ropes that bound her, she lifted her head. Rama stood in front of her.

"I have followed the path of dharma," he said, "but this is where the path ends. I cannot take you back. I have killed Ravana and set you free. You are free to go."

She looked from Rama to Lakshman, who stood by his side. But Lakshman avoided her eye. She looked at Hanuman, who stood on the other side, and saw in his face a mirror of her own. His eyes were filled with tears. She looked back at Rama.

"Why?"

"Ravana carried you away and kept you with him. Your dishonour would be my shame if I took you back. You are free to go."

She looked again at Lakshman and Hanuman, at Vibhishana who had brought her here, at the others who stood with Rama. When they met her eyes, they looked away. There was no one to speak for her but herself.

"There was no dishonour," she said, in a voice that was so quiet it sounded like a breath of wind. "He stole me from you. That's all."

Rama shook his head.

"It will not be believed."

"Not even by you?"

He looked away.

"I have done my duty. He is dead and you are free to go."

Lakshman, Hanuman and the others stood beside him in silence, their faces cast down, like mourners at a funeral. Sita looked at them all, then turned to Lakshman.

"Build me a pyre," she said, her voice quiet and calm. "Like a widow, let me die in the flames."

Lakshman waited for Rama to speak, but Rama said nothing and looked at no one. So Lakshman built the pyre and, when it was lit, Sita walked towards it and knelt down.

"If my devotion to Rama has never wavered," she said, "may the

Fire-god protect my body from the flames. If Rama has falsely accused me, may the God of fire keep me safe and prove my innocence."

Then she stood up and walked once around the fire before the flames engulfed her.

Hanuman and Sugriva held onto each other, both weeping. Vibhishana stared at Rama in disbelief. Lakshman covered his face with his hands. Rama did not move. When a tear ran down his cheek, it was like rain falling on stone.

"This is the act of a man," said Vibhishana, "an ordinary man."

"That's all I am," said Rama.

"We thought you were more than that," said Sugriva. "That's why we helped you to find her."

"You are more than that," said Hanuman. "I know you are!"

Their voices became lost in the roaring of the flames and they all looked again at the fire, which seemed suddenly to burn more fiercely. The flames blazed like the sun and they looked away.

"Who am I?" Rama cried to the fire. "Tell me who I am!"

The fire spoke with tongues of flame and the voice of a god. It was the voice of Brahma himself, a voice that only Rama could hear, a voice telling him who he really was.

"Look!" said Hanuman. "Look!"

A hand pulled back the flames, like someone parting a curtain, and the God of fire walked through, carrying Sita in his arms.

"Here is your beloved Sita," he said, carrying her to Rama and putting her down by his side. "Her innocence has been proved by fire and the gods return her to you. She is yours."

Rama wept when he saw her and took her in his arms.

"She's innocent!" said Hanuman, jumping on Sugriva's back. "I knew she was!"

Epilogue

The story ends with the journey back to Ayodhya.

Vibhishana gave them a chariot and they all rode in it together, Rama and Sita, Lakshman, Sugriva, Hanuman and Vibhishana, with the great monkey army marching behind.

On the way, they stopped at all the places they had visited during their exile, Kishkindha and the mountain where Rama had met Sugriva, the place where Jatayu had died trying to save Sita from Ravana, Agastya's ashrama, the beautiful river Godavari and Chitrakuta where Lakshman had built them a cottage to live in.

At last, they came to Ayodhya where Bharat came out to greet them, putting the sandals back on Rama's feet.

"The kingdom is yours again," he said.

Then began the time of Ram-raj, when Rama ruled in Ayodhya.

It was a time of peace and prosperity that lasted for ten thousand years. No widow mourned, no child died, no harvest failed. The trees were always in flower and there were rains in plenty. Rama ruled justly, following the path of dharma and everyone was happy.

ACKNOWLEDGEMENTS

Prince Half-a-son is adapted from a story in *Tales of the Punjab* by Flora Annie Steel (Macmillan & Co, 1894).

The Legend of Guru Nanak draws on stories by the anonymous author of *The Legends of Guru Nanak* with illustrations by R.M.Singh (Kapoor Investments Ltd, Canada.).

The version of *Heer Ranjha* that inspired my own comes from *Love Stories from Punjab* by Harish Dhillon (UBS Publishers' Distributors Ltd, 1998).

The version of *Ramayana* that I have followed is that by Dr B.R.Kishore in *Ramayana of Valmiki* (New Light Publishers, Delhi).

ILLUSTRATIONS

Pages 37, 39, 157: J. Lockwood Kipling, from *Tales of the Punjab* by Flora Annie Steel (Macmillan, 1894).

Pages 85, 89, 113: Mool Chund of Ulwar, from *Romantic Tales from the Punjab* by Rev Charles Swynnerton (Oxford University Press, 1928).